Discourse Analysis

Continuum Discourse Series

Series Editor: Professor Ken Hyland, Institute of Education, University of London

Discourse is one of the most significant concepts of contemporary thinking in the humanities and social sciences as it concerns the ways language mediates and shapes our interactions with each other and with the social, political and cultural formations of our society. The *Continuum Discourse Series* aims to capture the fast-developing interest in discourse to provide students, new and experienced teachers and researchers in applied linguistics, ELT and English language with an essential bookshelf. Each book deals with a core topic in discourse studies to give an in-depth, structured and readable introduction to an aspect of the way language in used in real life.

Other titles in the series (forthcoming):

Metadiscourse: Exploring Interaction in Writing
Ken Hyland

Using Corpora in Discourse Analysis
Paul Baker

Spoken Discourse: An Introduction
Helen de Silva Joyce and Diana Slade

Historical Discourse: The Language of Time, Cause and Evaluation
Caroline Coffin

Media Discourse
Joanna Thornborrow

Professional Discourse
Britt-Louise Gunnarsson

An Introduction to Critical Discourse Analysis
Carmen Rosa Caldas-Coulthard and Malcolm Coulthard

Discourse Analysis

An Introduction

Brian Paltridge

continuum

Continuum

The Tower Building   80 Maiden Lane
11 York Road   Suite 704
London SE1 7NX   New York, NY 10038

British Library Cataloguing-in-Publication Data
A catalogue record for this book is available from the British Library.

ISBN: HB: 978–0–8264–8556–4
      PB: 978–0–8264–8557–1

Typeset by YHT Ltd, London
Printed and bound in Great Britain by MPG Books Ltd, Bodmin, Cornwall

Contents

Contents

List of Boxes

List of Figures

List of Tables

Acknowledgements

I would like to thank the editor of this series, Ken Hyland, for his support for this project and for the detailed and helpful feedback he gave on each of the chapters of this book. Thank you also to Jenny Lovel at Continuum for her helpfulness and advice at each of the stages of the book's development. I also wish to thank two people who taught me so much about discourse analysis, Joy Phillips and Winnie Crombie. They both contributed in important ways to what I have learned about discourse. For feedback on individual parts of the book, I thank Angela Thomas, Neil England, Lynn Grant, Sally Humphrey and Ikuko Nakane. I am also grateful to my many very good students, particularly those whose work is cited in this book, Jianxin Liu, Jun Ohashi, Joanna Orr, Carmel O'Shannessy, Anne Prince, Kirsten Richardson, Neomy Storch, Wei Wang, Xiaoyong Zheng and Lan Yang. Thank you also to Eunjoo Song for the Korean example in Chapter 3. At Sophia University in Tokyo where I completed this book I especially thank Junichi Kasajima and Kensaku Yoshida for inviting me to come to Sophia. My thanks also to Keiko Adachi, Cheolgoo Bae and Anne Conduit for looking after me while I was there and for the many kindnesses that they showed me.

1 What is discourse analysis?

This chapter provides an overview of *discourse analysis*, an approach to the analysis of language that looks at patterns of language across texts as well as the social and cultural contexts in which the texts occur. The chapter commences by presenting the origins of the term discourse analysis. It then discusses particular issues which are of interest to discourse analysts, such as the relationship between language and social context, culture-specific ways of speaking and writing, and ways of organizing texts in particular social and cultural situations. It then discusses the notion of *communicative competence* and what this means for discussions of spoken and written discourse.

The chapter continues with a discussion of different views of discourse analysis. These range from more textually-oriented views of discourse analysis which concentrate mostly on language features of texts, to more socially-oriented views of discourse analysis which consider what the text is doing in the social and cultural setting in which it occurs. This leads to a discussion of the *social constructionist* view of discourse; that is, the ways in which what we say as we speak contributes to the construction of certain views of the world, of people and, in turn, ourselves. The relationship between language and identity is then introduced. This includes a discussion of the ways in which, through our use of language, we not only 'display' who we are, but also how we want people to see us. This includes a discussion of the ways in which, through the use of spoken and written discourse, people both 'perform' and 'create' particular social, and gendered, identities.

The ways in which 'texts rely on other texts' is also discussed in this chapter; that is the way in which we produce and understand texts in relation to other texts that have come before them as well as other texts that may follow them. The chapter concludes with a discussion of differences between spoken and written discourse. Examples are given throughout the chapter to illustrate each of the points being made. This chapter, then, introduces notions and lays the ground for issues that will be discussed in greater detail in the chapters that follow.

1.1 What is discourse analysis?

Discourse analysis focuses on knowledge about language beyond the word, clause, phrase and sentence that is needed for successful communication. It looks at patterns of language across texts and considers the relationship between language and the social and cultural contexts in which it is used. Discourse analysis also considers the ways that the use of language presents different views of the world and different understandings. It examines how the use of language is influenced by relationships between participants as well as the effects the use of language has upon social identities and relations. It also considers how views of the world, and identities, are constructed through the use of discourse. Discourse analysis examines both spoken and written texts.

The term *discourse analysis* was first introduced by Zellig Harris in 1952 as a way of analysing connected speech and writing. Harris had two main interests: the examination of language beyond the level of the sentence and the relationship between linguistic and non-linguistic behaviour. He examined the first of these in most detail, aiming to provide a way for describing how language features are distributed within texts and the ways in which they are combined in particular kinds and styles of texts. An early, and important, observation he made was that:

> connected discourse occurs within a particular situation – whether of a person speaking, or of a conversation, or of someone sitting down occasionally over the period of months to write a particular kind of book in a particular literary or scientific tradition.
>
> (Harris 1952: 3)

There are, thus, typical ways of using language in particular situations. These *discourses*, he argued, not only share particular meanings, they also have characteristic linguistic features associated with them. What

2

these meanings are, and how they are realized in language, is of central interest to the area of discourse analysis.

i. The relationship between language and context

By 'the relationship between linguistic and non-linguistic behaviour' Harris means how people know, from the situation that they are in, how to interpret what someone says. If, for example, an air traffic controller says to a pilot *The runway is full at the moment*, they most likely mean it is not possible to land the plane at the moment. This may seem obvious to a native speaker of English but a non-native speaker pilot, of which there are many in the world, needs to understand the relationship between what is said and what is meant, in order to understand that they cannot land their plane at that time. Harris's point is that the expression *The runway is full at the moment* has a particular meaning in a particular situation (in this case the landing of a plane) and may mean something different in another situation. If I say *The runway is full at the moment* to a friend who is waiting with me to pick up someone at the airport, this is now an explanation of why the plane is late landing (however I may know this), not an instruction to not land the plane.

Discourse analysis, then, is interested in 'what happens when people draw on the knowledge they have about language ... to do things in the world' (Johnstone 2002: 3). It is, thus, the analysis of language in use. Discourse analysis considers the relationship between language and the contexts in which it is used and is concerned with the description and analysis of both spoken and written interactions. Its primary purpose, as Chimombo and Roseberry (1998) argue, is to provide a deeper understanding and appreciation of texts and how they become meaningful to their users.

ii. Discourse analysis and pragmatics

A number of aspects of language use that are discussed by people working in the area of discourse analysis are also discussed in the area of *pragmatics*. Pragmatics is concerned with how the interpretation of language depends on knowledge of the real world, such as how *The runway is full at the moment* is understood as an instruction not to land a plane, rather than just a statement of fact. Pragmatics is interested in what people mean by what they say, rather than what words in their most literal sense might mean by themselves. It is sometimes contrasted with semantics which deals with literal (rather than pragmatic) meaning; that is, meaning without reference to users or the purpose of communication (Richards and Schmidt 2002). The view of discourse analysis presented in this book will include work in the area of pragmatics; that is, a consideration of the ways in which people mean more than what they say in spoken and written discourse.

iii. The discourse structure of texts

Discourse analysts are also interested in how people organize what they say in the sense of what they typically say first, and what they say next and so on in a conversation or in a piece of writing. This is something that varies across cultures and is by no means the same across languages. An email, for example, to me from a Japanese academic or a member of the administrative staff at a Japanese university, may start with reference to the weather saying, immediately after *Dear Dr Paltridge* something like *Greetings from a hot and sizzling Tokyo* or *Greetings! It's such a beautiful day today here in Kyoto.* I, of course, may also say this in an email to an overseas colleague but is it not a ritual requirement in English, as it is in Japanese. There are, thus, particular things we say, and particular ways of ordering what we say in particular spoken and written situations and in particular languages and cultures.

Mitchell (1957) was one the first researchers to examine the *discourse structure* of texts. He looked at the ways in which people order what they say in buying and selling interactions. He looked at the overall structure of these kinds of texts, introducing the notion of *stages* into discourse analysis; that is the steps that language users go through as they carry out particular interactions. His interest was more in the ways in which interactions are organized at an overall textual level than the ways in which language is used in each of the stages of a text. Mitchell discusses how language is used as, what he calls, *co-operative action* and how the meaning of language lies in the situational context in which it is used and in the context of the text as a whole.

If, then, I am walking along the street in Shanghai near a market and someone says to me *Hello Mister, DVD*, I know from the situation that I am in that they are wanting to sell me (most likely fake) DVDs. If I then go into a market and someone asks what seems to me to be a very high price for a shirt, I know from my experience with this kind of interaction that the price they are telling me is just a starting point in the buying and selling exchange and that I can quite easily end up buying the shirt for at least half the original price. I know, from my experience, how the interaction will typically start, what language will typically be used in the interaction, and how the interaction will typically end. I also start to learn other typical characteristics of the interaction. For example, a person will normally only say *Hello Mister, DVD* (or *Hello Mister, Louis Vuitton*, etc.) when I am between stalls, not when I am in a stall and have started a buying and selling interaction with someone.

Other researchers have also investigated recurring patterns in spoken interactions, although in a somewhat different way from Mitchell and others following in that tradition. Researchers working in the area known as *conversation analysis* have looked at how people open and close conversations and how people take turns and overlap their speech in conversations, for example. They have looked at casual conversations, chat, as well as doctor–patient consultations, psychiatric interviews and interactions in legal settings. Their interest, in particular, is in fine-grained analyses of spoken interactions, such as the use of overlap, pauses, increased volume and pitch and what these reveal about how people relate to each other in what they are saying and doing with language. They might, for example, look at how people 'speak over' what someone else is saying and what they are aiming to do in doing this. They may look at how this varies in different speech situations and what the speakers understand that this means in the particular situation. In an ordinary conversation, for example, the overlapping of speech may be an attempt by one speaker to take over the conversation from the other person. If the other person does not want them to take over the conversation, they may increase the volume of what they are saying and just keep on talking, not letting the other person interrupt them. In a different situation, however, overlapping speech may just be a case of co-operative conversational behaviour such as when one speaker gives feedback to another speaker, mirroring what they are saying as they speak. In some languages, such as Italian for example, overlap is tolerated much more in spoken interactions than it is in other languages, such as English.

iv. Cultural ways of speaking and writing

One useful way of looking at the ways in which language is used by particular cultural groups is through the notion of the *ethnography of communication* (Hymes 1964). Hymes started this work in reaction to the neglect, at the time, of speech in linguistic analyses and anthropological descriptions of cultures. His work was also a reaction to views of language which took little or no account of the social and cultural contexts in which language occurs. In particular, he considered aspects of *speech events* such as who is speaking to whom,

5

about what, for what purpose, where, and when, and how these impact on how we say and do things in culture-specific settings.

There are, for example, particular cultural ways of buying and selling things in different cultures. How I buy my lunch at a takeaway shop in an English-speaking country is different, for example, from how I might do this in Japan. In an English-speaking country there is greater ritual use of *Please* and *Thanks* on the part of the customer in this kind of interaction than there is in Japan. How I buy something in a supermarket in an English-speaking country may be more similar to how I might do this in Japan. The person at the cash register in Japan, however, will typically say much more than the customer in this sort of situation, who may indeed say nothing. This does not mean that by saying nothing the Japanese customer is being rude. It simply means that there are culturally different ways of doing things with language in different cultures. The sequence of events I go through may be the same in both cultures, but the ways of using language in these events, and other sorts of non-linguistic behaviour, may differ.

v. Communicative competence and discourse

Hymes's notion (1972) of *communicative competence* is an important part of the theoretical background to the ethnography of communication as well as, more recently, communicative perspectives on language teaching and learning. It is also an important notion for the discussion of spoken and written discourse. Communicative competence involves not only knowing a language, but also what to say to whom, and how to say it appropriately in a particular situation. That is, it includes not only knowing what is grammatically correct and what is not, but also when and where to use language appropriately and with whom. It includes knowledge of rules of speaking, as well as knowing how to use and respond to different *speech acts*; that is how, for example, to apologize or make a request, as well as how to respond to an apology or a request, in a particular language or culture.

All of this involves taking account of the social and cultural setting in which the speaking or writing occurs, speakers' and writers' relationships with each other, and the community's norms, values and expectations for the kind of interaction, or *speech event*. When I buy something in a shop, for example, I take account of the cultural setting I am in, the kind of shop I am in and the relationship between me and the person working there as I carry out the particular interaction. I do this at the level of language in terms of grammar, vocabulary, discourse structures and politeness strategies, as well as how I behave physically in the particular situation.

Communicative competence is often described as being made up of four underlying components: *grammatical competence, sociolinguistic competence, discourse competence* and *strategic competence*; that is, mastery of the language code (grammatical competence), knowledge of appropriate language use (sociolinguistic competence), knowledge of how to connect utterances in a text so it is both cohesive and coherent (discourse competence) and mastery of the strategies that speakers use to compensate for breakdowns in communication as well as the strategies they use to enhance the effectiveness of the communications (strategic competence) (Canale and Swain 1980; Canale 1983).

vi. Discursive competence

A further way of looking at cultural ways of speaking and writing is through the notion of *discursive competence* (Bhatia 2004). Discursive competence draws together the notions of *textual competence, generic competence* and *social competence*.

Textual competence refers to the ability to produce and interpret contextually appropriate texts. To do this we draw on our linguistic, textual, contextual and pragmatic knowledge of what typically occurs in a particular text, how it is typically organized and how it is typically interpreted. An example of this is how people use the Internet to communicate with each other. Someone using MSN Messenger, for example, learns sets of abbreviations that are commonly used in this sort of communication as well as how they are interpreted, such as *OIC* to mean *Oh I see* and *bb* to mean *Bye bye*. They also learn that starting a sentence without a capital letter is acceptable on MSN Messenger (as it is in text messaging) and that they should keep their exchanges short so they are easy to read at the other end.

Generic competence describes how we are able to respond to both recurring and new communicative situations by constructing, interpreting, using and exploiting conventions associated with the use of particular kinds of texts, or *genres*, much as I do when I send an email to a colleague or a text message to a friend. If I am an experienced text messager I do this with ease. If I am new to text messaging, however, I have to learn how to do this, what the 'rules' are for this kind of interaction, and what the possibilities and limitations are in terms of what I can say and how I can say it.

Social competence describes how we use language to take part in social and institutional interactions in a way that enables us to express our social identity, within the constraints of the particular social situation and communicative interaction. An example of this is how I present myself at a meeting at work, whether I want to be seen as someone who always has something to say about a point, or whether I want to keep my opinion to myself in this sort of situation. I may use language to show that I am in charge of the meeting, or I may use language to make it clear that I am not. That is, within the constraints of the particular situation, I may use language to show who I am and what my role is (and is not) in the particular social (and cultural) setting.

Discursive competence, then, incudes not only language-related and text-level knowledge. It also includes complex (and often changing) factors outside of the text which need to be taken account of for effective communication. As a user of MSN Messenger, I need to learn how to use language in this kind of event, how it is typically interpreted in this kind of event, the ways I can express who I am (or want someone to think I am) in this kind of event, as well as how factors outside of the text, such as the technology I am using, impacts on what I say and how I can say it. I will also learn that as the technology changes, or I discover more advanced technology (such as a more recent version of MSN Messenger, or a more expensive mobile phone), what I say and how I can say it will change even further.

1.2   Different views of discourse analysis

There are in fact a number of differing views on what discourse analysis actually is. Social science researchers, for example, might argue that all their work is concerned with the analysis of discourse, yet often take up the term in their own, sometimes different, ways (Fairclough 2003). Mills (1997) makes a similar observation showing how, through its relatively short history, the term discourse analysis has shifted from highlighting one aspect of language usage to another, as well as being used in different ways by different researchers. Cazden (1998) describes two main views on discourse analysis: those which focus on the analysis of stretches of naturally occurring language, and those which consider different ways of talking and understanding.

Fairclough (2003) contrasts what he calls 'textually oriented discourse analysis' with approaches to discourse analysis that have more of a social theoretical orientation. He does not see these two views as mutually exclusive, however, arguing for an analysis of discourse that is both linguistic and social in its orientation. Cameron and Kulick (2003) present a similar view. They do not take these two perspectives to be incompatible with each other, arguing that the instances of language in use that are studied under a textually oriented view of discourse are still socially situated and need to be interpreted in terms of their social meanings and functions.

We can see, then, that discourse analysis is a view of language at the level of text. Discourse analysis is also a view of language in use; that is, how, through the use of language, people achieve certain communicative goals, perform certain communicative acts, participate in certain communicative events and present themselves to others. Discourse analysis considers how people manage interactions with each other, how people communicate within particular groups and societies, as well as how they communicate with other groups, and with other cultures. It also focuses on how people do things beyond language, and the ideas and beliefs that they communicate as they use language.

i. Discourse as the social construction of reality

The view of discourse as the *social construction of reality* see texts as communicative units which are embedded in social and cultural practices. The texts we write and speak both shape and are shaped by these practices. Discourse, then, is both shaped by the world as well as shaping the world. Discourse is shaped by language as well as shaping language. It is shaped by the people who use the language as well as shaping the language that people use. Discourse is shaped, as well, by the discourse that has preceded it as well that which might follow it. Discourse is also shaped by the medium in which it occurs as well as it shapes the possibilities for that medium. The purpose of the text also influences the discourse. Discourse also shapes the range of possible purposes of texts (Johnstone 2002).

Wetherell's (2001) analysis of the BBC *Panorama* interview with Princess Diana (BBC 1995) provides an example of the role of language in the construction (and construal) of the social world. She shows how, through the use of language, Princess Diana 'construes' her social world, presenting herself as a sharing person and Prince Charles as 'a proud man who felt low about the attention his wife was getting' (Wetherell 2001: 15). That is, as she speaks, the Princess creates a view of herself, and the world in which she lives, in a way that she wishes people to see. As Wetherell points out:

> As Diana and others speak, on this and many other occasions, a formulation of the world comes into being. The world as described comes into existence at that moment. In an important sense, the social reality constructed in the *Panorama* interview and in other places of Diana's happy marriage bucking under media pressure did not exist before its emergence as discourse.
>
> (Wetherell 2001: 16)

A further example of this *social constructivist* view of discourse can be seen in the text on the cover of the December 2004 Asian edition of *Business Week*:

The three scariest words in U.S. industry: 'The China Price'

The feature story in this issue discusses China's ability to undercut production costs to the extent that, unless US manufacturers are able to cut their prices, they can 'kiss their customers goodbye'. This special report states that for decades economists have insisted that the US wins from globalization. Now they are not so sure. China, a former US trade representative says, 'is a tiger on steroids'. A labour economist from Harvard University says in this series of articles that the wages of white collar workers in the US 'could get whacked' as a result of this shift and that white collar workers in the US have a right to be scared that they may lose their jobs as they are displaced by this 'offshoring'. Ultimately, the report argues, more than half the 130 million US workforce could feel the impact of this change in global competition (Engardio and Roberts 2004). For someone reading about this for the first time, the competitive edge China has, with its combination of low prices and high tech, becomes not just part of their social stock of knowledge but also part of their social reality, a reality constructed (in part) through discourse.

In a further discussion of changes in contemporary China, Farrer (2002) describes changes in the use and meaning of the expression 'I love you' among young people in Shanghai. Whereas he says for people in the West saying 'I love you' may mean the beginning of commitment to each other, in the past, in China, the effect was just the opposite. He says that the verbal expression of love for Shanghainese before the reform era was looked upon with suspicion and suggested that the person who said it was unreliable. Nowadays, however, younger people, he says, have a much more positive attitude towards saying 'I love you' to each other, although sometimes using Cantonese, English or Japanese ways of saying this to avoid the embarrassment, still present for some, in talking romantically in everyday Shanghainese. Here we have an example of quite different social realities being created in different cultures by the use of the same (or seemingly same) expression.

Cameron and Kulick (2003: 29) in their discussion of the history of the terms 'gay', 'lesbian' and 'queer' provide a further example of this. As they argue:

words in isolation are not the issue. It is in *discourse* – the use of language in specific contexts – that words acquire meaning.

Whenever people argue about words, they are also arguing about the assumptions and values that have clustered around those words in the course of their history of being used. We cannot understand the significance of any word unless we attend closely to its relationship to other words and to the discourse (indeed, the competing discourses) in which words are always embedded. And we must bear in mind that discourse shifts and changes constantly, which is why arguments about words and their meanings are never settled once and for all.

ii. Discourse and socially situated identities

When we speak or write we use more than just language to display who we are, and how we want people to see us. The way we dress, the gestures we use, and the way/s we act and interact also influence how we display social identity. Other factors which influence this include the ways we think, the attitudes we display, and the things we value, feel and believe. As Gee (2005) argues, the ways we make visible and recognizable *who* we are and *what* we are doing always involves more than just language. It involves acting, interacting and thinking in certain ways. It also involves valuing and talking (or reading and writing) in appropriate ways with appropriate 'props', at appropriate times, in appropriate places.

Princess Diana, for example, knows in the *Panorama* interview, not only how she is expected to speak in the particular place and at the particular time, but also how she should dress, how she can use body language to achieve the effect that she wants, as well as the values, attitudes, beliefs and emotions it is appropriate for her to express (as well as those it is not appropriate for her to express) in this situation. That is, she knows how to enact the *discourse* of a Princess being interviewed about her private life in the open and public medium of television. This *discourse*, of course, may be different from, but related to, the *discourses* she participated in in her role as mother of her children, and the public and private roles and identities she had as wife of the Prince of Wales. A given discourse, thus, can involve more than just the one single identity (Gee 2004).

Discourses, then, involve the *socially situated identities* that we enact and recognize in the different settings that we interact in. They include culture-specific ways of performing and culture-specific ways of recognizing identities and activities. Discourses also include the different styles of language that we use to enact and recognize these identities, that is, different *social languages* (Gee 1996). Discourses also involve characteristic ways of acting, interacting and feeling, and characteristic ways of showing emotion, gesturing, dressing and posturing. They also involve particular ways of valuing, thinking, believing, knowing, speaking and listening, reading and writing (Gee 2005).

iii. Discourse and performance

As Gee explains:

> a Discourse is a 'dance' that exists in the abstract as a coordinated pattern of words, deeds, values, beliefs, symbols, tools, objects, times, and places in the here and now as a performance that is recognizable as just such a coordination. Like a dance, the performance here and now is never exactly the same. It all comes down, often, to what the 'masters of the dance' will allow to be recognised or will be forced to recognize as a possible instantiation of the dance.
>
> (Gee 2005: 19)

This notion of performance and, in particular, *performativity*, is taken up by authors such as Butler (1990, 2004), Cameron (1999), and Eckert and McConnell-Ginet (2003). The notion of performativity derives from speech act theory and the work of the linguistic philosopher Austin. It is based on the view that in *saying* something, we *do* it (Cameron and Kulick 2003). That is, we bring states of affairs into being as a result of what we say and what we do. Examples of this are *I promise* and *I now pronounce you man and wife*. Once I have said *I promise* I have committed myself to doing something. Once a priest, or a marriage celebrant, says *I now pronounce you man and wife*, the couple have 'become' man and wife.

Butler, Cameron and others talk about doing gender in much the way that Gee talks about discourse as performance. Discourses, then, like the performance of gendered identities, are socially constructed, rather than 'natural'. People 'are who they are because of (among other things) the way they talk' not 'because of who they (already) are' (Cameron 1999: 144). Social identities are, thus, not pre-given, but are formed in the use of language and the various other ways we display who we are, what we think, value and feel, etc. The way, for example, a rap singer uses language, what they rap about and how they present themselves as they do this, all contributes to their performance and creation of themselves as a rap singer. They may do this in a particular way on the streets of New York, in another way in a show in Quebec, and yet another way in a night club in Seoul. As they *do* being a rap singer, they bring into existence, or repeat, their social persona as a rap singer.

iv. Discourse and intertextuality

All texts, whether they are spoken or written, make their meanings against the background of other texts and things that have been said on other occasions (Lemke 1992). Texts may more or less implicitly or explicitly cite other texts, they may refer to other texts, or they may allude to other past, or future, texts. We thus 'make sense of every word, every utterance, or act against the background of (some) other words, utterances, acts of a similar kind' (Lemke 1995: 23). All texts are, thus, in an *intertextual* relationship with other texts.

Umberto Eco (1987) provides an interesting discussion of inter-textuality in his chapter 'Casablanca: Cult movies and intertextual collage'. Eco points out that the film *Casablanca* was made on a very small budget and in a very short time. As a result its creators were forced to improvise the plot, mixing a little of everything they knew worked in a movie as they went. The result is what Eco describes as an 'intertextual collage'. For Eco, *Casablanca* has been so successful because it is not, in fact, an instance of a single kind of film genre but a mixing of stereotyped situations that are drawn from a number of different kinds of film genres. As the film proceeds, he argues, we recognize the film genres that they recall. We also recognize the pleasures we have experienced when we have watched these kinds of films.

The first few scenes of *Casablanca*, for example, recall film genres such as the adventure movie, the patriotic movie, newsreels, war propaganda movies, gangster movies, action movies, spy movies and finally, with the appearance of Ingrid Bergman, a romance. The poster for this movie suggests a number of these film genres, but people who have seen the movie would most likely describe it as a romance. As Brown (1992: 7) observes, the chemistry between its two stars Humphrey Bogard and Ingrid Bergman 'was so thick it would make movie history' and defines *Casablanca* as movie romance for all time. It is not, however, just a romance. It is, rather, a mixing of types of film, in which one of the major themes is the relationship between the two lead players, set in a world of action, adventure, spies, gangsters and of course, romance.

1.3 Differences between spoken and written discourse

There are a number of important differences between spoken and written language which have implications for discourse analysis. Biber (1986, 1988) discusses a number of commonly held views on differences between spoken and written language, some of which are true for some spoken and written genres, but are false for others.

i. Grammatical intricacy and spoken discourse

The first commonly held view is that writing is more structurally complex and elaborate than speech. Halliday (1989) argues that speech is no less highly organized than writing. Spoken discourse, he argues, has its own kind of complexity. He presents the notion of *grammatical intricacy* to account for the way in which the relationship between clauses in spoken discourse can be much more spread out and with more complex relations between them than in writing, yet we still manage to keep track of these relations. The following extract by a judge on a television song competition contains sets of clauses that are long and spread out in the way that Halliday describes. The judge is talking about the winner of the show who came to the auditions dressed in a grunge outfit and who transformed herself throughout the show:

> You are fabulous, truly, truly fabulous. And you know what's fabulous about you? I believe that the real, true artists, the people that are around for a long time, who touch people's lives, are those artists that have lots of contradictions within them, and you had many contradictions within you when you first rocked up. You looked like a skate punk and you had this aura of 'Don't mess with me' about you, and, but every time you step in front of us you take another step towards being what we wanna create here, which is a superstar artist. That was a fantastic song for you. You just rocked the house and I can't believe they have got you in heels! Absolute class act, darling.   (Australian Idol Blog 2004)

ii. Lexical density in spoken and written discourse

Written discourse, however, according to Halliday tends to be more *lexically dense* than spoken discourse. Lexical density refers to the ratio of content words to grammatical, or function words, within a clause. Content words include nouns and verbs while grammatical words include items such as prepositions, pronouns and articles. In spoken discourse content words tend to be spread out over a number of clauses rather than being tightly packed into individual clauses which is more typical of written discourse. The following extract from Brown's (1992: 9) foreword to the book *Casablanca: Script and Legend* illustrates the higher lexical density that is typical of many written texts. In this extract, there are seven content words in each of the clauses. The content words in this extract are in italics. There are many more content words than function words in this extract:

> If *Casablanca defined true love* for a *generation* of *incurable romantics*, it also *defined* the *aesthetic possibilities* of *cinema* for a *generation* of *film lovers*.

In the following extract from the script of *Casablanca* (Koch 1996: 56) a woman who had a brief affair with the star of the film, Rick, is speaking. Here, there is an average of 1.6 content words per clause, fewer content words per clause than in the previous example of written text. The content words are italicized:

> Yvonne: Who do you *think* you are, *pushing* me around? What a
> *fool* I was to *fall* for a *man* like you.
> (TM & © Turner Entertainment Co. (s06))

iii. Nominalization in written and spoken discourse

There is also a high level of *nominalization* in written texts; that is, where actions and events are presented as nouns rather than as verbs. Halliday (1989) calls this phenomenon *grammatical metaphor*; that is, where a language item is transferred from a more expected grammatical class to another. Written texts also typically include longer noun groups than spoken texts. This leads to a situation where the information in the text is more tightly packed into fewer words and less spread out than in spoken texts. The following extract from an analysis of *Casablanca* by Corliss (1992: 233) illustrates this. The first two examples highlighted in text show long noun groups which are typical of much written discourse. The third example includes an example of grammatical metaphor. Here, the adjective 'turgid' (its more 'expected' grammatical class) is changed into the noun 'turgidity', an example of nominalization:

> Although Casablanca defines Bogey for all time as *the existential-hero-in-spite-of-himself, several of his roles just preceding this one (notably High Sierra and The Maltese Falcon)* had prepared his fans for *the misanthropy and climatic selflessness* he would embody as Rick Blaine. Bergman (as Ilsa Lund) and Henreid (as Victor Laszlo) are hardly incandescent lovers – neither are Bergman and Bogart, for that matter – but *their turgidity as sexual partners* works, intentionally or not, to the film's advantage.

This extract also includes two examples of *qualifiers* (Halliday 1985) following a noun which are also typical of much written discourse. In the following illustration of this extract, the first highlighted section of the text qualifies the noun group 'several of his roles'. The second highlighted section qualifies the noun group 'their turgidity'. This use of qualifiers is also typical of much written scientific discourse (Conduit and Modesto 1990) and adds to the length of noun groups in written discourse.

> Although Casablanca defines Bogey for all time as the existential-hero-in-spite-of-himself, several of his roles *just preceding this one (notably High Sierra and The Maltese Falcon)* had prepared his fans for the misanthropy and climatic selflessness he would embody as Rick Blaine ... their turgidity *as sexual partners* works, intentionally or not, to the film's advantage.

The next extract, also from *Casablanca* (Koch 1996: 127), is an example of the typically low level of nominalization and shorter noun groups in spoken discourse. The noun groups, shown in italics in this extract, are simpler and less dense than in the previous example. There are no examples of grammatical metaphor, nor any examples of qualifiers following a noun in this extract:

Ilsa:	Can I tell you *a story*, Rick?
Rick:	Has it got *a wow finish*?
Ilsa:	I don't know *the finish* yet.
Rick:	Well, go on, tell it. Maybe one will come to you as you go along

(TM & © Turner Entertainment Co. (s06))

iv. Explicitness in spoken and written discourse

A further commonly held view is that writing is more explicit than speech. This depends on the purpose of the text and, again, is not an absolute. A person can state something directly, or infer something, in both speaking and writing, depending upon what they want the listener or reader to understand, and how direct they wish to be. In the following extract from *Casablanca* (Koch 1996: 55), Yvonne asks if she will see Rick that evening. Rick clearly wishes her to infer 'probably not'. He has not said this explicitly, but it is most likely what he means:

Yvonne:	Will I see you tonight?
Rick:	(matter-of-factly) I never make plans that far ahead.

(TM & © Turner Entertainment Co. (s06))

Yvonne has to work out Rick's intended meaning from the situation she is in, what she knows about Rick, and the fact that she asked a 'yes/no' question but has not been given a 'yes/no' answer. That is, she works out what Rick means from the *situational context* they are in, from her *background knowledge* of this context, including what she knows about her relationship with Rick, and the *textual context* of what she has said.

v. Contextualization in spoken and written discourse

Another commonly held view is that writing is more decontextualized than speech. This view is based on the perception that speech depends on a shared situation and background for interpretation whereas writing does not depend on such a shared context. This is generally true of conversation but is not true of speech and writing in general (Tannen 1982). Spoken genres, such as academic lectures, for example, do not generally show a high dependence on a shared context, while written genres such as personal letters or memos do. Both written fiction and non-fiction may also depend on background information supplied by the reader and an active role of the reader to enter into the world of the text.

The opening lines in the best-seller *Eats, Shoots & Leaves* (Truss 2003) illustrates the role of the reader in providing the context to a piece of writing, in this case the author's horror at seeing signs that misuse the apostrophe:

> Either this will ring bells for you, or it won't. A printed banner has appeared on the concourse of a petrol station near to where I live. 'Come inside,' it says, 'for CD's, VIDEO's, DVD's, and BOOK's'.
>
> (Truss 2003: 1)

vi. The spontaneous nature of spoken discourse

A further view is that speaking is disorganized and ungrammatical, whereas writing is organized and grammatical. As we have seen, spoken discourse *is* organized, but it is organized differently from written discourse. Spoken discourse does, however, contain more half-completed and reformulated utterances than written discourse. This is because spoken discourse is often produced spontaneously and we are able to see the process of its production as someone speaks. This is not to say that written discourse is not at some stage half-completed or re-formulated. It is just that the text we see (apart from synchronous online chat and discussion boards) is simply the finished product and as Halliday (1989: 100) points out, 'a highly idealised version of the writing process.'

With spoken discourse, topics can also be changed and speakers can interrupt and overlap with each other as they speak. Speakers can ask for clarification and they can correct what they have said. Misunderstandings, further, can be cleared up immediately. Also, spoken discourse is able to use intonation, gesture and body language to convey meaning, whereas written discourse is more constrained in that ways of conveying meaning are more limited.

vii. Repetition, hesitation and redundancy in spoken discourse

Speaking also uses much more repetition, hesitation and redundancy than written discourse. This is because it is produced in real time, with speakers working out what they want to say at the same time as they are saying it. A further characteristic of spoken discourse is the use of pauses and 'fillers' like 'hhh', 'er' and 'you know'. Speakers do this to give them time to think about what they want to say while they are speaking. They also do this to hold on to their turn in the conversation while they are thinking about what they want to say, and how they will say it. The following extracts from the BBC *Panorama* interview between Princess Diana and Martin Bashir illustrate this. Here pauses are shown in brackets. The number in brackets indicates the length of the pause in seconds and (.) indicates a micro pause that is too small to count:

> Bashir: at this early stage would you say that you were happily married
> Diana: very much so (1) er the pressure on – on both as a couple (.) with the media was phenomenal (1) and misunderstood by a great many people (1) we'd be going round Australia for instance. hhh (2) and (.) you – all you could hear was oh (.) she's on the other side (1) now if you're a man (1) like my husband a proud man (.) you mind about that if you hear it every day for four weeks (.) and you feel (.) low about it y-know instead of feeling happy and sharing it.

viii. A continuum of differences between spoken and written discourse

As McCarthy (2001) argues, there is no simple, one-dimensional difference between spoken and written discourse. These differences are most usefully seen as being on a scale, or continuum; for example, from texts which are more involved interpersonally such as some casual conversations, to texts which are more detached such as some written public notices.

Some spoken texts may be more implicit and leave a lot of what is to be understood unsaid whereas written texts (in English at least) may often be more explicit. There is also a scale of real time to lapsed time for spoken and (most) written discourse. Some texts are also more fragmented than others in their performance such as casual conversations and online chat room discussions. Other texts, such as prepared academic lectures and published academic writing may be more tightly organized and integrated. This idea of a spoken to written scale, or continuum, 'avoids over-simplified distinctions between speech and writing but still brings out keys areas in which spoken and written discourse may be differentiated' (McCarthy 2001: 94).

Written discourse, then, is not just speaking written down. Speaking and writing draw on the same underlying grammatical system but in general they encode meanings in different ways depending on what they wish to represent. Biber's (1988) corpus-based study into differences between spoken and written texts found that there is no single absolute difference between speech and writing in English, but rather dimensions of variation where linguistic features tend to cluster, all of which varies for different kinds of texts, or genres. Equally, he found that considerable variation occurs even within particular genres, some of which he describes as surprising, and, sometimes, contrary to popular expectation.

Biber's work supports this notion of a spoken–written continuum. He has shown that there are no absolute differences between spoken and written language in terms of the predominance of certain linguistic features, but that spoken and written language are, rather, 'multidimensional constructs' with some spoken and written genres having a number of features in common with other spoken and written genres and a number of characteristics which show them to be quite different. Biber points out how certain linguistic features may cluster in texts that share a similar communicative function. These clusters, however, are often distributed differently in different types of spoken and written texts. Spoken and written styles, further, may intermingle with each other in that forms that are typically associated with spoken language may also occur in written language, such as in informal letters, email messages and advertising (McCarthy 2001).

1.4 Summary

Discourse analysis, then, focuses on knowledge about language and the world beyond the word, clause, phrase and sentence that is needed for successful communication. It considers the relationship between language and the social and cultural contexts in which it is used and looks at patterns of organization across texts. It considers what people mean by what they say, how they work out what people mean, and the way language presents different views of the world and different under-standings. This includes an examination of how discourse is shaped by relationships between participants, and the effects discourse has upon social identities and relations.

Discourse analysis takes us into what Riggenbach (1999) calls the 'bigger picture' of language description that is often left out of more micro-level descriptions of language use. It takes us into the social and cultural settings of language use to help us understand particular language choices. That is, it takes us beyond description to explanation and helps us understand the 'rules of the game' that language users draw on in their everyday spoken and written interactions. There are many ways in which one could (and can) approach discourse analysis. What each of these ways reveals is, in part, a result of the perspective taken in the analysis, and the questions that have been asked. The aim of this book is to provide an introduction to some of these perspectives.

1.5 Discussion questions

1. Think of examples of how people recognize your socially situated identity through your use of language. For example, in what ways does your use of language reflect your age, social class, gender, ethnic background or nationality? This might be through your use of vocabulary, your accent or the things you talk about and how you talk about them. Try to think of specific examples of each of these.

2. Think of a situation you have been in where someone has meant more than what they said in their use of language. For example, you may have asked someone a favour and not got a direct answer from them. How would the other person have expected you to work out their answer to your request? Or perhaps someone wanted to complain to you about something but thought it wouldn't be polite to do this directly. How did they do this indirectly, yet still feel sure you would get the point of what they are saying?

3. Think of rules of communication that people seem to follow when they are using language. For example what are some of the rules that students follow when talking to their teachers? Do they use a typical level of formality and typical forms of address (such as 'Sir', or 'Miss') when they speak to their teachers? Are there typical topics they talk to their teachers

about, and some topics they do not talk about? Are there typical ways they start and end a conversation with a teacher? Do some of these depend on the setting in which the conversation takes place, such as in a classroom, or in the teacher's office?

4. Think of some of the kinds of spoken or written discourse that you participate in, such as lunchtime conversations with your friends, tutorial discussions with other students, or email messages to friends. What are some of the characteristic ways in which you interact in this kind of situation? How do you typically express yourself in these situations? Is the way in which you communicate the same or different in each of these situations? Why do you think this is the case?

1.6 Directions for further reading

Cameron, D. (2001), *Working with Spoken Discourse*. London: Sage. Chapter 1. What is discourse and why analyse it?
While the focus of Cameron's book is on spoken discourse, it covers many issues that are of equal relevance to the analysis of written discourse. Cameron's first chapter discusses meanings of the term 'discourse' and goals and purposes in analysing discourse. The later part of this chapter talks about how social reality is 'discursively constructed' as people talk about things using the ways of speaking (or discourses) that they have access to.

Celce-Murcia, M. and Olshtain, E. (2000), *Discourse and Context in Language Teaching. A Guide for Language Teachers*. Cambridge: Cambridge University Press. Chapter 1. Introduction to discourse analysis
Celce-Murcia and Olshtain's book discusses discourse analysis and its importance for language teaching and learning. The chapter includes a framework for the processing and production of spoken and written discourse, a pedagogical perspective on communicative competence, and an overview of the authors' discourse approach to language teaching.

Jaworski, A. and Coupland, N. (1999), 'Introduction: perspectives on discourse analysis', in A. Jaworski and N. Coupland (eds), *The Discourse Reader*. London: Routledge.
Jaworski and Coupland's introduction to their book provides further details on a number of topics that have been presented in this chapter. This includes definitions of the term 'discourse', traditions in the

analysis of discourse, speech act theory and pragmatics, conversation analysis, the social constructionist view of discourse analysis and critical discourse analysis. Strengths and limitations of discourse studies are also discussed.

Riggenbach, H. (1999), *Discourse Analysis in the Language Classroom.* Volume 1: The Spoken Language. Ann Arbor: University of Michigan Press. Chapter 1. Overview: Discourse analysis in the language classroom.

Riggenbach's book provides many practical examples of how discourse analysis can be used in language learning classrooms. The introductory chapter to her book outlines the theoretical background to her book, covering a number of key topics in the analysis of spoken and written discourse. Riggenbach discusses what discourse analysis means for language teaching in terms of methodology, materials development and syllabus design.

2 Discourse and society

The previous chapter discussed the social-situatedness of discourse; that is, that spoken and written discourse occurs in particular social and cultural settings and is used and understood in different ways in different social and cultural settings. This chapter will discuss, in more detail, important aspects of the social and cultural settings of spoken and written discourse. It will start with a discussion of the notion of *discourse community* and the related notion of *speech community*. Both of these have an influence on what we say and how we say it. They also influence the *language variety* we choose to use as we speak or write in the setting we are in. Other factors which affect our use of language are the *social class* we are a member of (or the social class of the people we are communicating with) as well as the *social networks* we are part of. Within these social groups and social networks, there are various ways we express our *social identity* through discourse. One of the identities we express is our *gendered identity*. This is a topic that has been discussed at great length (and in changing ways) in the area of discourse analysis, and along with *discourse and identity*, is discussed in this chapter. The issue of *ideology and discourse*, a further important topic in the area of discourse analysis, is also discussed in this chapter.

2.1 Discourse communities and speech communities

A key notion in the area of discourse analysis is the concept of *discourse community* (see box below for definition). Swales (1990) provides a set of characteristics for identifying a group of people as members of a particular discourse community. The group must have some set of shared common goals, some mechanisms for communication, and some way of providing the exchange of information amongst its members. The community must have its own particular genres, its own set of specialized terminology and vocabulary, and a high level of expertise in its particular area. These goals may be formally agreed upon (as in the case of clubs and associations) 'or they may be more tacit' (Swales 1990: 24). The ways in which people communicate with each other and exchange information will vary according to the group. This might include meetings, newsletters, casual conversations or a range of other types of written and/or spoken communication. That is, the discourse community will have particular ways of communicating with each other and ways of getting things done that have developed through time. There will also be a threshold level of expertise in the use of the genres the discourse community uses for its communications for someone to be considered a member of that community.

A *discourse community* is a group of people who share some kind of activity such as members of a club or association who have regular meetings, or a group of students who go to classes at the same university. Members of a discourse community have particular ways of communicating with each other. They generally have shared goals and may have shared values and beliefs. A person is often a member of more than one discourse community. Someone may be a university student, a member of a community volunteer organization and a member of a church group, for example. The ways in which they communicate in each of these groups, and the values and beliefs that are most prominent in each of these groups may vary. There may also be discourse communities within discourse communities. Academic departments, for example, may differ in the ways that they do things and the beliefs and values that they hold, as indeed may other parts of the university.

A telephone call centre is an example of a discourse community. Cameron's (2000) study of telephone call centres in the UK suggests what some of the characteristics of this kind of discourse community might be. She found, for example, that the telephone operators in the call centres she examined were trained to communicate with customers on the phone in very particular ways. They were trained to answer the phone 'with a smile in their voice'. They were asked to pay attention to the pitch of their voice so that they conveyed a sense of confidence and sincerity in what they said. They were required to talk neither too loudly nor too quietly. They were trained not to drag out what they said, nor to speed through what they were saying. They were also required to provide sufficient feedback to their callers so that the callers knew they had been understood.

Call centre workers also have common goals, that of providing the service or making the sales the centre is set up for, common ways of sharing information amongst telephone workers, their own particular service call genres, and their own terminology and vocabulary for the product or service they are dealing with. There is also a specific level of expertise required for successful call centre workers, both in the knowledge of the product or service, and in the way call centre workers deal with their callers. New workers may be hired for a probationary period, for example, until it is clear that they have met the threshold level of performance required to be members of the particular call centre discourse community. If they do not meet this threshold level, their position with the company may be terminated.

People do, however, have different degrees of membership of discourse communities. That is, discourse communities may consist of close-knit networks of members such as writers of poetry and their readers, or loose-knit groups of members such as advertising producers, consumers and contributors to online discussion boards. Discourse communities may also be made up of several overlapping groups of people. People, further, may be (and normally are) members of more than just the one single discourse community. A person, thus, may be a call centre operator, a member of a poetry group, a member of school parent–teacher group and contributor to an online discussion board. A person may also have to operate in a number of different roles in the same discourse community. For example, a person may be working towards a doctoral degree in one part of a university and in another part of the university be a new (or indeed long-standing)

25

member of academic staff. The 'ways of belonging' may be quite different in each of these parts of the discourse community, as may be the genres that people use and the social relations within the different parts of the discourse community.

Discourse communities also interact with wider *speech communities*. For example, the academic discourse community of students and academics also interacts with the wider speech community of the town or city in which the academic institution is located (Swales 1993). It is for these reasons that some people prefer the term *communities of practice* (Wenger 1998; Barton and Tusting 2005) to the term 'discourse community'.

The notion of discourse community is not, however, as straightforward a concept as it might seem. There are often discourse communities within discourse communities. Swales' (1998) book *Other Floors, Other Voices* shows this well. Swales carried out a study of the building in which he was working at the time at the University of Michigan. He worked on the top floor of a small university building. The other floors were occupied by the computing resource site and a herbarium. He looked at the kinds of activities people working on each floor were engaged in and the kinds of texts they wrote. He also interviewed members of staff to get an understanding of why they wrote the kinds of texts they did. He found that people on each floor wrote quite different texts and were an example of a discourse community of their own. Swales proposes the notion of *place discourse community* to account for this kind of situation.

Devitt (2004: 42–4) adds to this discussion by proposing three types of groups of language user: *communities, collectives* and *networks*. Communities are 'groups of people who share substantial amounts of time together in common endeavors', such as a group of people who all work in the same office. Collectives are groups of people that 'form around a single repeated interest, without the frequency or intensity of contact of a community', such as people who are members of a bee-keeping group, or voluntary members of a community telephone advice service. Networks are groups of people that are not as tightly knit as speech communities with connections being made by one person 'who knows another person, who knows another person', such as connections that are made through email messages sent and received by people who may never have (or never will) met each other, but are participating in a common discourse.

2.2 Speech communities and spoken and written discourse

The term *speech community* is broader than the term discourse community. It is also important for the discussions of spoken and written discourse. A speech community, in general linguistics, refers to any group of people that speak the same language, such as French, English or German, etc. Sociolinguists, however, prefer to use the term speech community in a narrower sense to refer to people who not only use the same language, repertoire or varieties of a language, but who also have the opportunity to interact with each other (Spolsky 1998). As Spolsky (1998: 25) puts it:

> There is no theoretical limitation on the location and size of a speech community, which is in practice defined by its sharing a set of language varieties (its repertoire) and a set of norms for using them.

It is not essential, however, that all members of the speech community know and use all of these languages or language varieties. They will, however, 'recognise the conditions under which other members of the community believe it is appropriate to use each of them' (Spolsky 1998: 25). In a city such as Shanghai, for example, most local Chinese will know and use standard Mandarin. People who were born and grew up in Shanghai will also most likely know and speak Shanghainese as well, the local dialect of Shanghai, and know where and when to use this dialect. In some settings Mandarin may be more appropriate and in others Shanghainese. Members of the speech community will know this, even if they vary in their command of the different languages or language varieties. The notion of speech community, then, is broader than that of discourse communities. It includes discourse communities and the repertoire and varieties of languages that members of the speech community use to interact with each other.

The notion of speech communities is important for the effective use of spoken and written discourse. Sometimes communication may only succeed when speakers recognize (or believe) that they are part of the same speech community. The globalization of call centres has brought this particularly into focus. Japan, for example, recently sent some of its call centres offshore into parts of China where there are numbers of fluent second language speakers of Japanese. Callers from Japan did not realize, however, that they were speaking to someone in China. When they realized this, through, for example, a mistake in the use of honorifics, misunderstandings and even arguments occurred.

Some call centres in China have tried to overcome this problem by employing young Japanese to work in their call centres so that Japanese callers will think they are speaking to someone in the same country and, in turn, the same speech community (Aoki 2005). Call centres in India also have a similar problem when someone calls from the US, for example, not believing they are speaking to an American call centre operator. Some call centres in India, for example, now have the weather and US sports results displayed on TV monitors for the call centre workers to refer to as they take their calls to give the impression that callers are speaking to someone from their own speech community.

i. Defining a speech community

There are a number of factors which help to define a speech community other than just language. These might include social, geographical, cultural, political and ethnic factors, race, age and gender. Members of a speech community may share a particular set of norms for communication which reflect certain views on linguistic behaviour such as what is the most prestigious variety of the language in the particular setting, even if not all members of the community actually are able to use this variety. A person, further, may be a member of more than the one speech community (as they may be members of more than the one discourse community). They may switch from identifying with one speech community to another, 'even in the course of a single utterance' (Wardhaugh 1998: 124).

Speakers may not always, however, be full members of a particular speech community, just as they may not be full members of a discourse community. In a second language setting, for example, a speaker may participate, only to a certain degree, in the target speech community. The degree to which this occurs may be due to factors such as age of entry into the speech community, the speech community's attitudes and expectations towards the place of second language speakers in the speech community or other factors such as educational or occupational opportunities, or limitations, in the particular speech community. It may also depend on a person's degree of proficiency in the second language and the extent to which they want (or need) to be part of the second language speech community.

If, for example, I am a visiting professor for a semester at a Japanese university and have been invited to give classes in English, I may not need a lot of Japanese to survive for the period of time that I am there. I may decide to learn some Japanese phrases such as greetings and how to say thank you so I can establish some kind of social relationship with the Japanese staff that are looking after me and people I deal with in shops. If I have more complex needs, such as finding out the room I need to teach in and how to order stationery, I may need to rely on an English-speaking Japanese student or a member of staff that has been assigned to me to help with this sort of thing. In this case, I am only a very peripheral member of the local speech community, even though I am surrounded by it. This has important implications for the extent to which I will learn (or not) the genres of the institution I am working in; that is, the extent to which I need (and am expected) to participate in its genres. As a visiting professor, I am most likely not expected to attend meetings of the department I am working in. If I were working as a regular member of staff, however, I would be expected to attend and participate in departmental meetings (which most likely will be held in Japanese). My learning and genre needs, and my ability to participate in the spoken and written discourses of the speech and discourse community then would be quite different.

Speech communities, further, may be quite separate from each other or they may overlap or intersect with each other. Speakers often have a *repertoire* of social identities (see 'Discourse and identity' below) and speech community memberships each of which is associated with particular kinds of verbal and non-verbal expression (Wardhaugh 1998). As Saville-Troike (1996: 357) argues, which speech community or speech communities 'individuals orient themselves to at any given moment – which set of social and communicative rules they use – is part of the strategy of communication.' Indeed, much linguistic behaviour can be explained in terms of the various *social networks* (Milroy 1987) we are part of and the *communicative repertoire* or range of languages, language varieties, styles and registers we draw on when we participate in the spoken and written discourse of these networks.

2.3 Discourse and language choice

Speakers, then, often have a repertoire of social identities and discourse community memberships. They may also have a *linguistic repertoire* that they draw on for their linguistic interactions. That is, they may have a number of languages or language varieties they use to interact in in their particular communities. This kind of situation is common in many parts of the world. The choice of language or language variety may be determined by the domain the language is being used in, such as with family, among friends, and in religious, educational and employment settings. Social factors such as who we are speaking to, the social context of the interaction, the topic, function and goal of the interaction, social distance between speakers, the formality of the setting or type of interaction and the status of each of the speakers are also important for accounting for the language choice that a person makes in these kinds of settings (Holmes 2001).

The use of slang among teenagers in Singapore illustrates a deliberate choice in the use of a language variety to communicate with each other as well as to signal a particular group membership. In an article in the Singapore *Sunday Times* titled 'So steady pom pi pi', Tan (2005) discusses how teenagers in Singapore use slang in their speech as a way of bonding with their friends as well as to ensure their conversations will remain private. For example, one Singaporean teenager coined the acronym 'CCG' to mean 'cute cute guy' so that she could talk about (very cute) boys to her friend without anyone else understanding what she was saying. Another coined the term 'CMI' to describe someone who 'cannot make it' or is not up to standard. The expression 'steady pom pi pi' (a play on the words for whistle in Mandarin and Hokkien) means someone that is always cool and ready for any situation. One teenager interviewed described the use of homemade slang as 'a group thing', saying that people who go around in the same circles will use the same type of slang so that others will not understand what they are saying. As Peter Tan from the National University of Singapore explains these groups 'mark themselves by the way they dress, the activities they share, their hairstyle, and of course, the way they talk' (Tan 2005: 38).

A speaker or writer may also be the speaker of a particular language variety but be using that variety to communicate with a wider speech community than just their own. The best seller *Eats, Shoots & Leaves* (Truss 2003), for example, is written in standard British English but is clearly not aimed at just the one single speech community. It has been a best-seller in the US, the UK and Australia, all of which are different speech communities. The BBC *Panorama* interview with Princess Diana (BBC 1995), equally, had more than a single speech community in mind as it was made. It was broadcast worldwide and achieved an audience of over 200 million people (Kurzon 1996), well beyond the speech community in which it was originally located. *Casablanca*, like most Hollywood films, had a much broader audience in mind than just the US when it was made even if, in its early days, the US market was its main focus. The HBO show *Sex and the City* equally, is aimed at a viewership of different speech communities around the world, even though the cast of the show, Carrie, Samantha, Miranda and Charlotte, are clearly members of the same speech community, residents of New York City.

2.4 Discourse, social class and social networks

A further factor which influences the use of spoken and written discourse is social class. Social class is, however, somewhat difficult to define as its identification can be somewhat subjective. Factors which may help with this include occupation, education, income, housing and its location (Labov 1966). Other factors which may help with social groupings might include religious affiliation, leisure time activities and membership of community organizations (Wardhaugh 1998).

A group of speakers may appear to be very similar in terms of social class membership, however, but differ considerably in their use of language as they interact in the social networks they belong to and the spoken and written genres used by those networks. Social networks may be based, for example, on kinship ties, religious affiliations, neighbourhood membership, employee relations and leisure time activities. Milroy and Milroy's (1978) study of social networks in Belfast showed social networks to be important influences on the use of language. They saw, in particular, the stronger and more closeknit the network, and the more solidarity within the network, the greater the influence on language use and the maintenance of language varieties. As Milroy and Milroy (1997: 60–1) explain:

> Social networks and social class represent different orders of generalization about social organization. Class accounts for the hierarchical structure of society ..., whereas network deals with the dimension of solidarity at the level of the individual and his or her everyday contacts.

Each of these has an impact on how speakers represent themselves to each other in their use of spoken and written discourse. As Cameron and Kulick (2003: 11) observe, the use of language, 'whatever else it accomplishes, is an "act of identity", a means whereby people convey to one another what kinds of people they are'. These identities, further, are not 'natural'; they are social constructions. As speakers construct their gendered identities in interaction (Holmes 1997), so too do they construct their social (and other) identities.

2.5 Discourse and gender

Early work in the analysis of gender and discourse looked at the relationship between the use of language and the biological category of *sex*. This has now moved to an examination of the ways language is used in relation to the social category, or rather the *socially constructed* category, of *gender*. As Weatherall (2002: 102) explains gender 'is not just a natural and inevitable consequence of one's sex.' It is, rather, 'part of the routine, ongoing work of everyday, mundane, social interaction'; that is, 'the product of social practice' (Eckert and McConnell-Ginet 2003: 5). As Swann (2002: 47) has pointed out:

> gender as a social category has come to be seen as highly fluid, or less well defined than it once appeared. In line with gender theory more generally, researchers interested in language and gender have focussed increasingly on plurality and diversity amongst female and male language users, and on gender as performativity – something that is 'done' in context, rather than a fixed attribute.

Simone de Beauvoir famously said 'one is not born, but rather becomes a woman'. *Performativity* is based on the view that in saying something, we do, or 'become' it. A person learns, for example, how to do and, in turn 'display', being a woman in a particular social setting, of a particular social class. People perform particular identities through their use of language and other ways of expressing themselves in their interactions with each other. Mostly, this is done unconsciously as we 'repeat acts' such as gestures, movement and ways of using language that signify, or *index* a particular identity. These acts are not, however, natural nor are they part of the essential attributes of a person. They are part of what people acquire in their interactions with each other.

In her book *Language and Women's Place* Lakoff (1975) proposed what she called 'women's language'; that is, a use of language that is different from 'men's language' or, rather, what she termed 'neutral language'. This language, she argued, included features such as the use of overly polite forms, the use of question tags, rising intonation in declaratives, the avoidance of expletives, a greater use of diminutives and euphemisms, the use of more hedges and mitigating devices, more indirectness and the use of particular vocabulary items such as 'adorable,' 'charming' and 'sweet' (women's language) versus 'great', 'terrific' and 'cool' (neutral language). This use of language, she argued, made women's language tentative and, coupled with the use of demeaning and trivializing terms for women, works to keep women in their place in society. These differences, she argued, were the result of, and reinforced, men's dominance over women.

Lakoff's book led to two separate views of women's language, the *dominance* approach and the *difference* (or cultural) approach. Spender's (1980) *Man Made Language* is an example of the dominance approach which sees differences in the use of language as a result of men's domination over women. This view focuses on the distribution of power in society and argues that women's language reflects women's subordinate position in society and persists to keep them in that position (Eckert and McConnell-Ginet 2003). Participants in discourse, in this view, collude in sustaining and perpetuating male dominance and female oppression in society. West and Zimmerman (1983), for example, argued that men deny equal status to women in conversation and that linguistic gestures of power, although they might seem minor if viewed on their own, are an integral part of women's placement in the social scheme of things. These gestures, they argue, remind women, on a daily basis, of their subordinate position in society. That is, they are a way of *doing* power.

Tannen's (1990) *You Just Don't Understand* is an example of the difference approach. Tannen argued that boys and girls live in different subcultures in the way that people from different social and ethic backgrounds might be described as being part of different subcultures. As a consequence boys and girls grow up learning different ways of using language and communicating with people in other cultural groups (for example, men). Since then other researchers have argued that such a distinction is too simplistic and that power and subcultural factors are not in an either/or relationship with each other. Uchida (1992) and Lakoff (1990) in her more recent work, argue that gender, power and subculture are intertwined (Uchida) and inseparable (Lakoff) and that dominance and difference work together to simultaneously compose the construct of gender.

In a critique of both the dominance and difference views of language and gender, Cameron (1998) argues that expressions of gender and power are always context-specific and need to be understood in relation to who the person is speaking to, 'from what position and for what purpose' (Cameron 1998: 451); that is, what the use of language means in terms of the relationship between the speakers in the particular situation in which the interaction occurs. We need, then, a view of gender and discourse that looks at how people, in particular social and cultural interactions, do gender through their use of language.

Many of the conversations in the TV show *Sex and the City* are examples of the way the lead characters, through their use of language, do gender. In the following extract, Miranda asks Carrie why she accepted her boyfriend's proposal of marriage. In her response, Carrie both enacts and affirms, through her use of language, her gendered identity, that of a woman who, because she loves her boyfriend, has to accept his proposal of marriage:

> Miranda: I'm going to ask you an unpleasant question now. Why did you ever say yes?
> Carrie: Because I love him ... a man you love kneels in the street, and offers you a ring. You say yes. That is what you do.
>
> (Change of a Dress, 4: 15)

The discussion of how men and women speak, and what they do as they speak, has also been extended to how people speak about men and women. Holmes (2004), for example, compared the use of the terms *woman* and *lady* and found that the social significance of these terms has changed over the last 30 years. She found *woman*, for example, has moved from being marked as impolite at the time Lakoff was writing to a situation where this is no longer the case (although *woman* is more frequently used in written British English than in spoken British English). She also found that while *lady/ladies* may be used as a politeness marker in formal settings (as it was becoming at the time Lakoff was writing), nowadays, in informal settings, it is also used to trivialize and patronize.

As Holmes (2004: 156) argues, language choices are often enactments of who's in charge and 'whose values will prevail.' Richardson's (2000) study of the use of disparaging language and sexually humiliating formulae by male members of a cricket club to talk about women provides an example of this. Richardson found, as did Cameron (1999) in her study of talk between fraternity brothers in the US, that the men in her study used their talk, and the traditional 'women only' discourse of gossip, to create solidarity as a group, and to construct their heterosexual masculinity.

Mean's (2001) study of male football referees' use of language with men's and women's football teams shows a similar example of the use of language to 'do gender,' and to confirm masculine identity. She talks about sporting as a male category where values such as power and aggressiveness are highly valued, like in a form of combat. She found speed, loud talk and shouting to be ways in which these values were expressed in the male referee's language. She also found the male referees used fast continuous talk in a way that never occurred in women's football matches. The following extract, by a male referee, is an example of this. In this extract louder talk is in italics and shouting is in capitals. (.) represents a pause of less than a second.

> R: go *on* lads (.) keep going keep going keep going OH KEEP GOING LADS KEEP GOING LADS JUST INSIDE CARRY ON (.) INSIDE (.) KEEP GOING (.) (whistle blown) (.) go on play lads (.) play lads (.) keep going (.) right here mate (.) play lads.
>
> (Mean 2001: 795)

34

The male referees in Mean's data also frequently referred to the male players with address terms such as 'lads', 'fellas' and 'mates' as a way of showing group membership and solidarity with them. None of the female referees used address terms in this way.

Davies' (2003a) study of classroom storytelling activities shows further examples of gendered discourse. The girls in her study used what she calls 'friendship talk' in their storytelling as they collaborated and exchanged opinions and ideas about the stories they were telling. They worked with each other in a collaborative way, forming learning allegiances with each other as they did this. The boys, on the other hand, had to choose whether they would join in the 'macho discourse' of the young male group or not, and so be ostracized from the group. The boys used the word 'gay', for example, to defame boys they did not see as being part of the group (whether they were gay or not) and as a way of doing male 'macho gender'. Boys who wanted to be part of the group adjusted their behaviour so the term 'gay' would not be directed at them.

Hall's (1995) study of the use of language by telephone sex workers in the US provides a further example of how speakers create gendered identities through their use of language. She found many of the workers used language similar to Lakoff's' women's language as they talked to their clients on the phone. Not all of the sex workers in Hall's study were heterosexual, although this was the persona they were projecting, nor were they all female. One was a male Mexican American who took pride in being able to 'replicate' Asian, Latina and Black women's personas though his use of accent, intonation, voice quality and choice of vocabulary. The workers, thus, used 'gendered styles to construct sexual meaning' (Cameron and Kulick 2003: 59).

Gender, then, is 'not something a person "has", but something that a person does' (Cameron 2005a: 49). Gender (and in turn other identities) is not a result of who people (already) are but a result of, among other things, the way they talk and what they do.

As Eckert and McConnell-Ginet (2003: 4) argue:

> gender doesn't just exist, but is continually produced, reproduced, and indeed changed through people's performance of gendered acts, as they project their own claimed gender identities, ratify or challenge other's identities, and in various ways support or challenge systems of gender relations and privilege.

Sex and the City provides many examples of the lead characters *doing gender identity* of a certain kind (among other things, independent successful professional New York City women of a certain age and certain social class) not only in the way they talk, but also in the way they dress, and the way they behave as they speak to each other, their lovers and their friends. What to some people, then, may seem natural in their interactions is a result of what Butler (1990: 33) calls 'a set of repeated acts' and a 'repeated stylisation of the body'. These gendered identities are then 'reaffirmed and publicly displayed by repeatedly performing particular acts' (Cameron 1999: 444) in accordance with historically and socially constructed cultural norms which define (this particular view of) femininity.

Gender identity then is a complex construction. All levels of language and discourse, as well as aspects of nonverbal and other kinds of behaviour are involved in doing gender (Butler 2004). Gender, further, interacts with other factors such as social class and ethnicity. As Holmes observes:

> gender is only one part of a person's social identity, and it is an aspect which will be more or less salient in different contexts. In some contexts, for example, it may be more important to emphasise one's professional expertise, one's ethnic identity, or one's age than one's gender.

> (Holmes 1997: 9)

As Cameron and Kulick (2003: 57) argue, 'the relationship between language and gender is almost always indirect, mediated by something else'. The ways that people speak are, in the first instance, associated with particular roles, activities and personality traits, such as being a mother, gossiping and being modest (Cameron and Kulick 2003). The extent to which these roles, activities and personality traits become associated in a particular culture with being *gendered* lead to these ways of speaking pointing to, or *indexing* a particular gender in the same way that particular ways of speaking may point to, or index, a person's social class or ethnic identity (Cameron and Kulick 2003).

In some cases, a person's different identities may be difficult to separate. As Cameron and Kulick (2003: 58) point out:

> The actual balance between them is not determined in advance by some general principle, but has to be negotiated in specific situations, since meaning is not only in the language itself, but also in the context where language is used by particular speakers for particular purposes.

A person, then, will have a *multiplicity of identities* or *personae* (Eckert 2002) which may be at play, all at the same time, at different levels of prominence. They may not all be equally salient at a particular moment (Sunderland and Litosseliti 2002). Rather, one or more of these identities may be foregrounded at different points in time and for different (conscious or unconscious) reasons. Cameron's (2000) study of the use of language in telephone call centres in the UK is an example of this. Here there is a mix of both professional and gendered identities. Cameron talks about a process of styling the worker where male and female workers are trained to use what is popularly thought of as a feminine communication style and expressive intonation to project rapport and to establish empathy with their callers. The worker's supervisors, managers and 'mystery outside callers' in some cases use checklists as they listen to the workers' calls to ensure the training they have been given is producing a particular gendered style of speech.

The point here, then, is that:

> no way of speaking has only one potential meaning: the meanings it conveys in one context are not necessarily the same ones it conveys in another, and it may also acquire new meanings over time.
>
> (Cameron and Kulick 2003: 57)

People, further, '*do* perform gender differently in different contexts, and do sometimes behave in ways we would normally associate with the "other" gender' (Cameron 1999: 445) such as the case of the workers in Cameron's call centre study and the telephone sex workers in Hall's (1995) study.

2.6 Discourse and sexuality

The relationship between language and sexuality further complicates the topic of gender and discourse by adding the notion of *desire* to the discussion. While gender is something that is socially constructed, sexuality has a much more unconscious basis, based in the notion of desire; that is, a person's intimate desire for connection to others that exceeds their conscious control (Cameron and Kulick 2003). The lead characters' conversations about men in *Sex and the City*, for example, are guided by their sexual desire in just the same way as a personal ad on a gay website is guided by the gay man's desire for intimate connection with another man. So while Carrie and her friends' conversations index their gender, it is their unconscious desire that motivates their desire for intimate connections with men, and heterosexual men in general.

A person may, however, perform a certain identity in their conversation, as Carrie and her friends do in *Sex and the City*, where this may not, in fact, be the case. Rock Hudson, for example, did this famously in many of his movie roles (and in the performance of his public persona) where he 'played the straight man', displaying and maintaining male heterosexuality in his discourse (Kiesling 2002).

Jude Law gives a similar simulated gendered performance in the film *Closer* when he has online sex with Julia Roberts' future boyfriend. Masquerading as a heterosexual woman, Jude Law simulates (his view of) a woman having cybersex in an Internet chat room. The character at the other end of the line, played by Clive Owen, believes Jude Law's performance to the extent that he makes a date to meet his online sex object the next day, with the view of going to a hotel and having sex with 'her'.

Discussions of language and sexuality, then, take us beyond discussions of language and gender and into the world of language and desire. These desires, further:

> are not simply private, internal phenomena but are produced and expressed – or not expressed – in social interaction, using shared and conventionalised linguistic resources.
>
> (Cameron and Kulick 2003: 125)

Carrie and her friends do just this in *Sex and the City*. The meanings that they express are not just the result of their intentions, but are shaped by forces they 'have no conscious awareness of, let alone willed control over' (Cameron and Kulick 2003: 125). The woman at the bar in *Casablanca* is driven in the same way for intimate connection with Rick, as Carrie and her friends are in their relations with the men they meet throughout the show. Thus, whereas gendered identities may be socially inducted (and capable of being simulated or, indeed, faked as we have seen above), sexual desires are not, even though these desires may be displayed in linguistically recognizable (and regularly repeated) ways (Cameron and Kulick 2003).

2.7 Discourse and identity

A person may have a number of *identities*, each of which is more important at different points in time. They may have an identity as a woman, an identity as a mother, an identity as someone's partner and an identity as an office worker, for example. The ways in which people display their identities includes the way they use language and the way they interact with people. Identities are not natural, however. They are constructed, in large part, through the use of discourse. Identity, further, is not something that is fixed and remains the same throughout a person's life. It is something that is constantly constructed and reconstructed as people interact with each other. Part of having a

Come back to ethnolinguistic identity

certain identity is that it is recognized by other people. Identity, thus, is a two-way construction.

The earliest studies into the relationship between language and identity were based on a variationist perspective; that is, they looked at the relationship between social variables such as social class in terms of variation in the use of linguistic variables such as certain features of pronunciation, or the use of non-standard grammar. More recent work, however, has taken a *poststructural* perspective on language and identity, seeing identity 'as something that is in constant process' (Swann, *et al* 2004: 140–1) arguing that it is through language, or rather through discourse, that identity is principally forged.

The information a person 'gives off' about themself, and in turn, their identity, depends very much on the context, occasion and purpose of the discourse. It also depends on the 'space' and 'place' of the interaction (Blommaert 2005). Cameron (1999) gives an example of this in her discussion of how a group of male US college students construct heterosexual masculinity through the talk that they engage in while watching TV in their college dorm. Richardson (2000) shows something similar in her analysis of the language male cricket club members use to talk about women in the cricket club newsletter they contribute to. In both these studies the men involved perform and enact particular gendered (and sexual) identities which for that moment in time are, for them, socially salient.

It is not just through the performance of identities that they are created, however. It is also by the fact that they are recognized by other participants in the interactions. In Blommaert's (2005: 205) words, 'a lot of what happens in the field of identity is done by others, not by oneself'. In some cases this identity may only be temporary. Equally '[n]ot every identity will have the same range or scope' (Blommaert 2005: 211) nor be the same across time and physical space. As Blommaert says, people speak both in and from a place. Place, he argues 'defines people, both in their eyes and in the eyes of others' (Blommaert 2005: 223) as well as attributes certain values to their interactions. People can (and do) he argues, shift places 'frequently and delicately, and each time, in very minimal ways, express different identities' (Blommaert 2005: 224).

Thomas (2000, 2004) has explored the issues of language and identity in online chat environments, a very particular place and space. With a focus on adolescent 'cybergirls', she examines how girls use words and images to establish online identities which reflect both their fantasies and their desires in this particular setting. She does an analysis of both the words and the images that they use to create their identities. In their online environment, the cybergirls interacted with words, symbols for words, as well as various other symbols such as emoticons and 'avatars' (visual characters which express a certain identity) in order to establish their online identities. One of her participants, Violetta, talked about how she wrote online to convey a particular persona:

> Violetta: i'd have whole typing styles for people. like, if i were trying to trick someone i knew into thinking i was someone else, i'd type a lot differently than i do normally. a person's typing style can give them away like their voice does. (Thomas 2004: 367)

Thomas found that 'the girls who gain and exercise power in their online worlds are those who know how to use and manipulate words, images and technology' (Thomas 2004: 359). Some of what they did online she found reflected the kind of 'learned social accomplishments' that researchers in the area of language and gender have referred to. Some of what they did, however, reflected fantasies they had about themselves and their desired personae, the online medium giving them a safe and private place to establish these fantasized-about identities.

The identities that people establish online, then, provide an interesting example of how people create identities through their use of language (and other visual devices) that may, in some cases, be separate and distinct from their offline identity. Each of these identities are part of the ongoing process of establishing who we are, and who we want (at least at certain times) to be. It is for this reason that authors such as Thurlow *et al* (2004) prefer to talk about *identity online* rather than *online identity*. Some people communicating online may, indeed, change essential characteristics about themselves (such as their age, ethnicity, race or physical appearance) in order to present an identity online that will be more appealing to the audience they are wanting to communicate with. A Taiwanese user of online chat rooms in Tsang's (2000) study, for example, found he had more success in getting people to chat with him if he said he was Caucasian, rather than Chinese.

i. Identity and casual conversation

Many of the interactions in *Sex and the City* are examples of the use of discourse to create, express and establish social (and other) identities. A common way in which the characters in the show do this is through their use of the genre casual conversation. As Eggins and Slade (1997: 6) argue:

> Despite its sometimes aimless appearance and apparently trivial content, casual conversation is, in fact, a highly structured, functionally motivated, semantic activity. Motivated by interpersonal needs continually to establish who we are, how we relate to others, and what we think of how the world is, casual conversation is a critical linguistic site for the negotiation of such important dimensions of our social identity as gender, generational location, sexuality, social class membership, ethnicity, and subcultural and group affiliations.

Eggins and Slade argue that people do not engage in casual conversations just to 'kill time', but rather to negotiate social identities as well as to negotiate, clarify and extend interpersonal relations. As they put it:

> The apparent triviality of casual conversation disguises the significant interpersonal work it achieves as interactants enact and confirm social identities and relations.
>
> (Eggins and Slade 1997: 16)

They describe this as the central paradox of casual conversation. As they argue, casual conversation is the type of talk in which people feel most relaxed, most spontaneous and most themselves, 'yet casual conversation is a critical site for the social construction of reality'. Casual conversations do a number of things which are crucial to discussions of language and identity. They establish solidarity 'through the confirmation of similarities', and they assert autonomy 'through the exploration of differences' (Eggins and Slade 1997: 16).

The way in which language is used in casual conversations, like all spoken interactions, is influenced by the relationship between the people speaking, the frequency with which they come into contact with each other, the degree of involvement they have with each other, and their sense of affiliation for each other. In the case of *Sex and the City*, each of the four female characters knows each other extremely well. Although they are the best of friends, they are each quite different and from quite diverse backgrounds. As they meet together, they share their experiences and negotiate their understandings of (among other things) life, love, men and sex. As Carrie and her friends talk, they construct themselves in a way which signifies (their view of) desirable Western women, of a certain social class, in a certain physical and social setting through their use of the genre casual conversation.

Understanding the social and cultural context of the *Sex and the City* conversations is critical to understanding the identities that are

[handwritten marginal note: Matrix language]

being expressed and negotiated in many of the conversations. What to some people may seem natural in their interactions is a result of Butler's (2004) 'sets of repeated acts' and 'repeated stylisations of the body'; that is, the acts that they repeatedly perform which reaffirm and publicly display their views of themselves, and in turn their social identities as, among other things, independent successful professional New York City women of a certain age and certain social class.

When we speak (or write), then, we are telling other people 'something about ourselves' (Cameron 2001: 170) and relating to people in particular ways. Identity, thus, is a joint, two-way production. We may do this in a more or less active way (Sunderland and Litosseliti 2002) such as when we unconsciously perform a particular socially inducted identity, such as Carrie and her friends do in *Sex and the City*, or consciously, as the boys who wanted to be part of the group did in Davies' (2003a) study of storytelling events.

Identity, then, is not just a matter of using language in a way that reflects a particular identity. It is rather a socially-constructed self that people continually co-construct and reconstruct in their interactions with each other. This leads to different ways of doing identity with different people in different situations. A person's identity then:

> is not something fixed, stable and unitary that they acquire early in life and possess forever afterwards. Rather identity is shifting and multiple, something people are continually constructing and reconstructing in their encounters with each other in the world.
>
> (Cameron 2001: 170)

Identity is a 'negotiated experience' in which we 'define who we are by the way we experience our selves ... as well as by the ways we and others reify our selves' (Wenger 1998: 149). Identities are not fixed, but constantly being reconstructed and negotiated through the ways we do things and ways of belonging (or not) to a group (Casanave 2002). Our identities are further developed as we increase our participation in particular communities of practice. These identities, further, are based on shared sets of values, agreed-upon cultural understandings and the ideologies which underlie our use of spoken and written discourse.

ii. Identity and written academic discourse

Identity is as much an issue in written discourse as it is in spoken discourse. This is particularly the case in student academic writing. Hyland (2002c) discusses the view that is often presented to students that academic writing is faceless, impersonal discourse. Students are told, he says, 'to leave their personalities at the door' when they write and not use personal pronouns such as 'I' which show what is being said is the student's view or place in things. As Hyland (2002c: 352) argues, 'almost everything we write says something about us and the sort of relationship that we want to set up with our readers'. Indeed, one of the ways that expert academic writers do this, in some academic disciplines at least, is through the use of the pronoun 'I'.

Establishing writer identity is, however, something that is often difficult for second language writers. This is often complicated by students bringing a different writer 'voice' from their first language setting to the second language writing situation (Fox 1994). Students may come from backgrounds where they have considerable standing in their field of study and find it difficult to be told they need to take on the voice of a novice academic writer, and hide their point of view, as they write in their second language. Hirvela and Belcher (2001) argue that teachers need to know more about the ways students present themselves in their first language writing, and about their first language and culture identities, so they can help students deal with the issue of identity in their second language writing.

Prince (2000) carried out a study which examined just this issue. Her interest was in the ways in which second language thesis writers might be influenced (or not) by their experience of having written a thesis in their first language and culture. She looked at the experiences of a group of Chinese and Polish students, all of whom had written a thesis in their first language prior to writing a thesis in English. She found a major theme that emerged in her study was whether the students had to give up, or change, their personal identity in order to write a successful thesis in English. Prince tells how one of her Polish students, Ilona, fiercely fought to retain her personal and individual style of writing, but in the end found she had to give this away in order to pass. The Chinese students, on the other hand, did not have this experience and felt the way in which they presented themselves in their thesis was not dramatically different from how they had done this in Chinese.

Notwithstanding, all of Prince's students talked about the identity 'of being a non-English writer' that they had to deal with. Cadman (1997) also discusses this issue, arguing that the difficulty many second language students have with their writing goes far beyond being a non-English writer. A Chinese student in Cadman's study had exactly the same experience with her writing that Fox (1994) discusses. She found in her new writing environment that none of the expertise she brought with her was valued and she had no links with her past life that could help her succeed in the new academic setting.

Bartolome (1998: xiii) argues that learning to succeed in Western academic settings is not just a matter of language, but knowing the 'linguistically contextualised language' of the particular spoken and written discourses that are valued in the particular academic setting. Some students may choose to become part of this academic discourse and others may resist this. They may fear a loss of cultural identity, and not wish to be 'drowned' in the new academic culture (Prince 2000). Ilona, the Polish student in Prince's study, felt exactly this. She resisted rewriting her thesis because the thesis she was being asked to write did not reflect who she 'really was' and how she wanted to present her argument in the discourse. She wanted to wait to the very end of her thesis to reveal her findings, writing her thesis 'as a detective novel', as she described it. Revealing her findings any sooner, she felt, killed the excitement of the reading. She wanted to write a thesis with twists and turns, as she had done in Polish. She found, however, that she needed to revise her thesis so it would more closely fit the expectations of the readers of her text, the people that had been assigned to examine her thesis, in order to pass. She still asked at the end, however:

> For what reason I have to read the fifteen pages if I already know
> the answer? (Prince 2002: 76)

Ilona resisted then, as much as she could, the underlying values and ideologies that underlay the piece of writing that she was producing, a masters thesis in the field of engineering, written in an English-medium university. Her view of research was that it was something 'exciting, and should be presented as such, like the revealing of a mystery, a "closer and closer" progression towards an answer' (Prince 2000: 78).

As Casanave (2002: 23) argues in her book *Writing Games*, learning to belong to a community of practice can take time and a great deal of effort. It can be filled with tensions and conflict. As she points out:

> Newcomers inevitably feel the foreignness of unfamiliar practices,
> the unwieldiness of new forms and tools of communication, and
> relationships with more experienced practitioners that are not
> necessarily harmonious.

This is exactly what Ilona experienced as she struggled to write her thesis. Ilona found, as do many student writers, that the discourses and practices of the discipline in which she was writing was very different from what she had brought from her home culture and, unless she

44

revised her writing, would undermine her relationship with her readers (Hyland 2005a).

2.8 Discourse and ideology

The values and ideologies which underlie texts, such as the thesis that Ilona was writing, often tend to be 'hidden' rather than overtly stated. As Threadgold (1989) observes, texts are never ideology-free nor objective. Nor can they be separated from the social realities and processes they contribute to maintaining. For Threadgold, spoken and written genres are not just linguistic categories but 'among the very processes by which dominant ideologies are reproduced, transmitted and potentially changed' (1989: 107). In her view, a spoken or written genre is never just the reformulation of a linguistic model, but always the performance of a politically and historically significant process.

There are a number of ways in which ideology might be explored in a text. The analysis may start by looking at textual features in the text and move from there to explanation and interpretation of the analysis. This may include tracing underlying ideologies from the linguistic features of a text, unpacking particular biases and ideological presuppositions underlying the text and relating the text to other texts, and to readers' and speakers' own experiences and beliefs (Clark 1995).

One aspect that might be considered in this kind of analysis is the *framing* (Gee 2004; Blommaert 2005) of the text; that is, how the content of the text is presented, and the sort of angle or perspective the writer, or speaker, is taking. Closely related to framing is the notion of *foregrounding*; that is, what concepts and issues are emphasized, as well as what concepts or issues are played down or *backgrounded* (Huckin 1997) in the text. The following scene from *Sex and the City* is an example of this. Carrie had just discovered an engagement ring in her boyfriend, Aiden's, overnight bag. She then went into the kitchen and vomited. She is telling her friends about this incident:

Charlotte: You're getting engaged!
Carrie: I threw up. I saw the ring and I threw up. That's not
           normal.
Samantha: That's my reaction to marriage.
Miranda: What do you think you might do if he asks?
Carrie: I don't know.
Charlotte: Just say yessss!!!
Carrie: Well, it hasn't been long enough has it?
Charlotte: Trey and I got engaged after only a month.
Samantha: How long before you separated?

45

> Charlotte: We're together now and that's what matters. When it's right you just know.
> Samantha: Carrie doesn't know.
> Carrie: Carrie threw up.
> Samantha: So it might not be right ...   (Just Say Yes, 4: 12)

A key cultural value is foregrounded in this conversation: if a man asks a woman to marry him she should 'Just say yes' (the title of the episode). Other values are backgrounded, or rather omitted, such as Carrie's views on Aiden's occupation, ethnic background and social class, possibly because the audience of the show already knows this (not because, in this case, they are not relevant).

Equally important is what attitudes, points of view and values the text presupposes. A *presupposition* present in this conversation is that Aiden will formally propose to Carrie (which he later does). A further presupposition is that Aiden will ask her this directly and that she should give a direct response. This is very much an (English) culture-based assumption. Saville-Troike (2003), for example, discusses marriage proposals in Japanese showing that, in Japanese, a marriage proposal is not always directly stated and, if it is, it is not always directly responded to. An example of this is when the Japanese Crown Prince Naruhito proposed to his bride-to-be Masako (on a hunting trip). Masako did not accept the proposal immediately but took nearly three months to give a reply. When she did she said 'Will I really do?' and 'If I can be of any help to you, I will humbly accept'. The Crown Prince replied 'I will protect you throughout your life' (Asahi Newspaper 1993).

A further example of presupposition is the view expressed in the *Sex and the City* scene of marriage being based (among other things) in romantic love and desire. This is also a very culture-specific view of marriage. Farrer (2002) describes how this is only a recent phenomenon in China, for example, where marriage was, until recently, a family business, arranged by parents in accordance with social hierarchies, as Zhang in her (1986) book *Love Must Not be Forgotten* says, part of a mind-set passed down from feudal times. Arranged marriages (as opposed to 'love marriages') are still surprisingly popular on Japan. In earlier times, in Japan, as in China, marriage was a community-centred rather than a person-centred matter. Even today there is an Arranged Marriages Association in Japan which promotes the benefits of this kind of marriage (Davies and Ikeno 2002).

Recently, however, there has been a romantic revolution in China (Farrer 2002) with young urban people now expecting to be able to choose their own marriage partners and to marry for love. The award-winning movie *House of Flying Daggers* by the Chinese filmmaker Zhang Yimou (2005), for example, is a glorification of romantic love and desire, telling the story of three people who sacrifice everything for love. The overlying theme of this film suggests a change in the *social semiotic of desire* in present day Chinese society, in Eckert's (2002: 109) words, 'the most powerful force in the maintenance of gender order'.

A further presupposition underlying the *Sex and the City* conversation is the issue of who will propose to whom; that is, the *agency* of the action being discussed in the conversation. It is a clear assumption here that the man will propose to the woman, not the other way round. As independent as Carrie and her friends are, it is less likely that they would propose to a man (or that they would refuse him, should he ask). Even though the leading characters in the show take an active role in their pursuit of sex and many of the other things they want from life, it is the man who initiates the action and who has the most power in the situation. Carrie waits for Aiden to propose, not the other way round.

This, of course, is just a single reading of *Sex and the City*. People from other cultures and with different social, cultural and political points of view will, of course, read *Sex and the City* in quite different ways from how I have read it here. For some people, a show such as *Sex and the City* mirrors their social identities and ideologies. For others, however, it challenges social identities and ideologies. The critical framing of texts, where we stand back and look at them in relation to their social and cultural values, can help us unpack some of the assumptions underlying the use of language and what the text is aiming to do. It also helps remind us of the importance of considering the social, political underpinnings of spoken and written discourse, as well as helping us unpack the ideological thrust of seemingly ordinary, everyday genres (Johns forthcoming).

An analysis of this kind, then, takes us beyond the level of description to a deeper understanding of texts and provides, as far as might be possible, some kind of explanation of why a text might be as it is and what it is aiming to do. It looks at the relationship between language, social norms and values and aims to describe, interpret and explain this relationship. In doing so, it aims to provide a way of exploring and, perhaps challenging, some of the hidden and 'out of sight' social, cultural and political values that underlie the use of spoken and written discourse.

2.9 Conclusion

This chapter has looked at discourse analysis from a number of social and other perspectives. It has introduced several notions that are important for discussions of language from a discourse perspective. It has also aimed to show how some of these notions have changed since they were first introduced (such as language and gender and language and identity) and how these notions are currently viewed in discussions of the use of spoken and written discourse. The chapter which follows looks at discourse from a *pragmatics* perspective and provides further detail on how language does what it does, and means more than it says, in the context of our day-to-day communications.

2.10 Discussion questions

1. What discourse communities are you a member of? Do any of these communities overlap? How similar, or different, is your use of language in each these communities? Complete the chart below as you carry out your discussion.

Discourse community	*Use of language*

2. What factors influence the way you use language when you speak? For example, is your use of language influenced by your ethnic identity, your level (or kind) of education, your age, your gender or your occupation? How do you think your use of language reflects these sorts of categories? Complete the chart below as you carry out your discussion.

Factor	*Use of language*
Ethnic identity	
Education	
Age	

Gender	
Occupation	
Other identity	

3. Think of ways in which your identity has been constructed through ways of doing things and ways of belonging to a group. You may look at your identity as a student in your class, or as a member of another social group that you belong to. Complete the chart below.

Group	*Ways of belonging*	*Ways of doing things*

2.11 Data analysis projects

1. Think of ways in which how your use of language reflects the identity you have of yourself. Tape-record a conversation between you and someone else. Analyse your conversation and identify aspects of the conversation which you think reflect the way you are presenting yourself to the other person. These might, for example, include the use of particular vocabulary, the use of a particular voice quality, or through the way which you express a particular point of view.

2. Can you think of situations in which the way/s you interact is influenced by your gender? Tape-record a conversation between you and someone else where you think this is relevant. Analyse your conversation and identify aspects of the conversation which you think reflect your 'gendered identity'. This might, for example, be through the use of a particular voice quality, or the ways in which you interact linguistically with the person you are speaking to.

3. Think of a situation where your gender is less important than other factors in the way you interact. Tape-record a

conversation between you and someone else where you think this is relevant. Analyse your conversation and identify aspects of the conversation which you think reflect your most prominent identity in the conversation.

4. Choose a spoken or written text which you think reflects certain stereotyped (or otherwise) views of how people interact and their views on certain issues. Analyse the text according to the following categories:

    foregrounding
    backgrounding
    presuppositions
    agency

    To what extent do you think the text reflects certain presuppositions and ideologies?

2.12 Directions for further reading

Borg, E. (2003), 'Key concepts in ELT: Discourse community', *ELT Journal*, 57, (4), 398–400.
In this article Borg provides an accessible introduction to the notion of discourse community. He suggests ways in which the notion of discourse community is a useful one for language teachers, especially for people working in the area of English for specific purposes.

Cameron, D. (2001), *Working with Spoken Discourse*. London: Sage. Chapter 11. Identity, difference and power: locating social relations in talk.
This chapter of Cameron's book discusses identity and power in discourse. She focuses on the idea of 'socially constructed selves' and the ways in which people continually construct and reconstruct their identity through their encounters with other people and their use of discourse. Cameron also discusses the notion of 'co-constructed selves', pointing out that communication, and indeed identity construction, is a two-way process. It involves not only the construction of a particular identity, but also the recognition of that identity by others.

Eckert, P. and McConnell-Ginet, S. (2003), *Language and Gender*. Cambridge: Cambridge University Press.
While largely about language and gender, this book starts from a very broad base, elaborating on many of the social aspects of spoken and written discourse that have been presented in this chapter. Eckert and McConnell-Ginet discuss in detail the social constructionist view of

discourse; that is, the way in which what we say and do contributes to the construction of particular (in this case gendered) identities.

Sunderland, J. and Litosseliti, L. (2002), 'Gender identity and discourse analysis: Theoretical and empirical considerations,' in J. Sunderland and L. Litosseliti (eds), *Gender Identity and Discourse Analysis*. Amsterdam: John Benjamins, pp.1–39.

This chapter is a clear and accessible introduction to the topics of discourse and identity and discourse and gender. Sunderland and Litosseliti discuss identity as something that is both multiple and fluid and how identities are both realized and constructed as people 'do identity work' in their use of spoken and written discourse.

3 Discourse and pragmatics

This chapter presents an overview of research in the area of *pragmatics* that is of relevance to people interested in looking at language from a discourse perspective. It discusses the relationship between language and context, a key issue in the area of pragmatics as well as in the area of discourse analysis. It also looks at ways in which people typically perform *speech acts* (such as apologizing or requesting, etc.) in spoken and written discourse. The chapter discusses the reasons we choose to perform a speech act in a particular way such as, for example, reasons of *politeness*. The ways in which people perform speech acts across cultures is also discussed as well as what happens when people do not follow culture-specific expectations for performing particular speech acts.

3.1 What is pragmatics?

> *Pragmatics* is the study of meaning in relation to the context in which a person is speaking or writing. This includes social, situational and textual context. It also includes background knowledge context; that is, what people know about each other and about the world. Pragmatics assumes that when people communicate with each other they normally follow some kind of co-operative principle; that is, they have a shared understanding of how they should co-operate in their communications. The ways in which people do this, however, varies across cultures. What may be a culturally appropriate way of saying or doing something in one culture may not be the same in another culture. The study of this use of language across cultures is called *cross-cultural pragmatics*.

The relationship between linguistic form and communicative function is of central interest in the area of pragmatics and, as Cameron (2001) argues, is highly relevant to the field of discourse analysis. We need to know the communicative function of an utterance, that is, what it is 'doing' in the particular setting, in order to assign a discourse label to the utterance in the place of the overall discourse. For example, if someone says 'The bus was late,' they may be complaining about the bus service (and so we label the stage of the conversation 'complaint'), they may be explaining why they are late as a follow up to an apology (and so we label the stage of the conversation 'explanation') or they may be doing something else. We also need to know what this meaning is in order to understand, at a broader level, what people typically say and do as they perform particular genres in particular social and cultural settings.

3.2 Language, context and discourse

An understanding of how language functions in context is central to an understanding of the relationship between what is said and what is understood in spoken and written discourse. The *context of situation* of what someone says is, therefore, crucial to understanding and interpreting the meaning of what is being said. This includes the physical context, the social context and the mental worlds and roles of the people involved in the interaction. Each of these impacts on what we say and how other people interpret what we say in spoken and written discourse.

A conversation between two people in a restaurant may mean different things to the actual people speaking, something different to a 'side participant' in the conversation (such as someone sitting next to one of the speakers), something different to a 'bystander' (such as the waiter), and again something different to someone who may be eavesdropping the conversation (Verschueren 1999). Equally, a student's assignment written for a law course takes on a different meaning if it is re-typed on the letterhead of a law firm and addressed to a client. The text then takes on the status and function of 'a piece of legal advice' and the reader's interpretation of the text is significantly different from the way in which it would have been read by the student's professor (Freedman 1989). The linguistic context, in terms of what has been said and what is yet to be said in the discourse, also has an impact on the intended meaning and how someone may interpret this meaning in spoken and written discourse.

There are, then, a number of key aspects of context that are crucial to the production and interpretation of discourse. These are the *situational context* in terms of what people 'know about what they can see around them', the *background knowledge context* in terms of what people 'know about each other and the world' and the *co-textual context* in terms of what people 'know about what they have been saying' (Cutting 2002: 3). Background knowledge context includes cultural knowledge and interpersonal knowledge. That is, it includes what people know about the world, what they know about various areas of life, what they know about each other (Cutting 2002) and what they know about the norms and expectations of the particular *discourse community* in which the communication is taking place. Contextual knowledge also includes social, political and cultural understandings that are relevant to the particular communication (Celce-Murcia and Olshtain 2000).

As Thomas (1995: 22) explains:

> meaning is not something that is inherent in the words alone, nor is it produced by the speaker alone or the hearer alone. Making meaning is a dynamic process, involving the negotiation of meaning between speaker and hearer, the context of utterance (physical, social and linguistic), and the meaning potential of an utterance.

Meaning, thus, is produced *in interaction*. It is jointly accomplished, by both the speaker and the listener, or the writer and their reader. It involves social, psychological and cognitive factors that are relevant to the production and interpretation of what a speaker (or writer) says, and what a hearer (or reader) understands by what is said (Thomas 1995). Discourse, then, in the words of Jaworski and Coupland (1999: 49) is 'a form of collaborative social action' in which language users 'jointly collaborate in the production of meanings and inferences' as they communicate with each other in spoken and written discourse.

3.3 Speech acts and discourse

Two influential works in the area of pragmatics, and relevant to the area of discourse analysis, are Austin's (1962) *How to Do Things With Words* and Searle's (1969) *Speech Acts*. Austin and Searle argued that language is used to 'do things' other than just refer to the truth or falseness of particular statements. Their work appeared at a time when logical positivism was the prevailing view in the philosophy of language. The logical positivist view argued that language is always used to describe some fact or state of affairs and, unless a statement can be tested for truth or falsity, it is basically meaningless. Austin and Searle observed that there are many things that we say which cannot meet these kinds of truth conditions but which are, nevertheless, valid and which do things that go beyond their literal meaning. They argued that in the same way that we perform physical acts, we also perform acts by using language. That is, we use language to give orders, to make requests, to give warnings or to give advice; in other words, to do things that go beyond the literal meaning of what we say.

A central issue which underlies this is the relationship between the literal meaning, or *propositional content*, of what someone says and what the person intends by what they say. Thus, if someone says 'It's hot in here' they are not only referring to the temperature, they may also be requesting someone to do something, such as turn on the air conditioning. What we say, then, often has both a literal meaning and an *illocutionary meaning* (or *illocutionary force*); that is, a meaning which goes beyond what someone, in a literal sense, has said.

Austin argued that there are three kinds of act which occur with everything we say. These are the *locutionary act*, the *illocutionary act* and the *perlocutionary act*. The locutionary act refers to the literal meaning of the actual words (such as 'It's hot in here' referring to the temperature). The illocutionary act refers to the speaker's intention in uttering the words (such as a request for someone to turn on the air conditioning). The perlocutionary act refers to the effect this utterance has on the thoughts or actions of the other person (such as someone getting up and turning on the air conditioning).

The following example on a bus illustrates this. Clearly the bus driver is doing more than making a statement. He is also telling the boys to move. The locutionary act, in this case, is the driver saying he won't start the bus with people standing in the doorway, the illocutionary act is an order and the perlocutionary act is the boys moving inside the bus:

> Bus driver: This bus won't move until you boys move in out of the doorway.

It is not always easy, however, to identify the illocutionary force of what someone says, as it may also depend on the stage in the discourse, as well as the social context, in which the person is speaking. 'OK' for example may be an expression of agreement to what someone has just said, it may also be a 'continuer' in a conversation with no indication of agreement, or it may function as a 'pre-closing' signalling that a conversation is about to end. The illocutionary force of what someone says, thus, can really only be determined in relation to what has come before and what follows, rather than in isolation from the overall discourse (Flowerdew 1990).

An illocutionary force, further, might be spread over more than one utterance. The example below, where the sales request is spread over several utterances, illustrates this:

> A: Hello, welcome to Hungry Jack's. Can I take your order please?
> B: Can I have a Whopper with egg and bacon...
> A: Would you like cheese with that?
> B: Yes please ... and a junior Whopper with cheese ... and large fries please.
> A: Would you like any drinks or dessert with that?
> B: No thank you
> A: OK ... that's a Whopper with cheese, egg and bacon, a Whopper junior with cheese and large fries.
> B: Yes. Thank you.
> A: OK ... Please drive through.

It is also not unusual for what someone says to have more than a single illocutionary force. For example, 'What are you doing tonight?' might be both a question and an invitation. A person might reply 'I still haven't finished my homework' treating the utterance as both a question and invitation which they decide not to accept. They may equally reply 'Nothing special. What do you feel like doing?' providing an answer to the question but this time accepting the (as yet unspoken) invitation.

i. Direct and indirect speech acts

Sometimes when we speak we do mean exactly what we say. The following example from the BBC *Panorama* interview with Princess Diana is an example of this. Here, the interviewer asks Princess Diana if she allowed her friends to talk to the author of her biography, Andrew Morton:

> Bashir: Did you allow your friends, your close friends, to speak to Andrew Morton?
>
> Diana: Yes I did. Yes I did.
>
> (BBC 1995)

Often we do, however, say things indirectly. That is, we often intend something that is quite different from the literal meaning of what we say. For example a common expression on an invitation to a party is 'to bring a plate'. This may, to someone who is not familiar with this kind of cultural convention, be interpreted as a request to bring an (empty) plate to the party. In fact, it is asking someone to bring food to the party, not necessarily on a plate. Equally, if someone calls someone to ask them to come to their home for dinner and the person being asked says 'Can I bring anything?' in many countries the host will say 'No, just bring yourself' whereas, in fact, they expect the guest to bring wine (or in some countries something such as flowers for the host) with them to the dinner.

The example above of 'Can I have a Whopper with egg and bacon ...?' also illustrates this. Here, the customer is not asking about their ability to buy a hamburger – the literal meaning of the sentence – but making a sales request. This is very common in service encounters where 'can' is often used to refer to something other than ability or permission. This is further illustrated in the example below. Here, the first utterance is an offer of service, not about the sales person's ability to serve the customer. The second utterance is an acceptance of the offer and a sales request, not a question about ability or permission:

> A: Can I take your order now please?
>
> B: Can I have nine nuggets and chips with sweet and sour sauce and a can of Pepsi thanks?

In the following example a declarative form, the form most closely associated with making statements, is used to make a request:

> A: I'll have two boneless breast pieces, original recipe, half a dozen nuggets, a small chips with extra salt thanks.
>
> B: Any cold drinks or anything else with the order?

Indirect speech acts are often difficult for second language lear-ners to recognize as they may not necessarily know that in English 'This room's a real mess' might be a request for someone to help tidy up the room, or an order to tidy up the room. They also may not realize that an expression such as 'Would you mind helping me move the table?' is not asking about whether someone would mind doing something or not. It is a request for someone to do something, or it could indeed be an order.

ii. Felicity conditions and discourse

An important notion in speech act theory is the concept of *felicity conditions*. For a speech act to 'work', Austin argued that there are a number of conditions that must be met. The first of these is that there must be a generally accepted procedure for successfully carrying out the speech act, such as inviting someone to a wedding through the use of a formal written wedding invitation, rather than (for many people) an informal email message. Also the circumstances must be appro-priate for the use of the speech act. That is, someone must be getting married. The person who uses the speech act must be the appropriate person to use it in the particular context – such as the bride or groom's family, or in some cases the bride or groom, inviting the person to the wedding. A friend of the couple getting married cannot, for example, without the appropriate authority invite someone to the wedding.

Austin argued that this procedure must be carried out correctly and completely. And the person performing the speech act must (in most circumstances) have the required thoughts, feelings and inten-tions for the speech act to be 'felicitous'. That is, the communication must be carried out by the right person, in the right place, at the right time and, normally, with a certain intention or it will not 'work'. If the first two of these conditions are not satisfied, the act will not be achieved and will 'misfire'. If the third of these conditions does not hold, then the procedure will be 'abused.'

iii. Rules versus principles

Searle took Austin's work further by arguing that the felicity condi-tions of an utterance are 'constitutive rules'. That is, they are not just something that can 'go right' (or wrong) or be 'abused' – which was Austin's view – but something which make up and define the act itself. That is, they are rules that need to be followed for the utterance to work. They thus, in Searle's view, 'constitute' the particular speech act. In his view, the pragmatic use of language is rule governed and these rules can be precisely stated. He then attempted to classify speech acts into groups according to shared sets of conditions. He found this impossible to do, however, and proposed instead a set of criteria that might be used for classifying speech acts. The most important of these are the purpose of the utterance (in the sense of what we want the other person to do), the 'direction of fit' between the words we use and what we want the other person to do, and the amount of belief the speaker has in what they say.

Thomas (1995) critiques this notion of constitutive rules and suggests that the notion of *principles* is perhaps more helpful to this discussion. She suggests that Searle, in drawing on the notion of rules, was trying to describe communication in a manner that is more appropriate for grammatical, rather than pragmatic descriptions of language. In her view, the pragmatic use of language is constrained by maxims or 'principles' rather than by 'rules'.

Thomas points out that it is extremely difficult to devise rules which will satisfactorily account for the complexity of speech act behaviour. She presents five basic differences between rules and principles to support her argument. The first of these is that rules are 'all or nothing', whereas principles are 'more or less'. That is, rules are 'yes/no' in their application whereas principles can be applied partially. Thus, you can speak extremely clearly, fairly clearly, or not at all clearly, rather than simply 'clearly'. Thomas also argues that rules are exclusive whereas principles can co-occur. Thus, using one rule precludes another whereas a number of principles (rather than rules) might apply at the same time. Rules aim to define a speech act whereas principles describe what people do. Further, whereas rules are definite, principles are 'probabilistic'; that is, they describe what is more or less likely to be the case, rather than something which either does or does not apply. Finally Thomas argues that rules are arbitrary, whereas principles are 'motivated'. That is, people follow them for a reason, or purpose, to achieve a particular goal.

If, for example, someone apologizes for something (in English) there is the assumption that they were responsible for what has been done (or in a position to represent this on someone else's behalf), have actually said 'I'm sorry', are sincere in what they say and will do something to rectify the situation, if this is required (or possible). The person may not be completely responsible for what was done, however, so it is more helpful to see this as a case of more or less, rather than yes or no. Equally, an apology is often more ritual than 'sincere' but has been carried out for a very important reason, so that the person being apologized to will feel better about the situation and the tension that was there will be resolved. Taking a principles-based view of speech act performance, rather than a rule-based one, thus, describes what people often do, or are most likely to do, when they apologize, rather than what they 'must' do.

The analysis of speech acts then needs to take account of the fact that we are often dealing with approximations, or 'fuzzy' rather than discrete categories (Flowerdew 1990). Speech act analyses also need to take account of physical and social contexts of use, as well as the fact that meaning is not based on words alone but involves negotiation and interaction between users of a language. That is, it needs to take account of the different contributions that language users make to the meaning of interactions (Thomas 1995).

Work in the area of speech act theory was an important step forward towards understanding 'unspoken' aspects of what people mean by what they say. Speech act theory has also had a major impact on second and foreign language teaching. The notion of 'functions' in language teaching, for example, is a direct translation of the notion of a speech act. Work in the area of cross-cultural pragmatics, discussed later in this chapter, is also strongly influenced by research in the area of speech act theory.

iv. Presupposition and discourse

A further important notion in the area of speech act theory and pragmatics is *presupposition*. Presupposition refers to the common ground that is assumed to exist between language users such as assumed knowledge of a situation and/or of the world. This may come from sources such as books, television and the Internet, or through personal experiences with the world. A speaker says something based on their assumption (or presupposition) of what the hearer is likely to 'know', and what they will infer from what they say.

Two main kinds of presupposition are discussed in the area of pragmatics: conventional presupposition and pragmatic presupposition. Conventional presuppositions are less context-dependent than pragmatic presuppositions and are typically linked to particular linguistic forms. For example 'Would you like *some* coffee?' suggests the coffee is already prepared whereas 'Would you like *anything* to drink?' does not suggest a drink has already been prepared (Lo Castro 2003).

Pragmatic presuppositions, however, are context-dependent and arise from the use of an utterance in a particular context. The following example from the website of the television programme *Big Brother* illustrates this:

> This morning all the housemates are already awake and out of bed.
> The girls are in the bathroom and the boys are eating breakfast in
> the backyard. Ryan offers some bread to the birds. Paul says:
> 'Fryzie, You're not allowed.' The boys talk about birds. 'Crows, are
> like weak,' Ryan says. He corrects himself: 'Not like the football
> team, they rock. I mean the bird.'
>
> > (Extract courtesy *Big Brother* Series 4 website,
> > Endemol Southern Star Pty Ltd)

In this interaction, Ryan is talking about the birds he is feeding but is
concerned Paul will think he is talking about the local football team,
the Crows. Both speakers are in the same situation looking at the birds
while Ryan is speaking. They both know about the football team, the
Crows. Ryan assumes (or presupposes) that Paul will not want him to
criticize the Crows so makes it clear he is talking about the birds and
there is no double meaning in what he says.

The following example in the delicatessen section of a supermarket works in the same way. The customers know they need to take
a ticket from the ticket machine and wait their turn to be served. The
person with the ticket with '2' on it is the next person to be served. B
implicates what A has said as an offer of service to them (alone).

A: Customer number two!
B: Ah ..... could I have 250 grams of the honey smoked
           ham please?

These are examples of pragmatic presuppositions based on a shared
knowledge of the world.

Presuppositions are crucial to an understanding of what people
mean by what they say in spoken and written discourse. Often we
presuppose a person will have a similar understanding to us in terms
of what we mean by what we say. Ryan does this in the *Big Brother*
example, as does the sales person in the delicatessen section of the
supermarket. It is indeed because people make this assumption that
discourse (normally) proceeds as smoothly as it does.

3.4 The co-operative principle and discourse

In his paper, 'Logic and conversation', Grice (1975) argues that in order
for a person to interpret what someone else says, some kind of *co-
operative principle* must be assumed to be in operation. People
assume, he argued, that there is a set of principles which direct us to a
particular interpretation of what someone says, unless we receive some
indication to the contrary. The co-operative principle says we should
aim to make our conversational contribution 'such as is required, at the

stage at which it occurs, by the accepted purpose or direction' (Grice 1975: 45) of the exchange in which we are engaged.

Thus, when someone is speaking to us, we base our understanding of what they are saying on the assumption that they are saying what needs to be said, rather than more than needs to be said (as in the delicatessen example above), they are saying it at an appropriate point in the interaction (such as when the person working in the delicatessen has finished serving one person and is ready to serve another) and they have a reason for saying what they say (as both an offer of service as well as to make it clear whose turn it is to be served). The person working in the delicatessen follows these assumptions, assuming that their customers will follow them as well. In this way, both people involved in the service encounter co-operate in its production and interpretation.

Grice based his co-operative principle on four sub-principles, or *maxims*. These are the maxims of *quality, quantity, relation* and *manner.* The maxim of quality says people should only say what they believe to be true and what they have evidence for. Grice's maxim of quantity says we should make our contribution as informative as is required for the particular purpose and not make it more informative than is required. The maxim of relation says we should make our contribution relevant to the interaction, or we should indicate in what way it is not. His maxim of manner says we should be clear in what we say, we should avoid ambiguity or obscurity and we should be brief and orderly in our contribution to the interaction.

In the following example both speakers observe all of these maxims. Both say all that is required at the appropriate stage in the conversation. They both observe the purpose and direction of the conversation. What they say is relevant to the conversation and they are each brief, orderly and unambiguous in what they say:

A: Hi. What would you like?
B: Two hundred grams of the shaved ham thanks.

If someone is unsure of what they want to say, or wants to avoid someone inferring they have evidence for what they say, people often use *metadiscourse* (Hyland 2005b) to comment on what they are about to say, or have just said. This use of metadiscourse is central to the interpretation of texts as it shows both their attitude to what they are saying as well as their attitude to the audience of the text.

A speaker may, for example, say 'I may be mistaken, but ...' or end a sentence with 'maybe ...' to show they are aware of and are following the maxim of quality. Equally, a speaker may say 'I won't bore you with all the details' to show they are aware of the maxim of quantity. A speaker may indicate a change of topic using a device such as 'by the way' or use a marker such as 'anyway' to show they are aware of the maxim of relation. They may say something such as 'this may be a bit confused, but . . .' to show they are aware of the maxim of manner. That is, they comment on what they are saying not only to show they are aware of the conversational maxims, but also that they are trying to observe them.

We, thus, expect a person's contribution to an interaction to be genuine, neither more nor less than is required, as well as clear and appropriate to the interaction. Grice argues that we assume a speaker is following these maxims and combine this with our knowledge of the world to work out what they mean by what they say.

In the BBC *Panorama* interview, many of the people Princess Diana is referring to need to be inferred from what has gone before in the interview. In the following extract Princess Diana makes her contribution 'as informative as is required for the current purpose of the exchange' (Grice 1999: 78) showing she is obeying the maxim of quantity. Her interviewer Martin Bashir and the audience, she assumes, can clearly derive from her answer who she is talking about (Kowal and O'Connell 1997). Here Princess Diana uses 'people around me' and 'people in my environment' to refer to the royal household, expecting her audience will know who she is talking about:

> Diana: People's agendas changed overnight. I was now sepa-
>   rated wife of the Prince of Wales, I was a problem, I was
>   a liability (seen as), and how are we going to deal with
>   her? This hasn't happened before.
> Bashir: Who was asking those questions?
> Diana: People around me, people in this environment, and . . .
> Bashir: The royal household?
> Diana: People in my environment, yes, yes.

At other points in the interview, Princess Diana uses 'people' to refer to the press and at other points the British public. When she wants to make it clear exactly who she is referring to (and is obeying the maxim of quality) she adds a clarification, as in the extracts below:

> Diana: I'd like to be a queen of people's hearts, in people's
>   hearts, but I don't see myself being Queen of this
>   country. I don't think many people will want me to be
>   Queen.
>   . . . .
> Diana: The people that matter to me – the man on the street,
>   yup, because that's what matters more than anything
>   else.

There are times, however, when being truthful, brief and relevant might have different meanings. Indeed different contexts and situations may have different understandings of what 'be truthful, relevant and brief' means. There are, further, occasions where we cannot be brief and true at the same time (Cook 1989). This leads us to the 'flouting' of the co-operative principle and its maxims.

3.5 Flouting the co-operative principle

On some occasions speakers flout the co-operative principle and intend their hearer to understand this; that is, they purposely do not observe the maxim, and intend their hearer to be aware of this. In the following example a student goes to the library to collect books he had asked to be put on hold for him. The librarian knows, in his final line, what he is saying is not true (or physically possible), and intends the student to know this:

Librarian:	(raises his eyes, looks at the student with no facial expression)
Student:	Hi. Could you check for me whether I have any books to collect?
Librarian:	(swipes the student's card, clears his throat, wipes his nose with a tissue, glances at the computer screen, turns to the shelf to get a book, then another book)
Student:	Any more?
Librarian:	(turns and gets a third book, stamps them all with the return date)
Student:	Is that all?
Librarian:	Are you going to borrow all the books in the library?
Student:	OK .. I see .. thank you very much

People may also flout the maxim of relation, or be told they are flouting this maxim, in similar ways. The following extract is an example of this. An American student has asked a Chinese student directions to the station. As they are walking to the station, the following conversation occurs:

Chinese student:	What do you do in America?
American student:	I work in a bank.
Chinese student:	It's a good job isn't it?
American student:	Well, just so so.
Chinese student:	Then, how much is your salary every month?
American student:	Oh no ...
Chinese student:	What's wrong?
American student:	Why are you asking that?

| Chinese student: | Just asking, nothing else ... |
| American student: | The station isn't far is it? |

Here the question the Chinese student has asked does not observe the maxim of relation for an English conversation of this kind. He is not aware of this, although the American student clearly is. He then asks her if she is travelling alone and if she is married. The American student quickly hails a taxi and takes it to the station.

In the next example the serving person politely suggests the customer is flouting the maxim of quantity, saying more than is necessary, as the ham is already thinly sliced.

A:	Can I get six thin slices of Danish ham please?
B:	Six thin slices....
A:	Yep.
B:	They're all really thin, so....

i. Differences between flouting and violating maxims

Thomas (1995) and Cutting (2002) discuss differences between flouting and violating maxims. A speaker is flouting a maxim if they do not observe a maxim but has no intention of deceiving or misleading the other person. A person is 'violating' a maxim if there is a likelihood that they are liable to mislead the other person. For example 'Mummy's gone on a little holiday because she needs a rest' meaning 'Mummy's gone away to decide if she wants a divorce or not' violates, rather than flouts, the maxim of manner (Cutting 2002: 40). Here, the speaker intends the hearer to understand something other than the truth, on purpose.

A speaker may also 'infringe' a maxim when they fail to observe a maxim with no intention to deceive, such as where a speaker does not have the linguistic capacity to answer a question. A speaker may also decide to 'opt out' of a maxim such as where a speaker may, for ethical or legal reasons, refuse to say something that breaches a confidentiality agreement they have with someone, or is likely to incriminate them in some way (Thomas 1995; Cutting 2002).

ii. Overlaps between maxims

There is also often overlap between each of Grice's maxims. An utterance may be both unclear and longwinded, flouting the maxims of quality and quantity at the same time (Cutting 2002). Equally it may be socially acceptable, and indeed preferred, to flout a maxim (such as quality) for reasons of tact and politeness, such as when I ask someone if they like something I am wearing, and they don't.

It is important, then, for both the production and interpretation of spoken and written discourse to understand to what extent people are following these maxims, or not, in what they say. The Princess Diana interview is a good example of this. While Diana's contribution to the conversation is indeed co-operative, she very skillfully exploits Grice's maxims (especially the maxims of quality and quantity) to get her points across. Even when she pauses, or remains silent in the interview, she is observing the maxim of quantity, showing an appropriate reflectiveness and seriousness in her approach to the interview and not saying more than she should, or needs to (Kowal and O'Connell 1997). That is, she is making her contribution 'such as is required, at the stage at which it occurs', by the purpose and direction of the conversation.

3.6 Cross-cultural pragmatics and discourse

The ways in which people perform speech acts, and what they mean by what they say when they perform them, often varies across cultures. One of my Japanese students complained, for example, that he had had work done by a local (English-speaking) builder that was unsatisfactory and no matter how much he pushed the matter he could not get the builder to apologize. On reflection, he realized that this was, in part, due to the different implications that might be drawn from an apology in English as opposed to an apology in Japanese. For my Japanese student, he expected the builder to apologize as a matter of course and he was very disturbed that the builder would not do this. This did not mean for him, however, that the builder would be taking responsibility for the unsatisfactory work, or that, having apologized, he would then be obliged to do anything about it. In English, he discovered, the apology, for the builder, would mean that he was both taking responsibility for the faulty work and agreeing to do something about it – a situation the builder was most likely keen to avoid given the financial, and other, implications this might have had for him. In Japanese, the apology would not necessarily have had these implications.

i. Communication across cultures

Different languages and cultures, then, often have different ways of dealing with pragmatic issues, as well as different ways of observing Grice's maxims (Wierzbicka 2003). For example, speakers of different languages may have different understandings of the maxim of quantity in conversational interactions. Béal (1992) found in a communication in the workplace study that communication difficulties occurred between English and French speakers because the English speakers saw questions such as 'How are you?' or 'Did you have a good weekend?' as examples of 'phatic' communication and expected short, standard answers such as 'Fine thanks'. The French speakers, however, saw the questions as 'real' requests for information and, in the English speakers' eyes, flouted the maxim of quantity, by talking at length about their health or what they did at the weekend.

The same is a true of silence. Japanese, for example, has much greater tolerance for silence than does English. In a study of Japanese speakers' participation in English university tutorials, Nakane (2003) found that miscommunication occurred because native English speaker tutors interpreted the Japanese students' 'wait time' in answering questions as flouting the maxim of quantity. In this case, the Japanese students did not say enough, soon enough, in relation to the tutors' English speaking expectations for interactions in this kind of setting. What the tutors did not understand was that in Japanese communication silence is typically of longer duration than in Western countries and that silence can play quite a different role than it does, for example, in English. Silence, for Japanese students, does not necessarily mean they have nothing to say. It can, for example, represent thoughtfulness and a wish not to be seen as forward or selfish. Silence, thus, in Japanese has a very important role in the creation of group harmony which is quite different to its role in English spoken interactions (Davies and Ikeno 2002).

Austin's (1998) discussion of letters of recommendation in academic settings is a further example of cross-cultural pragmatic differences. As she points out, in English academic settings letters of recommendation may vary in strength of recommendation. Readers also take into account the prestige of the person writing the letter, where they work and the content and tone of the letter. They might also notice 'what has not been said' in the letter. In Japanese academic settings, however, the situation is quite different. Japanese letters of recommendation are often much shorter than they are in English and often there is no particular relationship between the length of the letter and the quality of recommendation. A reader may need to ask for more information about a candidate, rather than rely on the letter alone. An English-speaking academic, thus, may misread a Japanese letter of recommendation if they are not aware of the different pragmatic role and values these texts have in their particular cultural setting.

ii. Cross-cultural pragmatics

Studies which investigate the cross-cultural use of speech acts are commonly referred to as *cross-cultural pragmatics*. As Wierzbicka (2003) points out, different pragmatic norms reflect different cultural values which are, in turn, reflected in what people say and what they intend by what they say in different cultural settings. Wierzbicka gives the example of thanking in Japanese and English. The concepts encoded in the English word *thanks*, she argues, do not really fit Japanese culture. In English, she says, to thank someone means, roughly, to say we feel something good towards them because of something good they have done and we want them to feel good in return. But in Japanese culture with its stress on social hierarchy, moral duty and the repayment of favours, this situation is somewhat different. Japanese speakers of English, further, may frequently say *sorry* when they mean *thank you*, leading to a completely different interpretation of what they mean, from what they intend to mean. As Cameron (2001: 74) explains, the act of thanking is an expression of indebtedness in both English and Japanese. In the case of Japanese, however, 'a debt not yet repaid calls for an apology from the debtor'. Apologizing, thus, for a Japanese speaker, is one way of expressing indebtedness, and thanking someone.

iii. Pragmalinguistics and sociopragmatics

Two key notions in the area of cross-cultural pragmatics are *pragmalinguistics* and *sociopragmatics* (Leech 1983). Pragmalinguistics is 'the study of the more linguistic end of pragmatics – where we consider the particular resources which a given language provides for conveying particular illocutions' (Leech 1983: 11); that is, the study of speech acts in relation to typical linguistic structures. Sociopragmatics, on the other hand, refers to specific local conditions of language use; that is, the pragmatic performance of speech acts in specific social and cultural contexts.

iv. Cross-cultural pragmatic failure

The failure to convey or understand a pragmatic intention in another language and culture is what Thomas (1983) terms *cross-cultural pragmatic failure*. She describes two main types of cross-cultural pragmatic failure: *sociopragmatic failure* and *pragmalinguistic failure*. Sociopragmatic failure refers to a situation where a speaker of a second language assesses situational factors on the basis of the sociopragmatic norms of their first language and draws on these for the performance of a particular speech act.

An example of sociopragmatic failure is a foreign manager criticizing a Thai worker in front of their colleagues for being regularly late for work. In Thai culture, this should not be done in such a direct or public way. Doing this causes the person being criticized to lose face. A Thai person might do this by mentioning the problem in front of the whole group, rather than picking out an individual for criticism, or they might do it through an intermediary, such as a friend or colleague, rather then speaking directly to the person who is late for work (Gibson 2000).

Pragmalinguistic failure refers to a situation where a speaker transfers the procedure and linguistic means of realizing a speech act from their first language to their second language. Pragmalinguistic failure is, thus, essentially a linguistic problem, whereas sociopragmatic failure draws from the failure to understand different cultural perceptions and expectations of culture-specific speech act performance.

An example of pragmalinguistic failure is an English speaker failing to realize the importance of attaching an address form such as *chan* or *san* to someone's name when speaking to them in Japanese. An exchange student from the US, for example, may think she is being friendly by calling out her friend's name, *Akiko*, in a Japanese playground whereas for Japanese speakers, this is quite rude, even among friends. She needs to call her friend *Akiko-chan*. That is, she has transferred an (English) linguistic means of expressing involvement and friendship to a situation in which doing this, in fact, has the opposite effect.

Sometimes the results of this kind of miscommunication can be very serious, to say the least. The example of a Korean immigrant to the US who was sentenced to 20 years in prison for killing her son is a case in point. Her son was killed in an accident, but when asked by the police about this she constantly said 'I killed my son. It is my fault'. This was taken as evidence by the US court that she was guilty of the charge that was laid against her. In fact, what she was doing in saying this was in Korean culture quite understandable. She was, as a Korean mother, overstating her responsibility for the family problem and accusing herself of it. She, further, did not know how to use appropriate politeness strategies in English so was seen as rude and insulting in court, which also had an effect on the outcome of her case. It was not until five years later, when the case was aired on Korean television, that her case was reviewed and she was pardoned and released from prison (Cho 1992). In short, she did not know 'how, when and why to speak' in the target culture due to her lack of sociopragmatic and pragmalinguistic competence in the particular linguistic and cultural situation (Thomas 1983).

3.7 Conversational implicature and discourse

A further key notion in pragmatics which has implications for both the production and interpretation of discourse is the concept of *conversational implicature*. Conversational implicature refers to the inference a hearer makes about a speaker's intended meaning that arises from their use of the literal meaning of what the speaker said, the conversational principle and its maxims. For example, if I say 'There's nothing on at the movies' I do not mean 'nothing at all', but rather 'nothing that I'm interested in seeing'. The person I am speaking to will assume this and 'implicate' my meaning. Implicature is not the same, however, as inference. As Thomas (1995: 58) explains, an implicature 'is generated intentionally by the speaker and may (or may not) be understood by the hearer'. An inference, on the other hand, is produced by a hearer on the basis of certain evidence and may not, in fact, be the same as what a speaker intends.

To calculate an implicature, Grice (1975) argues, hearers draw on the conventional meanings of words, the co-operative principle and its maxims, the linguistic and non-linguistic context of the utterance, items of background knowledge and the fact that all of these are available to both participants and they both assume this to be the case. Given this basic process, implicature can be created in one of three ways. A maxim can be followed in a straightforward way and the hearer implicates what the speaker intends. The following example, where a customer orders a beer, illustrates this:

A: What'd you like?
B: A beer thanks.

Here, B has followed the maxim of quality by saying what he wants, the maxim of manner by answering clearly, the maxim of quantity by saying enough and no more, and the maxim of relation by providing an answer that is clearly relevant to the question. Here, no implicature is generated that is necessary for the interpretation of the utterance.

A maxim might also be flouted because of a clash with another maxim as in:

A: What time did your flight get in this morning?
B: Seven (when it actually arrived at 7.04 am)

Here B flouts the maxim of quality (the truth) in order to obey the maxim of quantity (be brief).

Or a maxim might be flouted in a way that exploits a maxim as in:

A: How are we getting to the airport tomorrow?
B: Well ... I'm going with Peter.

Here, B has given less information than is required and is flouting the maxim of quantity – from which B derives that he or she may have to make their own way to the airport.

i. Conventional and particularized conversational implicatures

Grice describes two kinds of conversational implicature: *conventional* and *particularized conversational implicatures*. With conventional implicatures, no particular context is required in order to derive the implicature. In the above example, the use of 'well' can conventionally implicate that what the speaker is about to say is not what the hearer is hoping to hear. Similarly, the use of 'anyway' conventionally implicates a return to the original topic of a conversation (Lo Castro 2003). The use of 'but' and 'on the other hand' to express contrast, 'even' to suggest something is contrary to expectation and 'yet' to suggest something will be different at a later time, are further examples of conventional implicatures.

Particularized conversational implicatures, however, are derived from a particular context, rather than from the use of the words alone. These result from the maxim of relation. That is, the speaker assumes the hearer will search for the relevance of what they are saying and derive an intended meaning. For example in:

A: You're out of coffee.
B: Don't worry there's a shop on the corner.

A derives from B's answer that they will be able to buy coffee from the shop on the corner. Most implicatures, in fact, are particularized conversational implicatures.

ii. Scalar implicatures

A further kind of implicature is *scalar implicature*. These are derived when a person uses a word from a set of words that express some kind of scale of values. Words such as 'all', 'most', 'something' and 'nothing' are examples of this. In the following conversation B is on a bus, talking on his mobile phone to A. A asks B about his private life:

> A: Have you been up to anything interesting lately?
> B: Not really, well ... nothing I can tell you about on the bus.

Here B has cancelled out 'nothing' from which B derives A has been doing 'something' interesting in his private life.

A speaker may choose one item from a scale, then correct it while they are speaking to cancel out another item in the scale. The following extract from the BBC *Panorama* interview is an example of this. Here Princess Diana cancels out 'full' with 'some', then cancels 'some' with 'half of', adding an explanation as to why she has done this (Abell and Stokoe 1999):

> Bashir: Looking back now, do you feel at all responsible for the difficulties in your marriage?
> Diana: Mmm. I take full responsibility, I take some responsibility that our marriage went the way it did. I'll take half of it, but I won't take any more than that, because it takes two to get in this situation.

3.8 Politeness, face and discourse

Two further key notions in the area of pragmatics and discourse are *politeness* and *face*. The notion of 'face' comes from Goffman's (1967) work on face and from the English 'folk' notion of face, which ties up with notions of being embarrassed, humiliated or 'losing face' (Brown and Levinson 1987). Politeness and face are important for understanding why people choose to say things in a particular way in spoken and written discourse.

In early work on this topic, Lakoff (1973) proposes three maxims of politeness. These are 'don't impose', 'give options' and 'make your hearer feel good'. For example, we apologize for imposing by saying 'I'm sorry to bother you but ...'. We make requests in an elaborate fashion by saying 'Do you think you could possibly ...' to give our hearer the option of refusal. Or we might make them feel good by saying something like 'You're better at this than me'.

The following example illustrates these maxims. Stephanie calls her mother from the train station to ask for a ride home:

> Mum: Is that you Steph?
> Stephanie: Yeah it's me
> Mum: Hi darling
> Stephanie: I'm at Town Hall Station. Do you think you could possibly come pick me up?
> Mum: Yep

Stephanie:	Or are you in a rush to have dinner so you can go out?
Mum:	Oh we've already got dinner ready. But I'll come and get you
Stephanie:	Oh that'd be great. I'm at Town Hall
Mum:	Yep
Stephanie:	And the train's not for ten minutes
Mum:	Yep. OK
Stephanie:	OK. Thanks Mum
Mum:	Bye.
Stephanie:	Bye.

In this example Stephanie asks for a lift in an elaborate fashion by saying 'Do you think you could possibly come pick me up?' She gives her mother an option by suggesting if she is busy cooking dinner then it is not necessary, and makes her mother feel good by saying 'Oh that'd be great'.

Politeness principles and co-operative principles, however, are often in conflict with each other. There are also situations in which one principle might become more important than another. In an emergency, for example, there is less need to be polite and 'make your hearer feel good' than, say, in a normal situation.

'Make your hearer feel good', further, may not always be a matter of words but 'how you say what you say'. For example Cameron's (2000) study of call centres found 'voice impression' and 'smiling while you talk' to be equally important politeness strategies. In her setting it wasn't just *what* the operators said, but *how* they said it that mattered in creating a positive impression and rapport with their callers.

i. Involvement and independence in spoken and written discourse

Two further issues in discussions of face and politeness are the notions of *involvement* and *independence* (Scollon and Wong-Scollon 2001). The term involvement refers to the need people have to be involved with others and to show this involvement; that is a person's right and need to be considered a normal, contributing, supporting member of society; in other words, to be treated as a member of a group. We might show this involvement by showing our interest in someone, by agreeing with them, by approving what they are doing or by using in-group identity markers such as given names, or nicknames. The independence part of face refers to a person's right not be dominated by others, not to be imposed on by others and to be able to act with some sense of individuality, or autonomy. We do this, for example, by not presuming other people's needs or interests, by giving people options, by not imposing on other people and by apologizing for interruptions. In order to maintain social relationships people acknowledge both of these aspects of a person's face at the same time. People thus aim to build up closeness and rapport with each other, while at the same time trying to avoid being a threat to each other's social distance; that is, maintaining each other's involvement and independence (Scollon and Wong-Scollon 2001).

ii. Choosing a politeness strategy

We draw on a number of considerations when we decide on a choice of politeness strategy. We may consider how socially close or distant we are from our hearer. For example, are we close friends, is the hearer older than I am, and are we 'social equals'? We may consider how much or how little power the hearer has over us. For example, am I talking to my boss or to my employee, to a policeman, to a service employee, or to a judge? We may also consider how significant what I want is to me, and to the person I am talking to. For example, am I asking for change, for a loan, or to borrow a car? We may consider how much emphasis both of us (in our culture or cultures) place on involvement and independence in circumstances like the one we are in. And we may consider whether both of us would have the same answers to these questions (Gee 1993).

3.9 Face and politeness across cultures

It is important to point out that the specific nature of face and politeness varies from society to society and from culture to culture. For example, in some cultures, the idea of personal space and independence may vary. In some societies, parents have more right to interfere in the domestic affairs of adult children than in others. In some cultures a bedroom is private and cannot be entered and in others it is not. In some cultures refusal of an offer may be merely polite (even if to an English speaker a refusal may seem like refusing involvement) and in others the opposite may be true (Cook 1989).

Gu (1990) discusses politeness in relation to Chinese culture while Ide (1982) discusses politeness in Japanese. Gu sees politeness in Chinese not so much in terms of psychological wants, but rather in terms of social norms. Face is threatened he argues, not when someone's needs are not met, but when someone fails to live up to social standards. Ide sees politeness in Japanese as something which helps to maintain communication. In Japanese politeness is less strategic and more a matter of socially obligatory linguistic choices through which social harmony is achieved (Eelen 2001).

Gift-giving is an example of a politeness strategy that varies across cultures. Brown and Levinson list gift-giving as a positive politeness strategy in English, or in Scollon and Wong-Scollon's (2001) terms an *involvement strategy*; that is, a strategy by which we show our closeness and rapport with someone else. We may spend a lot of time deciding what to buy for the gift, think about what the person receiving the gift will feel about what we have bought them, and what their reaction to our gift might be. In Japanese culture, however, there are times when gift-giving may mean something quite different from this and be more of a social ritual rather than a positive politeness strategy. Japanese have many gift-giving occasions throughout the year that cover many events in Japanese life where gift-giving is more ritual, or an expression of duty. The gift-giving may still have the function of maintaining social relationships, but be much less an expression of intimacy and rapport, than it might be in an English speaking country (Davies and Ikeno 2002).

The ways in which people express politeness also differs across cultures. On one occasion I asked a group of bilingual Japanese/English students how they would ask a friend to close the window if they were in the car with them and they were feeling cold. These students had all lived in an English-speaking country and were fluent in both English and Japanese. These are some of the examples they gave me of what they would say in English to an English speaking friend:

> Could you close the window for me?
> Can I close the window?
> Hey yo, close the window, would you?

This is what they said they would say in Japanese to a Japanese friend:

> Isn't it a little chilly?
> It's cold don't you think?
> I wonder why it's so cold today?

In the Japanese examples none of the students actually mentioned the window. When I asked them about this, one of the students told me that that in Japanese indirectness is a sign of intimacy and is often used between friends as a sign of mutual understanding and friendship. Indirectness, then, is often an involvement, or positive politeness, strategy in Japanese whereas in English it is often an independence, or negative politeness, strategy. My students also told me that in Japanese culture, involvement is much more important than independence. Thus, whereas in English a speaker may weigh up what they are saying in terms of both involvement and independence, a Japanese speaker may give much greater weight to what they are saying in terms of involvement, rather than independence.

3.10 Politeness and gender

Politeness strategies have also been shown to vary according to gender. Holmes (1995) discusses this at length, showing differences in the use of politeness strategies between men and women. Her work reveals that the relationship between sex, politeness and language is a complex one and that while research shows that, overall, women are more polite than men, it also depends on what we mean by 'polite' as well as which women and men are being compared and what setting or *community of practice* the interaction occurs in; that is, the particular local conditions in which the man or woman is speaking (Cameron 1998).

In her book *Gender and Politeness* Mills (2003) points out that context has an important role to play in terms of whether what someone says is interpreted as polite or not. She gives the example of 'street remarks' to illustrate this. If, for example, I say 'Hello gorgeous' to a long-time friend when I see her, this can be taken as an expression of intimacy and rapport; that is, as a positive politeness, or involvement strategy. If, however, someone calls this out from a building site to a woman walking by this can have the opposite effect. For the woman, it may be an act of harassment. For the men on the building site, it may be an act which shows solidarity and rapport among the group. It is not always the case that 'Hello gorgeous' is a positive politeness strategy, at least for the person it is being said to. We need, then, to consider who is saying what, to whom, from what position, where and for what purpose in order to come to a closer understanding of this (Cameron 1998).

This communities of practice view of politeness and gender is also discussed by Christie (2002) who looks at politeness and gender in parliamentary debate in the UK. Christie argues that while there are many instances of men and women publicly criticizing, ridiculing and challenging each other in parliamentary debates, these are not so much instances of gender specific impoliteness, but rather *politic verbal behaviour* (Watts 2003). In this case, Christie argues, the insults, etc. are part of the discourse expectations of a good parliamentary speaker, regardless of whether they are male or female. She also found in her data that female Members of Parliament rarely apologize, a finding that runs counter to other, more general politeness and gender research that suggests that women apologize more than men. Indeed, as with the work on language and identity, politeness and gender research suggests that it may not always be a person's gendered identity that is the most salient in a particular situation but perhaps some other aspect of their identity that more influences their linguistic behaviour (Mullany 2002).

A *community of practice* is a group of people who come together to carry out certain activities with each other. Parents doing volunteer work in a childcare centre, a group of high-school friends with a shared interest and Members of Parliament are examples of communities of practice. Members of a community of practice interact with each other in particular ways, have a common endeavour and share ways in which they express their group identity. The ways they talk, the ways they do things, and their common knowledges, values and beliefs emerge and develop as they carry out their activities. Researchers in the area of linguistic politeness argue for a communities of practice view of politeness; that is, an examination of the ways in which politeness is typically expressed, its function and what it means, in the particular social and communicative setting, place and time.

3.11 Face-threatening acts

Some acts 'threaten' a person's face. These are called *face-threatening acts*. In the earlier example between the librarian and the student, the librarian shows no signs of closeness or rapport and the student's face (in this case their involvement) is threatened. Often we use *mitigation devices* (Fraser 1980) in conversations to take the edge off face-threatening acts. One example is the use of a 'pre-sequence' as in the following invitation:

A: Are you doing anything after work? (a pre-sequence)
B: Why are you asking?
A: I thought we might go for a drink. (an indirect speech act)
B: Well, no, nothing in particular. Where would you like
        to go?

This example also uses an *insertion sequence* in the middle to take the edge off the face-threatening act of 'inviting someone out.'
We might also use an *off-record speech act* as in:

A: I'm dying for a drink (an off-record invitation)
B: Yes it's really hot isn't it? (an off-record rejection of the
        invitation)

Here, A never actually asked B to go for a drink so doesn't lose any face by being rejected. Equally, B hasn't rejected the invitation on record but simply 'commented' on the weather in their off-record rejection of the invitation.

3.12 Politeness and cross-cultural pragmatic failure

It is important to remember, then, that the particular nature of face varies across cultures and that politeness strategies are not necessarily universal. Equally, what may be a face-threatening act in one culture may not be seen the same way in another. Matsumoto (1989), for example, argues that the use of deference in Japanese is an indication of social register and relationship and not a politeness strategy. Gu (1990) and Mao (1994), equally, argue that the politeness model proposed by Brown and Levinson (1987) in their *Politeness. Some Universals in Language Usage*, for example, does not suit Chinese. As Gu (1990: 256) observes, while politeness, of itself, may be a universal phenomenon, 'what counts as polite behaviour (including values and norms attached to such behaviour) is ... [both] culture-specific and language-specific.'

Clearly, politeness strategies are not the same across languages and cultures and might mean different things in different linguistic and cultural contexts. A lack of understanding of politeness strategies in different languages and cultures can be a cause of cross-cultural pragmatic failure. As Tanaka (1997) and others have pointed out, native speakers of a language are often less tolerant of pragmatic errors in cross-cultural communication contexts than they are, for example, of grammatical errors. Different views of pragmatic appropriateness, then, can easily lead to misunderstandings and inhibit effective cross-cultural communication. In cross-cultural settings, in particular, people need an awareness, as well as an expectation, of sociopragmatic differences, as much as they need an understanding of how these differences might be expressed linguistically.

Learners at different levels of proficiency, further, may have difficulty in matching form with function in their use of politeness strategies. Learners often acquire the linguistic means of performing politeness strategies before they acquire pragmatic rules of use. Beebe and Waring (2005), for example, looked at different learners' responses to rudeness in English at different levels of proficiency. They found that the higher proficiency students were more aggressive in their response to rudeness than the lower proficiency students, and than a native speaker might be. In their view, the issue is not so much teaching pragmatic strategies, but working on 'linguistic aspects such as word choice or intonation manipulation that affect the way each strategy is executed in a more subtle and effective way' (Beebe and Waring 2005: 74).

3.13 Conclusion

This chapter has discussed key notions in the analysis of discourse from a pragmatics perspective. While many researchers discuss the importance of pragmatic competence as a component of communicative competence, much of the research in the area of pragmatics and language learning has examined pragmatic development in terms of the acquisition of particular speech acts or issues of politeness, rather than some of the other issues discussed in this chapter. As Tanaka (1997) observes, there is a paucity of research on the pragmatic aspect of second language learners' speech. What research there is, however, shows that language learners have difficulties in the area of pragmatics, regardless of their level of grammatical ability. As Tanaka argues, the development of second language learners' pragmatic competence needs to remain an important goal of language learning classrooms as pragmatic failure can 'deny learners access to valuable academic or professional opportunities' (Tanaka 1997: 15). Pragmatic competence, then, 'is not extra or ornamental, like the icing on the cake'. It is a crucial part of discourse competence and, in turn, communicative competence (Kasper 1997).

3.14 Discussion questions

1. Think of possible speech acts for each of the following situations. Compare the three sets of speech acts. In what ways are they different and why? For example is what you say influenced by your relationship with the person you are speaking to, their age or their gender? Or is it influenced by things such as how well you know the other person, or your view of their social position in relation to yours? If the person is your boss is that different, for example, than if the person you are speaking to is a co-worker? Or is what you say influenced by what you are talking about?
   * You and a close friend are having dinner together and you suddenly realize you have left your money at home. Ask your friend to lend you some money to pay for dinner.
   * You want to take a week off work to see a friend who is visiting you from overseas and you have no holidays owing

to you. You go to your boss's office to ask for the week's leave.

* You are in a restaurant. Your steak is over-cooked. You wanted it cooked rare. Ask the waiter to bring you another steak.

2. Choose a speech act (such as asking someone for a favour, or complaining about something) and discuss how it is performed in English and in another language. Discuss cross-cultural differences in the way the speech act is performed and how it is responded to, and why. For example, is what you say influenced by different views of politeness? Is it influenced by different views of appropriate social behaviour? Or is it influenced by different views of social relationships?

3. Think of a situation where you have experienced cross-cultural pragmatic failure; that is, a situation you think there has been a misunderstanding and the reason for this is cross-cultural. Explain what happened, why you think it happened and what you would tell someone else who found themselves in a similar situation.

4. Think of examples of face-threatening acts; that is acts (such as complaining, or refusing someone who has asked you out on a date). What are some ways you might respond to these acts, and why?

3.15 Data analysis projects

Collect several examples of spoken or written language. In each case, try to collect a complete example of the text, rather than just a section of it. Transcribe (in the case of spoken texts) and analyse the data you have collected from one of the following perspectives.

1. Carry out a speech act analysis of your texts to identify *direct speech acts* and *indirect speech acts*. Analyse in what way the speakers 'mean more than what they say'; that is, what is the difference between the literal meaning of what they say and what you think they mean by what they say. Why do you think they chose to use a direct or an indirect speech act?

2. Carry out an analysis of your sample texts concentrating on Grice's maxim of co-operative behaviour. Find examples where people are observing (or not) his maxims of quality (tell

the truth), quantity (say no more than you need to), relation (be relevant in what you say) and manner (be clear and unambiguous in what you say). Look at Schiffrin (1994) Chapter 6 for examples of this kind of analysis.

3. Carry out an analysis of your sample texts concentrating on *involvement* and *independence*. That is, look for strategies which show closeness, intimacy, rapport and solidarity (involvement strategies) and strategies which give the other person choices and allow them to maintain their freedom (independence strategies). How do the speakers use language to do this?

4. Carry out a *cross-cultural pragmatic analysis* of a particular speech act. That is, look at how someone performs a particular speech act in English and in another language. In what way/s are they similar and in what way/s are they different? Why do you think this might be the case? Lo Castro (2003) Chapter 11 is a useful starting point for this analysis.

Directions for further reading

Cameron, D. (2001), *Working with Spoken Discourse*. London: Sage. Chapter 6. Doing things with words: pragmatics.
This chapter discusses the history of speech act theory, the relationship between form and function, Grice's principles of co-operative communication, politeness and face. The chapter then takes one example of a speech act, complements and considers it from a politeness perspective. Challenges to the view that pragmatic strategies are universal are also discussed.

Celce-Murcia, M. and Olshtain, E. (2000), *Discourse and Context in Language Teaching. A Guide for Language Teachers*. Cambridge: Cambridge University Press. Chapter 2. Pragmatics in discourse analysis.
This chapter of Celce-Murcia and Olshtain's book discusses central issues in the area of pragmatics. This includes contextual meaning, Grice's co-operative principle, the relationship between speech acts and social functions and politeness theory.

Eslami-Rasekh, Z. (2005), 'Raising the pragmatic awareness of language learners', *ELT Journal*, 59, 3, 199–208.
Eslami-Rasekh's article discusses the stereotyped labelling of learners as insensitive or rude as a result of cross-cultural pragmatic failure. She then presents suggestions for raising learners' pragmatic awareness in language learning classrooms.

4 Discourse and genre

One of the key ways in which people communicate with each other is through the participation in particular communicative events, or *genres*. Richards and Schmidt (2002: 224) define the term genre as:

> a type of discourse that occurs in a particular setting, that has distinctive and recognizable patterns and norms of organization and structure and that has particular and distinctive communicative functions.

A letter to the editor is an example of a genre. Letters to the editors occur in a particular setting such as in newspapers and magazines. They have distinctive and recognizable patterns of organization and structure. That is, they typically have a heading at the top, the body of the letter and the name of the author of the letter at the end. They are typically fairly short and they usually aim to comment, or present a particular point of view, on a topic of current interest to the readers of the newspaper or magazine. Other examples of genres are news reports, business reports, parliamentary speeches, summing up in a court of law and weather reports. Each of these occurs in a particular setting, is organized in a particular way and has a distinctive communicative function, or purpose.

In recent years there has been increased attention given to the notion of genre in discourse studies as well as in the area of language teaching and learning. The approach to genre analysis commonly applied in the teaching of English for specific purposes is based on Swales' (1981, 1990) analyses of the discourse structure of research article introductions. Swales uses the notion of *stages* to describe the discourse structure of texts. The notion of genre has also been used in the teaching of writing in the work of the *Sydney School* (Hyon 1996) of genre studies. Here the term *schematic structure* (or *generic structure*) is often used to describe the discourse structure of texts.

The following example of a letter to the editor shows the stages, or schematic structure, of a sample text. This letter was sent to a local newspaper, a typical setting for a letter to the editor. It is laid out in a typical manner for a letter, and has a typical communicative function, or purpose, for a letter to the editor; that is, to argue a point. On the left of the text is the discourse structure of the text which is typical of letters, in general. On the right of the text is the discourse structure which is typical of an argument-type text (see Hartford and Mahboob 2004; Wang 2004 for further discussions of letters to the editor).

Sender's address	34 Victoria St Lake's Entrance 3099	
Telephone number	Tel – 9380 7787	
Date	20 April 1995	
Receiver's address	Letters to the Editor The Sunday Age	
Salutation	Dear Sir/Madam	
Body of the letter	I feel compelled to write to you about the appalling way Stephen Downes denigrates restaurants and, in fact, the very food which he is, sadly, in the position of 'judging'.	Thesis statement
	He has a happy knack of putting the reader completely off by his disgusting descriptions. He also completely disregards the joy that simplicity brings to the customer, who after all are the whole reason for the restaurants in the first place.	Argument
	I do speak with a great deal of knowledge as my husband and I, until recently, owned and were chefs at our two restaurants, Sartain's at Metung and Sally's, Lakes Entrance.	Evidence 1

83

	Mr Downes' snide remarks about the entrees **Evidence 2** at the Pavilion, St Kilda Beach, just indicate he has absolutely no idea of the wishes of even the most discerning customers. Then, when he mentioned the 'subtle slime' to go with the 'massive scrum' of yabbies, I felt it was time to act! How dare he describe a dish so badly, then call it a quality product. He insults the chef.
	The Main Event. Well, I was sad to hear that **Evidence 3** for $21.50 the garfish were not boned, but that is the restaurant's choice and I don't cri- ticise. He describes two tiny potatoes as being 'tired', when obviously it is the receiver who is 'spoilt' and 'tired' of judging so much food.
	Don't let Stephen Downes destroy descriptions **Summing up** of good food. Having made these derogatory remarks about the restaurant, he then awards them three stars. Very strange.
Sign off	Yours faithfully
Signature	*Sally Sartain*
Sender's name	Sally Sartain

Figure 4.1   *The discourse structure of a letter to the editor* (Sartain 1995)

4.1   What is a genre?

What indeed then are genres? Genres are ways in which people 'get things done' through their use of spoken and written discourse. In the previous example, Sally Sartain chose a letter to the editor to make her point, rather than a phone call to the editor of the newspaper, or indeed a letter or phone call to the reviewer she is complaining about. She did this, no doubt, because she wanted to make her point in the public manner of a letter to the editor, and get maximum coverage for the point she wanted to make.

A *genre* is a 'kind of' text. Academic lectures and casual con-versations are examples of spoken genres. Newspaper reports and academic essays are examples of written genres. Instances of a genre often share a number of features. They may be spoken or written in typical, and sometimes conventional, ways. They also often have a common function and purpose (or set of functions and purposes). Genres may typically be performed by a particular person aimed at a particular audience, such as an academic lecture being delivered by a lecturer to a group of undergraduate students. There may be certain contexts in which a genre typically occurs, such as a lecture taking place in a university lecture theatre, and certain topics that are typically associated with the use of a genre, such as particular academic course content. Genres change through time. This may, for example, be in response to changes in technologies or it may be as a result of changes in values underlying the use of the particular genre. The office memo is an example of a genre that has changed in response to technological changes. An office meeting may change when a new person takes over chairing the meeting who has a different idea from their predecessor as to how the meeting should be run, what is important to discuss, and how this should be discussed.

We use language in particular ways according to the content and purpose of the genre, the relationship between us and the person we are speaking to, or the audience we are writing for. The way we use language in a particular genre also depends on whether the text is written or spoken, and the social and cultural context in which the genre occurs. When we do this, we draw on our previous experience with the genre to know how we should normally do this, as Sally Sartain has clearly done in her letter to the editor. This does not mean, however, that every instance of a genre is the same, nor that genres do not change. Genres in fact vary in terms of their typicality. That is, a text may be a typical example of a genre, or a less typical one, but still be an example of the particular genre.

People, further, may deliberately place one genre within another. Bhatia (1997) calls this 'genre embedding'. Genre embedding refers to where one genre, for example, a letter, a story or a newspaper article, is used for another 'conventionally distinct' genre, such as an advertisement to sell a product, or a job advertisement.

Examples of genre change can be seen in the way the Internet has influenced existing forms of communications, such as internal office memos, and has introduced new forms of communication such as Internet chat rooms, blogs and online discussion forums. The introduction of new technologies can also bring with it new genres, such as the way mobile phones have introduced the new genre of text messaging.

i. Defining genre

Martin's (1984: 25) definition of genre as 'a staged, goal-oriented, purposeful activity in which speakers engage as members of our culture' has been extremely influential in the work of the Sydney School of genre analysis. Martin and Rose (2003: 7), elaborating on this definition, add:

> Social because we participate in genres with other people; goal-oriented because we use genres to get things done; staged because it usually takes us a few steps to reach our goals.

Swales (2004: 61) says he prefers the notion of 'metaphor' for talking about genres, rather than 'definition', saying that definitions are often not 'true in all possible worlds and all possible times' and can 'prevent us from seeing newly explored or newly emerging genres for what they really are'.

ii. Choice and constraint in the use of spoken and written genres

Drawing on the work of Devitt (1997), Swales (2004) discusses the view of genre in which there are both choices and constraints, regularity and chaos. Genres are dynamic and open to change, but it is not a case of 'free for all' or 'anything goes'. As Devitt (2004: 86) explains, conformity among genre users 'is a fact of genre, for genres provide an expected way of acting'. As she argues, there are often consequences for violating genre expectations, and these consequences cannot always be predicted. Both constraint and choice, she argues, are necessary and positive components of genres. It is not necessarily the case that choice (or creativity) is good and constraint is bad. Both need to be valued.

In Bhatia's (1998: 25–6) words:

> Practicing a genre is almost like playing a game, with its own rules and conventions. Established genre participants, both writers and readers, are like skilled players, who succeed by their manipulation and exploitation of, rather than a strict compliance with, the rules of the game. It is not simply a matter of learning the language, or even learning the rules of the game, it is more like acquiring the rules of the game in order to be able to exploit and manipulate them to fulfil professional and disciplinary purposes.

iii. Assigning a text to a genre category

A key issue underlying this discussion is how we define a text as an instance of a particular genre, or in other words, how we assign it to a 'genre category'. Cook (1989) argues that we draw on many aspects of language and context to do this. We may consider the author (or speaker) of the text and the intended audience of the text. We may also consider the purpose of text, the situation in which the text occurs, the physical form and, in the case of written texts, the title of the text. We may be influenced by a pre-sequence to the text, such as 'Once upon a time' as well as the discourse structure of the text. Other factors that might help us decide what genre the text is may include the content of the text, the level of formality of the text, particular uses of language in the text, the style or register of the text and whether it is a spoken or a written text. Some of these may be more important than others in helping us to decide what genre a text is. Some may also be difficult to determine, such as the purpose (or purposes) of the text. Figure 4.2 summarizes this using the letter to the editor from Figure 4.1 as an example.

Author	Member of the public
Audience	Editor of the newspaper, the wider public
Purpose	To argue a point
Situation	A local newspaper
Physical form	Written on a sheet of paper
Pre-sequence	Dear Sir/Madam
Internal structure	sender's address + date + editor's address + salutation + body of the letter + sign off + signature + sender's name
Content	Topic of relevance to the readership of the newspaper
Level of formality	Medium level of formality
Style	Typed, use of the first person
Written language	Mostly complete sentences
Requirements	Letter must be signed, contact details must be given

Figure 4.2 *Typical features of a letter to the editor*

Morton's (1999) book about Monica Lewinsky, *Monica's Story*, provides an interesting example of genre classification. The following conversation between a customer and the sales assistant in a bookstore in Los Angeles tries to get at the question 'What genre is it?':

| Customer: | What kind of book would you say this is? Where would you put it on your bookshelves? |
| Sales assistant: | Well .. I suppose you'd call it a biography because it's got some of her earlier life in it. It's not a memoir... I don't know ... It's not very interesting. She got someone else to help her write it. It should have been in the first person, I only read about half of it ... I don't know... Maybe it's an exposé... |

On the cover of the taped version of the book, *Monica's Story* is classified as 'a candid intimate biography of a young woman whose life holds some surprising secrets'. In this case, the sales assistant sees the book as an instance of a slightly different genre from that of the publisher, and perhaps even the author. In her case she draws on her expectations for different genres and what she already knows about the particular text. She draws on formal features of the genre, such as the use of the third person, the content and bias of the text, the author of the text, the purpose of the text and the physical form and situation in which the text occurs. What to one person, then, may be an instance of a particular genre may, to another person, be more like an instance of another.

Linguists such as Hasan (1989a) have suggested that the crucial properties of a genre can be expressed as a range of possible textual structures. Martin (1992), equally, puts forward the view that genres can be defined in terms of similarities and differences in the discourse structures of the texts. While discourse structure is clearly a characterizing features of some genres, it is not always the case that every instance of a particular genre will have exactly the same discourse structures (nor indeed the same communicative purpose) (Askehave and Swales 2000). An academic essay, for example, may be an 'explanation', 'evaluation' or 'argument' type text, or a combination of these, as indeed may be a summing up in a court of law. Equally, advertisements may serve not only to inform, but also to persuade, cajole, frighten, shock, worry or arouse (Cook 1989).

Communicative purpose is an important (although complex) criterion for deciding whether a text is an instance of a particular genre. That is, a text may be presented in an unusual way (for that particular genre) but still have the same communicative aim as other instances of the particular genre. In some cases, the text might be considered a 'best example' of the particular genre, and in others, it might be so atypical as to be considered a 'problematic' example of the genre. Shopping lists, responses to letters of recommendation and company brochures, for example, may have more than a single communicative purpose (Askehave and Swales 2000). A book review may describe and evaluate a book but may also 'promote' the book. Book introductions which introduce the work may also promote it (Bhatia 1997).

The issue of genre identification is, thus, a complex one and requires a flexible, rather than a static view of what it is that leads users of a language to recognize a communicative event as an instance of a particular genre. A key factor in this process lies in a perspective on genre based on the notion of *prototype* rather than on sets of *defining features*. Genres are most helpfully seen as 'resources for meaning' rather than 'systems of rules' (Swales 2002: 25). There may be typical ways in which they are organized at the discourse level, typical situations in which they occur, and typical things they 'aim to do'. It is not always the case, however, that these will necessarily be the same in every instance, even though they may be in the majority of cases.

Assigning a text to a genre category, then, does not necessarily involve an exact match in terms of characteristics or properties. Rather, it involves the notion of 'sufficient similarity' (Swales 1990) to have a relationship with other examples of the genre in the particular genre category. Genres, further, may overlap in some ways, and still remain members of the same genre category. A text may also belong to more than the one genre category, such as a book review being used as an advertisement.

4.2 Relationships between genres

A recent development in genre theory has been the notions of *genre networks*, *genre chains*, *genre sets* and *repertoires of genres* (Tardy 2003; Devitt 2004; Swales 2004). A key issue here is the way the use of one genre may assume, or depend on the use of a number of other interrelated genres. An example of this is the academic essay which may draw from and cite a number of other genres such as academic lectures, specialist academic texts and journal articles. Academic essays also interrelate closely with assignment guidelines, statements of assessment criteria, tutorial discussions and teacher–student consultations.

i. Genre chains and genre networks

A further example of the interrelatedness of genres can be seen in the job interview which interacts in a *genre chain* with a number of other genres in a particular *genre network* which includes the job advertisement, the position description, the letter of application and the resume. The job interview may then be followed by an offer of appointment and, perhaps, a negotiation of offer, each of which interrelate closely with the genres which precede them. The typical sequence for these genres is shown in Figure 4.3.

job advertisement	position description	letter of application	resume	job interview	offer of appointment	negotiation of offer

Figure 4.3 *A genre chain: applying for a job*

At times people may draw on a *repertoire of genres* to carry out a particular task. A company may, for example, seek further information on a job applicant by means of a telephone call, an email, a letter, a fax or (in some circumstances) a casual conversation. Further information may also be sought by asking a question in passing at lunch or dinner, over a drink, or in a casual corridor conversation with the applicant. In some countries the genre network for job applications may be more complex than this. When applying for certain jobs in Italy, for example, it is often helpful to have someone who knows you who can 'put in a word for you' when you apply for the position; that is, what in Italian is called a 'raccomandazione'. Some public positions in Italy, including very senior ones, also require the applicant to take part in a public written examination, or 'concorso', something which occurs much less often in English-speaking job application settings.

Knowledge about genres, thus, includes an understanding of 'the totality of genres available in the particular sector' (Swales 2004: 22), how these genres interact with each other, which genres a person might choose to perform a particular task, and what the typical sequence and *hierarchy* of these genres might be; that is, which genres might have the most value in the particular setting. In Italy, for example, a 'raccomandazione' may have higher value than a letter of recommendation, or public examination, in the job application process. In other cultures, someone 'putting in a word' for a job applicant may have much less influence or, indeed, a negative effect.

ii. An example of a genre chain: letters to the editor

Letters to the editor provide a useful example of genre chains in that they often refer to and assume a knowledge of other genres and other preceding events. They may refer to another instance of the same genre – that is, a previous letter to the editor – or to a range of different genres (and other knowledges). The letter to the editor from the beginning of

---

DINING: Critic ignores the discerning diners

I feel compelled to write to you about the appalling way Stephen Downes denigrates restaurants and, in fact, the very food which he is, sadly, in the position of 'judging'.

He has a happy knack of putting the reader completely off by his disgusting descriptions. He also completely disregards the joy that simplicity brings to the customer, who after all are the whole reason for the restaurants in the first place.

I do speak with a great deal of knowledge as my husband and I, until recently, owned and were chefs at our two restaurants, Sartain's at Metung and Sally's, Lakes Entrance.

Mr Downes' snide remarks about the entrees at the Pavilion, St Kilda Beach, just indicates he has absolutely no idea of the wishes of even the most discerning customers. Then, when he mentioned the 'subtle slime' to go with the 'massive scrum' of yabbies, I felt it was time to act! How dare he describe a dish so badly, then call it a quality product. He insults the chef.

The Main Event. Well, I was sad to hear that for $21.50 the garfish were not boned, but that is the restaurant's choice and I don't criticise. He describes two tiny potatoes as being 'tired', when obviously it is the receiver who is 'spoilt' and 'tired' of judging so much food.

Don't let Stephen Downes destroy descriptions of good food. Having made these derogatory remarks about the restaurant, he then awards them three stars. Very strange.

Sally Sartain,
Lakes Entrance

Figure 4.4 *Letter to the editor (Sartain 1995)*

this chapter, as it appeared in the newspaper (shown in Figure 4.4), is an example of this.

In this letter, Sally Sartain refers to a review of a restaurant published in a previous edition of the same newspaper. An examination of this review (an extract from which is shown in Figure 4.5), however, confuses Sartain's argument: the restaurant was given a three

---

THE JUDGEMENT   SCORE: ***

....

The Pavilion breaks Melbourne's habit of matching poor   ****   Excellent
restoration and bay views.   ***   Very good
Hallelujah! Its prices are at the high end of the bistro spectrum,   **   Good
but the servings are enormous and well-made from   *   Acceptable
fine ingredients. Professionals are in charge. And you've got   #   Fail
the view. And good service.
And, by the time you read this, a lunch menu with a few
cheaper mains. The wine list is excellent, its prices ranging well.

Figure 4.5 *Review of The Pavilion restaurant (Downes 1995).*

out of four star rating, yet Sally Sartain describes the review as 'appalling'.

However, the opening section from a subsequent newspaper article (see Figure 4.6 below) about the particular food reviewer starts to show a more complex picture of the situation. In this article, the reporter writes about an occasion where the reviewer was refused entry to a restaurant he had come to review. He returned a month later with his company lawyer and was again refused entry. The restaurant owner told him 'You're welcome to eat, but not to write'.

Restaurateur shows food critic the door

BY JAMIE WALKER

They call him 'Close 'em Downes'. It hardly matters to Stephen Downes, who has dined out for 20 years on the fear and loathing he provokes.
Until now, that is. A Melbourne restaurant has banned Downes and the repercussions are being felt far and wide.

Figure 4.6 *Restaurateur shows food critic the door* (Walker 1997)

The notes shown in Figure 4.7 are addressed to the same reviewer, this time pinned to a noticeboard in a Thai restaurant that the reviewer had previously reviewed. The writers of these notes – and the many others on the same board – are clearly referring to a number of previous texts, including a 'one star' review of the Thai restaurant written by the reviewer which was attached to the board alongside the notes.

Dear Stephen Downes
Lovely meal, great service. Will be back
Amanda and Jenna
XXX

S. Downes's review is proof of how useless these reviews are.

Great food, place, service and staff

Stephen, you're very mean!

Figure 4.7 *Notes to the food reviewer*

The letter to the editor shown in Figure 4.1, then, is clearly more than just a reaction to a single text. It is a reaction to a number of previous texts and previous events. Looking at the letter, in isolation, does not provide sufficient information to make a judgement about whether the writer's argument is reasonable or not.

What is interesting about this letter is that the review being written about is really very positive and gives a different view of the reviewer than the letter does. But looking at other reviews done by the same reviewer and the newspaper article about him presents another view on the situation. Each of these texts, thus, interacts with each other within their own particular genre network. Looking at the texts in isolation removes them from this context as well as removes much of the information needed to more fully interpret the texts and to make a judgement about them.

iii. An example of a genre network

Figure 4.8 is an example of a genre network based on the genres students engaged in graduate study at a US university need to be familiar with. This network shows genres outside of the typical ones university students might assume they need to be able to take part in, in order to succeed in (and beyond) their university studies. The sequence in which they take part in these genres may vary, and may not be necessarily the same for every student, but they are part of a typical repertoire of genre needs for many graduate students. A further issue for students in this kind of setting is that many of the genres they need to be able to participate in are what Swales (1996) terms *occluded* or *supporting genres* (Swales and Feak 2000); that is, genres which are 'closed', not public in nature and often difficult to access examples of. Swales and Feak contrast these with *open genres*; that is, genres that are public, are often published, and are easily visible or audible. As they point out supporting genres often pose particular problems for graduate students and beginning researchers.

iv. An example of genre sets

Figure 4.9 shows the genre chains and *genre sets* around the writing of Swales's (1998) book *Other Floors, Other Voices*. It shows the relationship between his original book proposal and the other genres that he was involved in, and which influenced the production of the final text of his book. Other genres not included here would no doubt include the interviews that were conducted for the study the book is based on (most by Swales, but in the case of his own case study, the interview with Swales by Tony Dudley-Evans), the other data that was examined for the writing of the book, the publisher's contract, any

Figure 4.8 *A genre network for graduate students* (Swales and Feak 2000: 8)

permissions or ethics application that were required for carrying out the research and publication of the book, and any other conversations that may have taken place between the author and the study participants in the process of carrying out the study the book is based on.

4.3 Written genres across cultures

The area of research known as *contrastive rhetoric* (Connor 1996) or more recently *intercultural rhetoric* (Connor 2004) which looks at the use of genres across cultures also has implications for discussions of

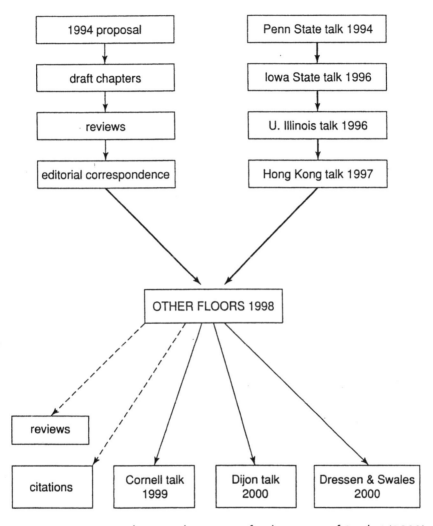

Figure 4.9 *Genre chains and genre sets for the writing of Swales' (1998)
Other Floors, Other Voices* (Swales 2004: 24)

genre. Many studies in the area of contrastive rhetoric have focused on
the discourse structure of academic writing in different languages and
cultures.

Contrastive rhetoric has its origins in the work of Kaplan (1966)
who examined different patterns in the academic essays of students
from a number of different languages and cultures. Although Kaplan
has since revised his strong claim that differences in academic writing

in different languages are the result of culturally different ways of thinking, many studies have found important differences in the discourse structure of academic texts in different languages and cultures.

Other studies, however, have found important similarities in the discourse structure of academic writing across cultures. Cahill (2003), for example, argues that in Chinese and Japanese essay writing, for example, the discourse structure is not always as different from English essay writing as is sometimes supposed. Some Western teachers, he argues, influenced by contrastive rhetoric discussions may expect to see 'Asian ways of writing' in their Asians students' essays 'when they are in fact not there at all' (Cahill 2003: 187). Kubota (1997) argues that just as Japanese expository writing has more than one typical discourse structure, so too does English, and that it is misleading to try to reduce discourse types to the one single norm and to overgeneralize the cultural characteristics of academic writing from a few specific examples.

Leki (1997) argues that many stylistic and discourse devices that are said to be typical of Chinese, Japanese and Thai writing, for example, also occur in certain contexts in English. Equally, features that are said to be typical of English writing appear, on occasion, in other languages as well. Contrastive rhetoric, she argues, can most usefully be seen, not as the study of culture-specific thought patterns, but as the study of 'the differences or preferences in the pragmatic and strategic choices that writers make in response to external demands and cultural histories' (1997: 244).

Canagarajah (2002: 68) argues that contrastive rhetoric research needs 'to develop more complex types of explanation for textual difference' if it is to enjoy continued usefulness in the teaching of academic writing. Genre analysis, he suggests, is able to help provide some of this explanation, as long as it keeps away from normative, rule-governed and 'value-free' descriptions of genre-specific discourse patterns.

4.4 Spoken genres across cultures

Much less attention has been given, however, to differences in spoken genres across cultures. One interesting study that does do this is Nakanishi's (1998) examination of 'going on a first date' in Japanese, which in his study meant mostly having dinner with someone for the purpose of getting to know them better. Nakanishi collected data from 61 Japanese women and 67 Japanese men. He then compared his findings with similar research carried out in the US. Nakanishi was interested in the typical sequence of events in the lead up to, the carrying out and the closing of this genre in Japanese. He was also interested in how Japanese men and women acted during, and at the end of, the first date. He found the way men and women conceptualized this genre in Japanese was very similar. He found, however, gender specific behaviour in the performance of this genre such as the Japanese women avoiding silence during the date and asking a lot of questions to find out more about their dating partner. The Japanese women were also much less hesitant in expressing their ideas and feelings on a first date than they would be in many other genres in Japanese. This was especially interesting as in other genres silence and reticence are perfectly acceptable in Japanese and, indeed, quite normal. If the Japanese women had been silent he found, they often thought the date had not been a success. What is especially interesting about this study is that the women in Nakanishi's study behaved in a way during the date that is not typical of what someone familiar with Japanese culture and communication styles might expect.

In the US study, the men took proactive roles in setting up the date and deciding where it would be, as they did in the Japanese study. The men in both sets of data were also more proactive and the women more reactive in the closing of the date. The role of conversation in the two sets of data differed remarkably however. In the US data the women saw their role as following their dating partner's lead in the conversation, and helping to keeping the conversation going, whereas the Japanese women much more often initiated the conversation and the choice of topics in the conversation. There was also an important role for non-verbal behaviour during the date in the Japanese data that was quite different from the US data. The Japanese women observed their dating partner's behaviour as a way of finding out more about them. They looked at the way the men ate (my Japanese students tell me they can tell a lot about a person's upbringing from the way they eat) and their use of eye contact. The American women commented more on what the men physically did, or did not do on the date, saying things such as 'He lost points for not opening my car door' and 'He never touched me the whole night ... I began to wonder about him' (my Japanese female students tell me they would be horrified if a boy touched them on the first date). The role of conversation and non-verbal behaviour in the two settings, thus, was quite different. It is important to remember, then, that while there may be ways of performing the same genre across cultures that are quite similar, there may also be parts of the genre that are significantly (and importantly) quite different.

4.5 Steps in genre analysis

Bhatia (1993) presents a number of steps for carrying out the analysis
of genres. He does not argue that we need to go through all the stages
he lists, nor in the order in which he presents them. For example, we
may decide to take a 'text-first' or a 'context-first' approach to the
analysis of a particular genre (Flowerdew 2002). That is, we may
decide to start by looking at typical discourse patterns in the texts we
are interested in (a text-first approach), or we may decide to start with
an examination of the context of the texts we want to investigate (a
context-first approach).

The steps, then, should be used flexibly and selectively
depending on the starting point of the analysis, the purpose of the
analysis, the aspect of the genre that we want to focus on, and the level
of prior knowledge we already have of the particular genre.

The first step is to consider what is already known about the
particular genre. This includes knowledge of the situational and cultural context in which it occurs as well as any conventions that are
typically associated with the genre. For information on this, we can go
to existing literature such as guide books and manuals as well as seek
practitioner advice on the particular genre. It is also helpful to look at
what analyses have already have been carried out of the particular
genre, or other related genres, by looking at research articles or books
on the topic.

The next stage is to refine the analysis by defining the speaker or
writer of the text, the audience of the text and their relationship with
each other. We also need to consider the goal, or purpose, of the texts.
We should think about the networks of texts that surround the genre as
well as identify the subject matter of the text and how this relates to the
context of the text.

The next step is to select the collection of texts we wish to
examine. Bhatia suggests taking a few randomly chosen texts for
exploratory investigation, a single typical text for detailed analysis, or
a larger sample of texts if we wish to investigate a few specified
features.

4.6 The social and cultural context of genres

An important further stage is the examination of the social and cultural
context in which the genre is used. In the case of a written text, factors
that might be considered include:

- the setting of the text;

- the focus and perspective of the text;
- the purpose/s of the text;
- the intended audience for the text, their role and purpose in reading the text;
- the relationship between writers and readers of the text;
- expectations, conventions and requirements for the text;
- the background knowledge, values and understandings it is assumed the writer shares with their readers, including what is important to the reader and what is not;
- the relationship the text has with other texts.

Each of these aspects are important to consider as they all, in their way, have an impact on what a writer writes, and the way they write it.

i. A context analysis of theses and dissertations

Figure 4.10 is an analysis of the social and cultural context of theses and dissertations. It shows the range of factors that impact on how the text is written, how it will be read and, importantly, how it will be assessed.

4.7 The discourse structure of genres

It is then necessary to decide on the linguistic analysis to be carried out on the particular text/s. This may include the discourse structure of the texts. It may also include an examination of language features typically found in the texts. The function that the discourse structures and language features typically perform in the texts may also be considered.

i. An example: the discourse structure of theses and dissertations

Figure 4.11 is an analysis of the typical discourse structure of theses and dissertations. This analysis comes from a study (Paltridge 2002) that examined theses and dissertations written in a range of different study areas. The texts were collected and analysed in terms of the overall organizational structure of each of the texts. A comparison was then made between the texts in order to see if there was a recurring pattern of structural organization across the set of texts. The study showed that, rather than there being just the one single type of discourse pattern that is typical for theses and dissertations, there are at least four different types of pattern that writers typically choose from,

99

Setting of the text	The kind of university and level of study, the kind of degree (e.g. honours, master's or doctoral, research or professional) Study carried out in a 'hard' or 'soft', pure or applied, convergent or divergent area of study (Becher and Trowler 2001)
Focus and perspective of the text	Quantitative, qualitative or mixed method research Claims that can be made, claims that cannot be made Faculty views on what is 'good' research
Purpose of the text	To answer a question, to solve a problem, to prove something, to contribute to knowledge, to display knowledge and understanding, to demonstrate particular skills, to convince a reader, to gain admission to a particular area of study
Audience, role and purpose in reading the text	To judge the quality of the research Primary readership of one or more examiners, secondary readership of everyone else the student shows their work to How readers will react to what they read, the criteria they will use for assessing the text, who counts the most in judging the quality of the text
Relationship between writers and readers of the text	Students writing for experts, for admission to an area of study (the primary readership), students writing for peers, for advice (the secondary readership) Writer identity, authority and positioning
Expectations, conventions and requirements for the text	An understanding and critical appraisal of relevant literature A clearly defined and comprehensive investigation of the research topic Appropriate use of research methods and techniques for the research question Ability to interpret results, develop conclusions and link them to previous research Level of critical analysis, originality and contribution to knowledge expected Literary quality and standard of presentation expected Level of grammatical accuracy required How the text is typically organized, how the text might vary for a particular research topic, area of study, kind of study and research perspective What is typically to be contained in each chapter The amount of variation allowed in what should be addressed and how it should be addressed The university's formal submission requirements in terms of format, procedures and timing
Background knowledge, values and understandings	The background knowledge, values and understandings it is assumed students will share with their readers, what is important to their readers, what is not important to their readers How much knowledge students are expected to display, the extent to which students should show what they know, what issues students should address, what boundaries students can cross
Relationship the text has with other texts	How to show the relationship between the present research and other people's research on the topic, what counts as valid previous research, acceptable and unacceptable textual borrowings, differences between reporting and plagiarizing

Figure 4.10 *The typical social and cultural context of theses and dissertations*

Traditional: simple	Topic-based
Introduction Literature review Materials and methods Results Discussion Conclusions	Introduction Topic 1 Topic 2 Topic 3, etc. Conclusions
Traditional: complex	**Compilation of research articles**

Introduction
Background to the study and review
of the literature
(Background theory)
(General methods)
Study 1
   Introduction
   Methods
   Results
   Discussion and conclusions
Study 2
   Introduction
   Methods
   Results
   Discussion and conclusions
Study 3, etc.
   Introduction
   Methods
   Results
   Discussion and conclusions
Discussion
Conclusions
	Introduction
	Background to the study
	Research article 1
	   Introduction
	   Literature review
	   Materials and methods
	   Results
	   Discussion
	   Conclusions
	Research article 2
	   Introduction
	   Literature review
	   Materials and methods
	   Results
	   Discussion
	   Conclusions
	Research article 3, etc.
	   Introduction
	   Literature review
	   Materials and methods
	   Results
	   Discussion
	   Conclusions
	   Discussion
	   Conclusions

Figure 4.11 *Typical discourse structures of theses and dissertations (Paltridge 2002: 135)*

depending on the focus and orientation of their thesis or dissertation. Following previous research on the topic, these four thesis and dissertation types were labelled 'simple traditional', 'complex traditional', 'topic-based' and 'compilations of research articles'. The four types are shown in Figure 4.11. The sequence of items in the chart shows the typical sequence in the sections of the texts. The sections in brackets are 'optional' in the texts. That is, they occurred in some instances of the genre, but not in all of them.

4.8 Applications of genre analysis

Writers such as Hammond and Macken-Horarick (1999) argue that genre-based teaching can help students gain access to texts and discourses which will, hopefully, help them participate more successfully in second language spoken and written interactions. Other writers, such as Luke (1996), argue that teaching 'genres of power' (such as academic essays or dissertations) leads to uncritical reproduction of the status quo and does not necessarily provide the kind of access we hope it might provide for our learners. Others, such as Christie (1993) and Martin (1993) argue that not teaching genres of power is socially irresponsible in that it is the already disadvantaged students who are especially disadvantaged by programmes that do not address these issues.

Other issues that have been raised include the extent to which the teaching and learning of genres might limit student expression if this is done through the use of model texts and a focus on audience expectations. This is clearly something teachers need to keep in mind in genre-based teaching. Teachers equally need to think about how they can help students bring their own individual voices into their use of particular genres (Swales 2000). Students also need to be careful not to overgeneralize what they have learnt about one genre and apply it inappropriately to their use of other genres (Hyon 2001).

Gee (1997) argues that it is simply good teaching to help learners learn what they need to know. She sees the explicitness of genre-based teaching as one of its strengths in that it provides a discourse-based framework for learners to draw on as they need. She argues that a development of genre awareness in terms of types of genres and their characteristic features is essential for learners so that they are aware of the purposes that different genres serve in society and culture, and can learn to gain control of these genres.

Kay and Dudley-Evans (1998) discuss teachers' views on genre and its use in second language classrooms. Some of the teachers Kay and Dudley-Evans spoke to were concerned that a genre-based approach may become too prescriptive. The teachers pointed to the need to highlight the kind of variation that occurs in particular genres as well as consider why this might be. Care, then, needs to be taken to avoid a reductive view of genres and the textual information that is given to students about them.

The teachers Kay and Dudley-Evans spoke to also stressed the importance of contextualizing genres in the classroom by discussing purpose, audience and underlying beliefs and values, before moving on to focus on the language features of a text. They said learners should be exposed to a wide range of sample texts and that these should be both authentic and suitable for the learners. They also felt a genre-based approach should be used in combination with other approaches, such as process and communicative approaches to language teaching and learning. They said, however, they thought a genre-based approach was especially suitable for beginner and intermediate level students in that the use of model texts gave them confidence as well as something to fall back on. They concluded that genre provided a useful framework for language teaching and learning as long as it was made clear that the examples of genres they presented with were just possible models and not rigid sets of patterns.

Scott and Groom (1999) present a similar view, saying that genres are not fixed codes but just one of the resources students need for the expression and communication of meaning. The teaching of generic forms, for Scott and Groom, does not discount the use of models, but rather sees models as part of a of wider repertoire of resources that students can draw on and adapt, as appropriate, to support their meaning making.

Genres, then, provide a *frame* (Swales 2004) which enables people to take part in, and interpret, particular communicative events. Making this genre knowledge explicit can provide learners with the knowledge and skills they need to communicate successfully in particular situations. It can also provide learners with access to socially powerful forms of language.

Discussion questions

1. Bazerman (1988: 7) argues that 'attempts to understand genre by the texts themselves are bound to fail'. Select several examples of a genre. Consider what there is 'beyond the text' (Freedman 1999) that you need to know about in order to fully understand the texts. For example, what is it you need to know about the social and cultural setting of the text, the people involved in the text, or the social expectations and values which underlie the particular text. Read Paltridge (2004) for an example of an analysis which examines some of these issues.

2. Read Johns (1993) on genre and audience. Consider what Johns has to say about audience in relation to a genre that is important for university students. How might the notion of audience help the students with their written work? For example, how useful is it for students to think about who they are writing for, and what that person expects of them?

3. Look at a number of newspaper reports in several different newspapers which are all on the same topic. What background knowledge do the reports assume? That is, what do they expect you already know (and don't know) about the topic of the article? Also, in what way is each of the newspaper reports different? That is, how does the intended readership of the newspaper effect how the article is written? How can you explain these differences?

4. Find several instances of a genre which seem to you to be prototypical of the particular genre. What are some features of the genre that seem to you to be typical for the particular genre? Then find one text which is not so typical for the genre. Try to explain these differences.

4.10 Data analysis projects

1. Look at examples of essays written in different subject areas. Have a look for similarities and differences in the way they are written. For example, are they all laid out the same way? Do they use headings or are they just continuous text? How do the writers support their arguments? Do they refer to published sources, or do they refer to their own personal experiences? Consider what the reason might be for these differences.

2. Collect a number of examples of a genre that has developed, or changed, in response to changes in technology. For example, look at email messages and consider what some of the characteristics are that are particular to them. Consider why they are written this way.

3. Do a context analysis of a spoken or written genre based on the following set of headings:
   - the setting of the genre;
   - the focus and perspective of the genre;
   - the purpose/s of the genre;
   - the intended audience for the genre;
   - the relationship between participants in the genre;
   - expectations, conventions and requirements for the genre;
   - the background knowledge, values and understandings it is assumed genre participants will share

with each other, including what is important to them and what is not;

- the relationship the genre has with other texts and genres.

Look at a number of sample texts to help you with this. Also interview people who take part in the genre and ask them about each of these points.

4. Collect a number of examples of a particular genre and analyse the schematic structure of each text. Look at Hyland (2004a) Chapter 2 for suggestions on how to do this. What is common to all of the texts and what is not? Why might some of the texts be different?

4.11 Directions for further reading

Hyland, K. (2004a), *Genre and Second Language Writing*. Ann Arbor: University of Michigan Press.
Hyland's book on genre and writing is a clear and accessible introduction to theory and research in the area of written genres, and as well as the application of these understandings to the practical concerns of second language classrooms.

Johns, A. M. (1997), *Text, Role and Context: Developing Academic Literacies*. Cambridge: Cambridge University Press.
The book describes Johns' socio-literate approach to genre-based teaching and, in particular, the teaching of academic writing. She discusses how teachers can work with students and academic staff to help students write texts that consider the goals, role and purpose of their pieces of writing, as well as the academic institutions in which they are writing.

Paltridge, B. (2001), *Genre and the Language Learning Classroom*. Ann Arbor: University of Michigan Press.
This book presents an overview of approaches to genre in the area of language teaching and learning. Practical activities for language teachers to consider are presented in each of the chapters.

Swales, J. M. (1990), *Genre Analysis: English in Academic and Research Settings*. Cambridge: Cambridge University Press.
This book is a seminal work in the area of genre studies and especially in the area of English for specific purposes. It provides an extensive definition of the term genre as well as outlines key theoretical issues in the area of genre analysis. This work is continued in Swales' (2004) book *Research Genres: Explorations and Applications*.

5 Discourse and conversation

A major area of study in the analysis of discourse is conversation analysis. Conversation analysis looks at ordinary everyday spoken discourse and aims to understand, from a fine-grained analysis of the conversation, how people manage their interactions. It also looks at how social relations are developed through the use of spoken discourse. This chapter discusses the principles underlying conversation analysis. It then outlines procedures in transcribing and coding data. The chapter gives examples of the kinds of conversational strategies speakers use as well as providing examples of these in a number of different kinds of conversational interactions.

Conversation analysis is an approach to the analysis of spoken discourse that looks at the way in which people manage their everyday conversational interactions. It examines how spoken discourse is organized and develops as speakers carry out these interactions. Conversation analysis has examined aspects of spoken discourse such as sequences of related utterances (*adjacency pairs*), preferences for particular combinations of utterances (*preference organization*), *turn taking, feedback, repair, conversational openings and closings, discourse markers* and *response tokens*. Conversation analysis works with recordings of spoken data and carries out careful and fine-grained analyses of this data.

5.1 Background to conversation analysis

Conversation analysis originated in the early 1960s at the University of California with the work of Sacks, Schegloff and Jefferson. Conversation analysis comes from the field of sociology. It, thus, takes less of a 'linguistics' view of spoken discourse than some other forms of discourse analysis. This draws from its interest, in particular, in how language goes about performing social action. Conversation analysts are interested, in particular, in how social worlds are jointly constructed and recognized by speakers as they take part in conversational discourse. Early work in conversation analysis looked mostly at everyday spoken interactions such as casual conversation. This has since been extended to include spoken discourse such as doctor–patient consultations, legal hearings, news interviews, psychiatric interviews and interactions in courtrooms and classrooms.

i. Issues in conversation analysis

A key issue in conversation analysis is the view of ordinary conversation as the most basic form of talk. For conversation analysts, conversation is the main way in which people come together, exchange information, negotiate and maintain social relations. All other forms of talk-in-interaction are thus derived from this basic form of talk. It is not the case that other forms of talks are the same as ordinary conversation. They do, however, exploit the same kinds of resources as 'ordinary conversation' to achieve their social and interactional goals.

A further key feature of conversation analysis is the primacy of the data as the source of information. Analyses, thus, do not incorporate speakers' reflections on their interactions, field notes or interviews as ways of gathering information about the discourse. In the view of conversation analysts, the use of this kind of data represents idealizations about how spoken discourse works and is, thus, not valid data for analysis. Conversation analysis, thus, focuses on the analysis of the text for its argumentation and explanation, rather than consideration of psychological or other factors that might be involved in the production and interpretation of the discourse.

One of the aims of conversation analysis is to avoid starting with assumptions about analytical categories in the analysis of conversational data. Conversation analysts, rather, look for phenomena which regularly occur in the data and then make that the point of further investigation. Interest is, in particular, in fine-tuned analysis of the sequence, structure and coherence of conversations.

In this view, conversation is seen as being 'context-shaped' and 'context-renewing' in the sense that 'anything anyone says in conversation both builds on what has been said or what has been going on ... [as well as] creates the conditions for what will be said next' (Gardner 1994: 102). Conversation analysts, thus, aim to demonstrate how participants both produce and respond to evolving social contexts, using conversational, rather than contextual data, as the source for the claims it wishes to make.

ii. Transcribing and coding conversation analysis data

In conversation analysis, the transcription of the data is also the analysis. Texts are, thus, recorded (either on tape or by video) then analysed at the same time as they are transcribed. If a particular feature such as the use of increased pitch, or particular sequences of utterances, becomes apparent in the analysis, this then becomes the starting point for further analysis. The analyst listens and transcribes to see how frequently this aspect of the conversation occurs and, importantly, if speakers respond to it in the same way each time it occurs. In this way, the analysis aims to understand how speakers manage their conversational interactions.

5.2 Transcription conventions

Particular transcription conventions are used in conversation analysis. The extract from *Sex and the City* that was discussed in Chapter 2 is presented here, transcribed from a conversation analysis perspective. The transcription conventions that are used in this analysis are based on the work of Jefferson (2004) and are shown as a key to the analysis at the end of the conversation:

Charlotte: you're getting enga↑ ged.
Carrie: I threw up I saw the ring and I threw up (.5) that's not normal.
Samantha: that's my reaction to marriage.
Miranda: what do you think you might do if he asks.
Carrie: I don't know.
Charlotte: just say ye:::s::
Carrie: well (.) it hasn't been long enough (.5) has it?
Charlotte: Trey and I got engaged after only a month=
Samantha: =how long before you separated.
Charlotte: we're together NOW and that's what matters. (.) when it's right you just know
Samantha: Carrie doesn't <u>know</u>.
Carrie: Carrie threw up=
Samantha: =so it might not be right

(Just Say Yes, 4: 12)

Key

↑	shift into especially high pitch
NOW	especially loud sounds relative to the surrounding talk
::	prolongation of the immediately prior sound
(.)	a brief interval (about a tenth of a second) within or between utterances
(0.5)	the time elapsed (by tenths of seconds) between the end of the utterance or sound and the start of the next utterance or sound
<u>now</u>	stress
=	latched utterances – no break or gap between stretches of talk
?	rising intonation
.	falling intonation
,	unfinished intonational contour

The analysis, thus, shows a rising pitch in Charlotte's exclamation 'You're getting engaged!' The . at the end of this utterance indicates an ending with falling intonation, as with most of the other utterances in the conversation. There is no delay between Charlotte's statement and Carrie's response. There is, however, a .5 second pause in Carrie's response before she adds 'That's not normal'. Another speaker could have taken the conversation away from her at the point of the pause but they chose not to, allowing her to comment on what she had previously said.

Charlotte's lengthened vowel in 'Just say yes' emphasizes the point she is making before Carrie replies with 'well' followed by a microsecond pause which allows her to hold the floor in the conversation, and a further .5 second pause before she invites a response from the others with her use of rising intonation and the tag question 'has it?' The next two lines are examples of latched utterances. That is, Samantha adds her comment to Charlotte's statement without allowing anyone else to intervene.

The underlining and use of capitals in '<u>NOW</u>' in Charlotte's response to Samantha indicates both loud talk and word stress. Charlotte's microsecond pause, again, enables her to hold the floor so that no one is able to intervene and she is able to complete what she wants to say. If she had not done this, one of the other speakers could have taken the turn from her as her completed syntactic unit, intonational contour and 'completed action' would have indicated a point at which another speaker could taken the turn; that is, a *transition-relevance place* (TRP) in the conversation. The final example of latched utterances shows that Samantha is able to project, in advance, that a TRP is approaching as Carrie is speaking and takes the floor from Carrie with her consent, and without difficulty.

This analysis, thus, shows how Carrie and her friends manage their conversation in a co-operative manner. They let each other continue with what they want to say, rather then compete for a place in the conversation. It also shows the strategies they use when they want to take a turn in the conversation, such as not letting too much time to lapse before speaking, in case another speaker should take the turn.

5.3 Sequence and structure in conversation

A particular interest of conversation analysis is the sequence and structure of spoken discourse. Aspects of conversational interactions that have been examined from this perspective include conversational openings and closings, turn taking, sequences of related utterances ('adjacency pairs'), preferences for particular combinations of utterances ('preference organization'), feedback and conversational 'repair'.

i. Opening conversations

One area where conversational openings have been examined in detail is in the area of telephone conversations. Schegloff analysed a large data set of telephone openings to come up with the following 'canonical opening' for American private telephone conversations:

		summons/answer
((ring))		sequence
Recipient:	Hello	
Caller:	Hi Ida?	identification/recognition
		sequence
Recipient:	Yeah	
Caller:	Hi, this is Carla=	greeting sequence
Recipient:	=Hi Carla.	
Caller:	How are you.	how are you sequence
Recipient:	Okay:.	
Caller:	Good.=	
Recipient:	=How about you.	
Caller:	Fine. Don wants to know..	reason for call sequence

(Schegloff 1986: 115)

A study carried out by O'Loughlin (1989) in Australia found a similar pattern for opening telephone conversations, except that in the Australian data the caller most frequently self-identified in their first turn after they had recognized their recipient rather than in the second turn, as in the American data.

In a study of telephone openings in Mandarin Chinese, Yang (1997) found the speakers in her study also began their calls with summons/answer and identification/recognition sequences. The greeting and 'how are you' sequences found in American and Australian phone calls, however, were less common or even absent in her data. The majority of the telephone openings she examined went straight from the identification/recognition sequence to the first topic of the conversation. Below is a typical example of the opening of telephone calls in Chinese. The double brackets surrounding the ring of the telephone indicates a sound that is not transcribed:

	((ring))		summons
Recipient:	Wei?	(Hello)	answer
Caller:	Jinghong.	(Jinghong)	identification
Recipient:	Ei.	(Yes)	recognition

(Yang 1997: 25)

The following example from a radio call-in programme illustrates a further way of opening a conversation:

Announcer:	For husband Bruce of twenty-six years Carol has this dedication (.) So how are things going.
Caller:	Absolu::tely wonderful.
Announcer:	That's great to hear you're still happy.
Caller:	Oh yes (.5) very much so.
Announcer:	And what's your dedication all about for Bruce.
Caller:	Well:: we're going away tomorrow to the

> Whitsundays (.) and (.5) umm:: I'm looking for-
> ward to it very much and I know he is too:: for a
> break.

In this conversation the announcer opens the conversation by saying who is on the line and what the conversation will be about. That is, his utterance introduces the caller to the listening audience and readies the speaker for being on-air and for discussing the topic of the call. The middle stage of the conversation is devoted to the topic of the call, finding the dedication that the caller will make. The conversation ends when the caller has provided the dedication and all the information that was asked for, completed a syntactic unit, and employs falling intonation as a signal that she has completed her turn. The announcer does not take the opportunity to take another turn but instead plays the music dedicated to the caller's husband as his way of closing the conversation. He, thus, constrains what the caller can say, excluding the possibility of her bringing up other things that would cause a delay in moving on with the programme (Thornborrow 2001).

ii. Closing conversations

Schegloff and Sacks (1973) have also looked at conversational closings. This work has since been continued by Button (1987) who, in his discussion of telephone closings, points out that telephone closings usually go over four turns of talk, made up of pre-closing and closing moves. The pre-closing is often made up of two turn units consisting of items such as 'OK' and 'all right' with falling intonation. The closing is made up of two further units, such as 'bye bye' and 'goodbye.' Button (1987: 102) calls this an *archetype closing*. In this closing both speakers mutually negotiate the end of the conversation. Other material, how-ever, in the form of an *insertion sequence*, can be introduced between the two units which make up these turns, before the closing finally takes place.

The closing may also be preceded by a number of pre-sequences, such as the making of an arrangement, referring back to something previously said in the conversation, the initiation of a new topic (which may not be responded to), good wishes (such as 'give my love to Jane'), a restatement of the reason for calling and thanks for calling. Sometimes, however, the closing may be foreshortened when the archetype closing is skipped over and a foreshortened closing takes place. Equally the closing may be extended by continued repetition of pre-closing and closing items (such as 'bye', 'bye', 'love you', 'love you', 'sleep well', 'you too', etc.). Closings are, thus, complex interactional units which are sensitive to the speaker's orientation to continuing, closing (or not wanting to close) the conversation (Button 1987; Thornborrow 2001).

iii. Turn taking

Conversation analysis has also examined how people take and manage turns in spoken interactions. The basic rule in English conversation is that one person speaks at a time, after which they may nominate another speaker, or another speaker may take up the turn without being nominated (Sacks *et al* 1974; Sacks 2004). There are a number of ways in which we can signal that we have come to the end of a turn. This may be through the completion of syntactic unit, or it may be through the use of falling intonation, then pausing. We may also end a unit with a signal such as 'mmm' or 'anyway', etc. which signals the end of the turn. The end of a turn may also be signalled through eye contact, body position and movement and voice pitch.

By contrast, we may hold on to a turn by not pausing too long at the end of an utterance and starting straight away with saying something else. We may also hold on to a turn by pausing during an utterance rather than at the end of it. We may increase the volume of what we are saying by extending a syllable or a vowel, or we may speak over someone else's attempt to take our turn.

The previous examples of conversational openings show how speakers give up turns by the completion of syntactic units and falling intonation. The final utterance in the telephone call-in extract shows how the speaker holds on to her final turn, until she has said everything she wants to. She lengthens the syllable in 'well' and 'umm', pauses during her utterance and lengthens the vowel in 'too'. She then indicates she is ready to end her turn.

When speakers pause at the end of a turn, it is not always the case, however, that the next speaker will necessarily take it up. In this case, the pause and the length of the pause become significant (in English, at least). In the following example of a university tutorial discussion, the nominated speaker, Wong Young, does not respond so after a one second pause the lecturer asks again. Wong Young pauses again before he actually takes the turn, during and at the end of the turn. He then extends the syllable in 'uh' and the vowel in 'so', when the lecturer overlaps with 'comments?' as her way of insisting he provide a response to her question. Here the square brackets indicate the point of overlap in the utterances. The normal brackets indicate barely audible speech, and the symbol 'o' indicates speech that is noticeably quieter than the surrounding talk:

113

```
Lecturer:      OK, let's move on, =Tadashi: and (.) Wong Young can
               you,
               (1.0)
Lecturer:      The last, (.) Eleven,
               (0.6)
               What is a profession. (0.3) What distinguishes profes-
               sion from trade, (0.2)
               What does it mean to be a professional? (0.4) Does being
               a pro-professional affect the way you dress (0.2) speak
               behave towards others at work?
               (0.7)
Wong           Uh: o [ (so:) ] o
Young:
Lecturer:              [Comm]ents?
```

(Nakane 2003: 185)

A speaker may also use overlap as a strategy for taking a turn, as well as
to prevent someone else from taking the turn. The following example,
from the same data set, shows this. Here the lecturer has asked Tadashi
a question but another student, Kylie, wants to take the turn and
constantly uses overlap to do this.

```
Lecturer:      There are hundred and forty-nine HSC courses, how
               many languages cour[ses].
Kylie:                             [thi]rty ei[ght]?
Tadashi:                           [uh:];
Kylie:         [thir]ty eight?
Tadashi:       [ uh:]
               (0.3)
Lecturer:      no there are thirty eight langu[ages],
Tadashi:                                      [(lan]guage)=
Lecturer:      =but each language is more than one [cour]se.
Tadashi:                                           [ye:h]
Kylie:         ah [that's right. Yeah that's right yeah]
Lecturer:         [many languages ha[ve mo]re than one]
Tadashi:                            [ uh: ]
Kylie:         [that's]
Lecturer:      [course.]
Kylie:         right.=
Tadashi:       =uh huh huh=
Lecturer:      =all right? (.) do you remember?
Tadashi:       I don't remember.= ((giggling))
Lecturer:      =no? (0.2) okay.
```

(Nakane 2003: 192)

Turn taking, then, varies according to particular situations. In a
classroom, for example, it is often the teacher who nominates who can

take a turn. A student may, or may not respond, or students may compete to take the turn (as in the example above). Students may also put up their hand to ask permission to take a turn. Turn taking may also depend on factors such as the topic of the conversation, whether the interaction is relatively co-operative, how well the speakers know each other, and the relationship between, and relative status of, the speakers (Burns and Joyce 1997).

A *turn constructional unit*, further, can be made up of a single word such as in the above example where the lecturer simply says 'Comments?', or it may be an extended *multi-unit turn*. The unit may simply be a sound such as 'uh' or it may be made up of a word, a phrase, a clause or a sentence with change between speakers occurring at the end of any of these units or during them if another speaker succeeds in talking the floor (Gardner 2004).

iv. Adjacency pairs

Adjacency pairs are a fundamental unit of conversational organization and a key way in which meanings are communicated and interpreted in conversations. Adjacency pairs are utterances produced by two successive speakers in a way that the second utterance is identified as related to the first one as an expected follow-up to that utterance. The following example, again from a radio call-in programme, illustrates speakers using adjacency pairs in a typical and expected way. In each of the pairs of utterances in this interaction the first speaker stops and allows the second speaker to produce the expected second part to the pair of utterances:

Announcer:	Sharon Stone's on the phone. (.) how are yo:::u.
Caller:	very good.
Announcer:	I bet you get hassled about your surname.
Caller:	yes I do::
Announcer:	and what do you want to tell Patrick.
Caller:	umm that I love him very much (.5) and I (.5) and I wish him a very happy birthday for today.

Arguments show a similar pattern in that once a point of view has been expressed, a possible follow-up is a 'challenge' followed by a 'response'. The following examples from an argument about the need for a bouncer at a party show this:

Ryan:	I'm gonna have to get Peter ta come over too (0.1)	Point of view
Marie:	why=	Challenge
Ryan:	=so people don't crash the pa::rdy	Response (Orr 1996: 35)

115

Marie:	Oh they won't crash the [pardy sweetheart]	Challenge
Ryan:	[OH YEAH (.)	Response
	YEAH]	
	Maybe twenty years ago mmm (.) you know	
	(0.2) like today (0.1) I- I- (.) th- there be ea-	
	easy another forty people if ya didn't have a	
	person at the gate	(Orr 1996: 36)

v. Adjacency pairs across cultures

It is important to point out that what is an expected follow-up to a seemingly everyday utterance in one language and culture might be quite different in another. Béal's (1992) study of communication problems in a workplace setting between French and English speakers provides an example of this. Béal found that the French workers often responded to the everyday greeting 'Did you have a good weekend?' by stopping and telling the English-speaking workers all about their weekend. The English-speaking workers were irritated by this and did not realize that a French speaker would not ask this question if they did not want a real (and complete) answer. They did not realize, further, that this is not a typical question French speakers would ask each other in an everyday conversational situation and, even though they sometimes responded by telling them about their weekend, they also saw the question as an invasion of their privacy. Expected follow-ups in the use of adjacency pairs, then, varies across language and cultures.

vi. Adjacency pairs and stage of the conversation

The particular context and stage of the conversation are especially important for assigning an utterance the status of a particular pair part. For example, 'Hello' can perform many different functions in a conversation. It can be a summons in a telephone call and it can be response to a summons in a telephone call. It can also be a way of greeting someone in the street, although clearly not the only way. An utterance such as 'thanks' equally can be a response to a compliment, a congratulation or a response to an offer of service. An utterance, thus, may play more than one role in a conversation.

5.4 Preference organization

The basic rule for adjacency pairs, then, is that when a speaker produces a first pair part they should stop talking and allow the other speaker to produce a second pair part. There is, however, a certain amount of freedom in responding to some first pair parts. For example a compliment can be followed be an 'accept' or a 'reject'. Thus, some second pair parts may be *preferred* and others may be *dispreferred*. For example a question may be followed by an expected answer (the preferred second pair part) or an 'unexpected or non-answer' (the dispreferred second pair part). When this happens, the dispreferred second pair part is often preceded by a 'delay', a 'preface' and/or an 'account'. The following example illustrates this:

A: Are you going out with anyone at the moment? (Question)
B: Uhhh ... (Delay)
       Well, kind of ... (Preface)
       There is someone I met a while back ... (Account)
       Actually, I'm getting married at the end of the year (Unexpected answer)

Table 5.1 is a summary of some common adjacency pairs, together with typical preferred and dispreferred second pair parts.

Table 5.1 *Common adjacency pairs and typical preferred and dispreferred second pair parts* (Levinson 1983).

First pair parts	Second pair parts	
	Preferred	**Dispreferred**
request	acceptance	refusal
offer/invite	acceptance	refusal
assessment	agreement	disagreement
question	expected answer	unexpected answer or non-answer
blame	denial	admission

A study carried out by O'Shannessy (1995) looked at preference organization in barrister–client interactions where the barrister was collecting his clients' history in preparation for presenting their case in court. O'Shannessy found there was a preference for 'other-correction' (rather than 'self-correction') in these interactions. That is, when one of the speakers said something that contained an inaccuracy, it was corrected by the other person rather than the person who had made the error. If an inaccuracy was not corrected, it formed the basis of an inference – that the information provided was correct. The following example shows 'other correction' by the client. The barrister follows the correction with a 'correction accept', then a 'correction confirm', again, preferred responses:

> Barrister: the twins Michael and Allan (.) live with the wife (1.0)
>   Michael in employed as an apprentice butcher.=
> Client: oh not MIChael, ALLan=
> Barrister: <u>ALLAN</u>. Ye:s.
> Solicitor: alrigh.
> Barrister: (0.1) ALLAN is employed as an apprentice but[cher]
>   (O'Shannessy 1995: 56)

The following example, a continuation of the above extract, shows an example of the client not providing an expected answer to the solicitor's question. The solicitor asks his question again to try to get his preferred response, his 'expected answer'. The client does not want (or is unable) to provide the detail the solicitor asks for and draws the set of pairs to a close with 'just leave it that's fine':

> Solicitor: [How] long has he been an apprentice butcher.=
> Client: not very long.
> Solicitor: o how long. o
> Client: maybe three four months I'm not sure=
> Solicitor: is now employed?
> Client: no just leave it that's fine
>   (O'Shannessy 1995: 56)

i. Insertion sequences

Sometimes speakers use an insertion sequence; that is, where one adjacency pair comes between the first pair and the second pair part of another adjacency pair. In the following example Ryan asks his mother, Marie, if he can have a DJ for his party. She doesn't reply but, by means of an insertion sequence, passes the question on to her husband, John:

> Ryan: and (0.2) can I have a DJ too (0.1) is that OK (0.2)
> Marie: John
> John: what
> Marie: can he have a DJ (.) DJ=
> Ryan: =cause you won't be spending much on foo:d so I
>   thought (0.2)
> John: well how much does a DJ cost
> Ryan: yeah I've got to find out
>   (Orr 1996: 59)

5.5 Feedback

Another aspect of spoken interactions that has been examined by conversation analysts is the ways speakers provide each other with feedback; that is, the ways in which listeners show they are attending to what is being said. This can be done, for example, by the use of 'response tokens' such as 'mmm' and 'yeah', by paraphrasing what the other person has just said, or through body position and the use of eye contact. In the following example from the tutorial discussion, the students, Tadashi and Kylie, provide feedback to each other by use of the token 'yeah', the repetition of key words, falling intonation and latched utterances:

Lecturer:	And the middle one (.) i:s:
Tadashi:	Co[mmunity ?] community.
Kylie:	[community] ?
Kylie:	Community, I think it is?
Tadashi:	o Yeah o.=
Kylie:	=Yeah,=
Tadashi:	= o Oh yeah, o (0.4)
Kylie:	Communi – self community. [yeah] .=
Tadashi:	o [yeah]. o =

=Community french community
(Nakane 2003: 182)

It is not always the case, however, that an item such as 'yeah' or 'mm' performs an acknowledging function in a conversation. Gardner (2001), for example, shows that the item 'mmm' can perform many other functions as well. Where it does provide an acknowledging function, it may also serve to prompt a topic change, a recycling of a topic, or it may solve a dispreferred action, for example. The function response items such as 'mmm', 'yeah' and 'OK' perform are also influenced by the intonation, place and timing of the utterance.

5.6 Repair

An important strategy speakers use in spoken discourse is what is termed *repair*; that is, the way speakers correct things they or someone else has said, and check what they have understood in a conversation. Repair is often done through *self repair* and *other repair*. The following example from O'Shannessy's study of barrister–client interactions shows an instance of *self-repair*. In this case, there was no apparent error to the other speaker that needed to be corrected in what had been said:

Client:	because (1.0) he's got a girlfriend – oh (0.5) a woman and ah (0.5)

Other repair occurs where the error is apparent to the other speaker. The following example from the same data set shows this:

> Barrister: Michael is employed as an apprentice butcher.=
> Client: oh not MIChael, ALLan=

5.7 Gender and conversation analysis

Conversation analysis has, in recent years, made a major contribution to discussions of language and gender. With the move from the view of language as a reflection of social reality to a view of the role of language in the construction of social reality (and in turn identity) a number of researchers have examined the social construction of gender from a conversation analysis perspective.

Conversation analysis is able to reveal a lot about how, in Butler's terms, people 'do gender', that is, the ways in which gender is constructed, as a joint activity, in interaction. Weatherall (2002: 114) discusses the concept of *gender noticing* for accounting for gender when 'speakers make it explicit that this is a relevant feature of the conversational interaction'.

The analysis of data from a conversation analysis perspective can help reveal aspects of gendered interactions that might, otherwise, not be considered. Stokoe (2003), for example, does this in her analysis of gender and neighbour disputes. Using *membership categorization analysis* she shows how, in the neighbourhood disputes she examined, the category *woman* was drawn on by people engaged in the interactions to legitimate complaints against their neighbours as well as to build defences against their complaints. The following examples from her data illustrate this. In these examples, Edgar and Vernon are talking about their neighbours for a television documentary called *Neighbours at War*. In their view 'bad' women are foul mouthed, argue in the street and are bullies. Edgar and Vernon, thus, engage in 'gender noticing' in their negative evaluation of their female neighbours:

> Edgar: well (.) she just <u>flew</u> at me (.) <u>a</u>nd (.) the language it was
> and er oh it was <u>incredible</u> for a lady I mean she's only
> a small (.) old la<u>dy</u> (.) I really couldn't believe what was
> happening (.) and then
> Vernon: she's a bully (0.5) that's the best word a b<u>u</u>lly (.) and
> she's a foul mouthed woman (.) she's got no<u>th</u>ing going
> for her as far as I'm concerned (.) she wants to get
> herself sorted out
>
> (Stokoe 2003: 337)

5.8 Conversation analysis and second language conversation

While most studies in the area of conversation analysis have examined native speaker talk, in recent years attention has also shifted to non-native speaker talk. Markee (2000), for example, shows how conversation analysis can be used as a tool for analysing and understanding the acquisition of a second language. He discusses the importance of looking at 'out-lier' data in second language acquisition studies pointing out that, from a conversation analysis perspective, all participants' behaviour makes sense to the individuals involved and must be accounted for, rather than set aside, in the analysis.

Storch (2001a, 2001b) carried out a fine-grained analysis of second language learner talk as her students carried out pair work activities in an ESL classroom. She found this analysis allowed her to identify the characteristics of the talk, and the nature of the interactions they engaged in that contributed to, or impeded, their success in the acquisition of the language items they were focusing on. She also found how the grouping of pairs in the class were important for the nature of their discourse and the extent to which the discourse was collaborative, and facilitated their learning or not.

5.9 Criticisms of conversation analysis

While conversation analysis has very many strengths, it has also attracted criticism. Baxter (2002: 853), while describing conversation analysis as an invaluable tool for the analysis of spoken discourse, also describes it as somewhat 'monolithic'. Hammersley (2003) argues that conversation analysis's view of itself as self-sufficient research tool is problematic; that is, the view that it does not need data other than the conversation to explain and justify its claims. In Hammersley's view the rejection in conversation analysis of what people say about the world they live in and their conversational interactions as sources of insight into the data is a major weakness. He suggests that when we analyse data from a conversation analysis perspective, we are working as 'spectators' not 'participants' in the interaction. It is, thus, not really possible for us to know how the participants view the conversation unless we ask them. It is also not, in reality, possible for an analyst to start on the analysis of their text, completely unmotivated; that is, just looking at the text to see 'what's there' without any preconceived notions of what this might be.

A recent debate (Billig 1999) that took part in the journal *Discourse and Society* on the relationship between conversation analysis and critical discourse analysis further illustrate these points. In this debate Schegloff criticizes critical discourse analysis (see Chapter 8 of this book) for relying on the analyst's view of what is happening in the text rather than looking at how the participants 'take up' what is said in a text. Schegloff also criticizes critical discourse analysts for drawing on what they know about people engaged in an interaction for their interpretation of the data. As Hammersley points out in this debate, however, even Schegloff does this to some extent in his analyses. He gives the example of a study by Schegloff of two parents in a strained relationship, either separated or divorced, talking about their son on the telephone. As Hammersley shows, there is no information about the relationship between the people involved in the conversation in the transcript. This information is, however, crucial to an understanding of the conversation and is, in fact, drawn on by Schegloff in his analysis and interpretation of the data. Just because something is not observable in the data, then, does not mean that it is not relevant. Hammersley's view is that conversation analysis could be more usefully combined with other qualitative, and even quantitative, approaches to discourse analysis to help us further understand how people use conversation to engage in, and construct, their social lives. Conversation analysis, on its own, he argues, does not tell us all there is to know about human social life.

Wooffitt (2005) in his book *Conversation Analysis and Discourse Analysis* outlines further criticisms of conversation analysis. The first of these is conversation analysis's lack of attention to issues of power, inequality and social disadvantage. The second is the lack of attention in conversation analysis studies to wider historical, cultural and political issues. Wetherell (1998) argues that conversation analysis would benefit from considering post-structuralist views on discourse, such as *agency* and the *subject positions* speakers take up in the discourse, rather than just looking at the text itself. That is, the analyses would be enhanced by considering the positions speakers take and the social and cultural values that underlie how they perform in the discourse. Post-structuralist discourse analysis, equally, she adds, would be improved by greater attention to the details of conversational interaction that is typical of work in the area of conversation analysis.

Feminist researchers such as Kitzinger (2000), however, argue that conversation analysis is not incompatible with work that examines issues of power and the wider social and political implications of discourse. She argues that if researchers want to 'understand what people are saying to each other, and how they come to say it, and what it means to them' (Kitzinger 2000: 174) they have to attend to the data at the same level of detail and attention that the speakers do in their talk. She is optimistic, then, of the potential of conversation analysis for feminist and other forms of socially engaged discourse analysis research.

5.10 A sample study: refusals

Kitzinger and Frith (1999) provide an example of a study which draws on conversation analysis and other data sources to examine what speakers say, why they say it, and how what they say is taken up by other people. Their study is about how women communicate (as well as fail to communicate) to men that they do not want to have sex with them; that is, how women refuse unwanted sex.

Their study commences with an examination of how the conversation analysis literature says that people typically refuse offers. As we have seen earlier in this chapter an offer may be followed by one of two possible second pair parts: an acceptance or a refusal. The acceptance is the preferred second pair part to an offer so is less complex than a refusal. It is usually immediate and involves the use of a direct speech act, such as 'Yes, I'd love to'. A refusal, however, is a face-threatening act and is the dispreferred second part to an offer. It is, thus, usually more complex, often indirect and less immediate. The refusal often involves the use of delays, accounts, hedges and prefaces before the speaker gets to the actual refusal of the offer. Thus, telling a woman to 'Just say no' to unwanted sex goes against how people normally carry out refusals, and may not indeed be 'read' by the other person as a refusal, for just this reason.

Kitzinger and Frith outline how conversation analysis shows how people typically accept an offer giving the following as an example of this:

A: Why don't you come up and <u>see</u> me some[time
B: [I would like to
                                            (Atkinson and Drew 1979: 58)

Here, there is no delay. Indeed the acceptance starts before the offer is completed. The reply also uses a direct speech act (I would like to).

The following is an example of how people typically refuse an offer. The second pair part in this example includes an outbreath as a delay (hehh), a preface (Well that's awfully sweet of you), before it gets to the refusal, which is hedged (I don't think I can make it this morning), a further delay (hh uhm) before it gets to the account, or reason, for the refusal (I'm running an ad in the paper and-and uh I have to stay near the phone):

123

A: Uh if you'd care to come and visit a little while this morning I'll give you a cup of <u>coffee</u>

B: hehh Well that's awfully sweet of you. I don't think I can make it this morning.. hh uhm I'm running an ad in the paper and-and uh I have to stay near the phone.

(Atkinson and Drew 1979: 58)

Kitzinger and Frith then interviewed women who talked about having refused unwanted sex. In response to advice to 'Just say no' the women showed an awareness of how they should normally perform a face-threatening act such as a refusal in conversation and that this required much more conversational work than just a simple 'no'. One of the respondents said:

It just doesn't seem right to say no when you're up there in the situation.

(Kitzinger and Frith 1999: 303)

As Kitzinger and Frith point out:

Telling a man that you do not want to have sex by saying things like 'I really don't know if we should do this', or 'not now, can't we wait', or 'I really like you but I'm not sure' ... can be misconstrued that you need a little more urging to become cooperative.

(Wiseman 1994: 65)

The women in their study knew that 'just saying no' was not enough for a refusal in this kind (or indeed most kinds) of situation. Kitzinger argues that men who claim, in a date rape situation, that the woman's delay in refusing them meant they really meant 'yes', are:

claiming not to understand perfectly normal conversational inter-actions and laying claim to an implausible and clearly self-interested ignorare of normative conversational patterns.

(Kitzinger 2000: 180)

As Kitzinger and Frith (1999: 306) argue, the women's experience tells them that 'just saying no' in refusing an offer is rude and that 'the word "no" is neither sufficient, nor necessary, for a refusal to be heard as such'. It is not, they argue, the adequacy of the women's communication in these kinds of situations that should be questioned, 'but rather their male partner's claims not to understand that these women are refusing sex' (Kitzinger and Frith 1999: 310). Their study, then, is one that exploits the level of detail provided in conversation analytic work, as well as data from other sources for social, educational and political purposes; that is, talking to women about how they can say no to unwanted sex.

5.11 **Summary**

Conversation analysis, then, provides a way of carrying out fine-grained analyses of spoken discourse which can help not just describe the social word, but understand how, through the use of language, it is constructed. There are differing views, however, as to whether looking at the data alone is sufficient to explain what is going on in conversational interactions. Many conversation analysts would argue that it is. Others, however, suggest combining conversation analysis with more ethnographic descriptions in a kind of 'multi-method/multi-level' analysis which combines the strengths of the insights that can be provided by conversation analysis with data that can be gathered using procedures such as interviews, questionnaires and participant observations (Wodak 1996). Cicourel (1992) supports this view, arguing that what is most important is for researchers to justify explicitly what has been included and what has been excluded in an analysis and how this relates to their particular theoretical and analytical goals.

5.12 **Discussion questions**

1. Read Schegloff (2004) on answering the telephone in English. How do you typically answer a telephone call in English? How similar or different is this to Schegloff's 'canonical opening' for telephone conversations? Why do you think this might be the case?

2. Think of ways in which you signal that it is someone else's turn to speak in a conversation. Do you finish a syntactic unit and pause? Do you use falling intonation to show you are coming to the end of what they are saying? Do you look at the person you want to take up the turn? What do you do if the other person does not take up the turn?

3. If you have learnt a second language, think of an example of the kinds of things that conversational analysis looks at that you have found difficult in your second language. For example, have you found refusing an offer of food difficult in your second language? Have you sometimes not been sure how to participate in a conversation? Why do you think this might be the case?

5.13 Data analysis project

Collect an example of naturally occurring spoken data and carry out a conversation analysis of it. Look at Jefferson (2004) for guidance on how to write up your transcription. The main categories you could explore in your analysis, depending on your interests, and the texts, are adjacency pairs, sequence organization, turn taking, feedback, repair organization, openings, pre-closings and closings. Look for regular patterns in what you observe in your analysis. What could your analysis explain about the particular interaction?

5.14 Directions for further reading

Cameron, D. (2001), *Working with Spoken Discourse*. London: Sage. Chapter 7. Sequence and structure: Conversation analysis.
In this chapter Cameron discusses and gives examples of research that examines turn taking, adjacency pairs, telephone closings, as well as institutional talk (as opposed to ordinary talk). The chapter includes suggestions for further reading on the topic of conversation analysis.

Hutchby, I. and Wooffitt, R. (1998), *Conversation Analysis: Principles, Practices and Applications*. Cambridge: Polity Press.
This book is a very detailed guide to the principles and practice of conversation analysis. Background theories are extensively outlined and many examples are given of each of the aspects of analysis that are discussed. The book includes a review of applications of conversation analysis in a range of different settings such as courtrooms, classrooms, the media and medical consultations.

Schegloff, E. A., Koshik, I., Jacoby, S. and Olsher, D. (2002), 'Conversation analysis and applied linguistics,' *Annual Review of Applied Linguistics*, 22, 3–31.
This paper provides an overview of some of the kinds of talk that conversation analysts have examined. It discusses, in particular, turn taking, repair and word selection in conversational interactions. The paper concludes with a discussion of what conversation analysis has to offer applied linguistics research.

6 Discourse grammar

In recent years discussions of grammar have moved from sentence-based perspectives to more of a discourse-based perspective. Hughes and McCarthy (1998), for example, have argued that traditional explanations of grammar do not adequately capture grammatical selection in longer, real-world texts. As they have shown, a number of linguistic items show quite different patterns of use when looked at from a discourse perspective. Linguists such as Halliday and Hasan have also done work in the area of discourse grammar, although from rather a different perspective. Their interest has been in patterns of grammar and vocabulary that combine to tie meanings in the text together as well as connect the text to the social context in which it occurs; that is, items that combine together to make the text *cohesive* and give it *unity of texture.* This chapter discusses both these views of discourse grammar, starting with the first of these perspectives.

6.1 Grammar from a discourse perspective

A number of linguistic items such as *it, this* and *that* have been shown to have quite different patterns of use when looked at from a discourse, rather than a sentence perspective. McCarthy (1994) found that *it* often signals reference to a continuing or ongoing topic in a text, rather than just something inside or outside the text, as more traditional explanations might suggest. *This* often indicates the raising of a new topic or a new focus in the current topic, and *that* has a distancing or marginalizing function in a text, rather than just demonstrative functions. McCarthy (1998) has also found similar differences in relation to the use of tenses such as the past perfect, the use of *be to* with future meaning, and other language items such as *wh-* cleft constructions (as in 'What you need is . . .').

Celce-Murcia has, for some time, argued for contextual analyses that look at grammatical form in relation to where, why and how frequently it is used in written and spoken discourse rather than in isolated sentences. She makes a similar argument to McCarthy about *this* and *that* showing how, in extended texts, *this* and *that* function in ways other than just pointing to something (Celce-Murcia 1997). She also shows how tense and aspect choices differ in extended discourse. Celce-Murcia and Olshtain (2000) discuss how *be going to* and *will*, when looked at from a discourse perspective, show different functions other than just the expression of future time. They found 'be going to' is typically used when English speakers narrate future scenarios, which they then follow with a contracted form of 'will', for example. They also found the present simple is often used alongside 'will' to add descriptive details to the future event being recounted.

i. Grammar and discourse from a contextual perspective

Hilles (2005) describes the process of examining grammar and discourse from a contextual perspective. The first stage in this process is to make a decision as to what aspect of language to investigate. A good starting point for this is the difference between what ESL textbooks tell students they should say and what it seems that native speakers of the language actually do say. It may be that different ESL texts present different views on the use of the language item, or that expert speakers differ in their view of how the particular language item should be used.

The next stage is to look at as many sources as possible, from reference grammars, style manuals to ESL textbooks, to see what is already known about the language item. This may include looking at how the item is used in other languages, and how use of the item has changed over time. The next step is to look at real-life native speaker examples of the particular item in spoken or written discourse. These examples can be collected individually, or a corpus can be consulted for texts which contain the particular language item.

The data then needs to be analysed, 'paying special attention to the various contexts in which the form(s) in question appear, and to develop hypotheses regarding when, where and why a particular form is used' (Hilles 2005: 4). A key point here is the role the language item plays in the overall discourse and other affective or socio-interactional, or contextual factors that may influence the use of the item in the discourse.

The final step is to test the hypotheses that have been formed by asking native speakers if they would make the same choices that the research suggests they would make. This may be done by asking native speakers to role-play an activity where the language item might be used in a particular way, or by carrying out a survey asking native speakers about the use of the language item in the particular spoken or written situation.

ii. Comparing discourse and sentence-based grammars

Hughes and McCarthy (1998) make a helpful comparison between discourse and sentence-based grammars. A discourse-based grammar, they argue, makes a strong connection between form, function and context and aims to place appropriateness and use at the centre of its descriptions. Larsen-Freeman (2003) makes a similar argument in her view that form, meaning and use need to be at the basis of all grammatical descriptions. A discourse-based grammar, Hughes and McCarthy continue, acknowledges language choice, promotes awareness of interpersonal factors in grammatical choice and can provide insights into areas of grammar that, previously, lacked a satisfactory explanation. Aspects of language they feel are especially suitable to this view include ellipsis and tense-function correlations. Discourse-based analyses are also useful for looking at the relationship between vocabulary items in texts, the relationship between items such as 'it' and 'others' and the items they are referring to inside or outside of the text, and conjunction.

6.2 The texture of a text

Hasan (1989a, 1989b) discusses two crucial attributes of texts and which are important for the analysis of discourse. These are *unity of structure* and *unity of texture*. Unity of structure refers to patterns which combine together to create information structure, focus and flow in a text, including the schematic structure of the text. The notion of schematic structure was presented in Chapter 4 of this book. This chapter will introduce the notions of *theme*, *rheme* and *thematic progression*, another way in which information flow and focus take place in texts. It will also discuss *patterns of cohesion*, a further way in which unity of texture is achieved in a text.

i. Unity of texture

Unity of texture refers to the way in which resources such as patterns of *cohesion* create both cohesive and coherent texts. Texture results where there are language items that tie meanings together in the text as well as tie meanings in the text to the social context in which the text occurs. An example of this is where the meaning of items that refer outside of the text, such as 'it' and 'that', can be derived from the social context in which the text is located.

Texture, then, is a result of the interaction of these kinds of features. In her chapter 'The texture of a text', Hasan (1989b: 71) describes texture as being 'a matter of meaning relations'. A crucial notion in this discussion is that of a *tie* which connects the meanings of words to each other as well as to the world outside the text. The basis for cohesion, and in turn texture, thus, is semantic. It is both explicit and implicit and is based in the ways in which the meanings of items are tied in a semantic relationship to each other. The interpretation of these items is found by reference to some other item, or source, within or outside the text. In the following sentence, for example, I use my knowledge of the text and the context in which it is located to work out what 'it' (in this case, gravy) is referring to in the text:

> Waiter: Where would you like <u>it</u> sir?
> Customer: Just a little on the meat thanks.

6.3 Cohesion and discourse

An area of language in which grammar and discourse are highly integrated is in *patterns of cohesion* in texts. The main patterns of cohesion are *reference*, *lexical cohesion*, *conjunction*, *substitution* and *ellipsis*. These are discussed in the sections which follow.

Cohesion refers to the relationship between items in a text such as words, phrases and clauses and other items such as pronouns, nouns and conjunctions. This includes the relationship between words and pronouns that refer to that word (*reference* items). It also includes words that commonly co-occur in texts (*collocation*) and the relationship between words with similar, related and different meanings (*lexical cohesion*). Cohesion also considers semantic relationships between clauses and the ways this is expressed through the use of *conjunctions*. A further aspect of cohesion is the ways in which words such as 'one' and 'do' are used to substitute for other words in a text (*substitution*) and the ways in which words or phrases are left out, or ellipsed, from a text (*ellipsis*). All of this contributes to the *unity of texture* of a text and helps to make the text cohesive.

6.4 Reference

Reference refers to the situation where the identity of an item can be retrieved from either within or outside the text. The main reference patterns are *anaphoric*, *cataphoric*, *exophoric* and *homophoric* reference.

i. Anaphoric reference

Anaphoric reference is where a word or phrase refers back to another word or phrase used earlier in a text. In the following example, from a review of the book *He's Just Not That Into You: The No-excuses Truth to Understanding Guys* (Behrendt and Tuccillo 2004), examples of anaphoric reference are shown in italics in the text. The identity of *the* and *it* are retrieved by reference to an earlier mentioned item (the name of the book) in the text:

> It seems everyone's read that self-help book: Greg Behrendt and Liz Tuccillo's He's Just Not That Into You ... First in the US, then all over the world, women became converts to *the* book's tough-love message. When *it* was published late last year, Oprah sang *its* praises, tearful women called *it* 'the Bible', and others declared *it* had changed their lives forever.
>
> (Cooper 2005: S38)

Once the title of the book has been mentioned, the author assumes that the reader will be able to work out what she is referring to in her use of 'it' further on in the text. Equally, she assumes the reader will know

131

'which book' she is referring to when she says 'the book's tough-love message'. If a reader is not sure what is being referred to, they will typically read back in the text to find the answer.

ii. Cataphoric reference

Cataphoric reference describes an item which refers forward to another word or phrase which is used later in the text. In the following example, from the same extract, the identity of the italicized item follows, rather than precedes, the reference item. It is thus an example of cataphoric, rather than anaphoric, reference:

> It seems everyone's read *that* self-help book: Greg Behrendt and Liz Tuccillo's He's Just Not That Into You.   (Cooper 2005: S38)

In this case, the reader knows the item being referred to is yet to come in the text and reads forward to find the meaning of 'that'.

iii. Exophoric reference

Exophoric reference looks outside the text to the situation in which the text occurs for the identity of the item being referred to. The following example from Chapter 3 illustrates this. Both speakers clearly know what book is being referred to in this conversation (*Monica's Story*). 'You' and 'your' are also examples of exophoric reference. Both speakers know, from outside the text, who these items are referring to:

> Customer: What kind of book would *you* say *this* is? Where would you put *it* on *your* bookshelves?

iv. Homophoric reference

Homophoric reference is where the identity of the item can be retrieved by reference to cultural knowledge, in general, rather than the specific context of the text. An example of this, again from the review of *He's Just Not That Into You*, follows:

> First in *the* US, then all over *the* world, women became converts to the book's tough-love message.   (Cooper 2005: S38)

This is different from the final use of 'the' in this sentence. To answer 'which book' we know it is the one being discussed in the text. We know, however, from our cultural knowledge 'which' United States and 'which' world are being referred to in the text.

v. Comparative and bridging reference

Further types of reference include *comparative* and *bridging* reference. With *comparative reference*, 'the identity of the presumed item is retrieved not because it has already been mentioned (or will be mentioned) in the text, but because an item with which it is being compared has been mentioned' (Eggins 2005: 98). 'Others' and 'opposite' in the following extracts are examples of this:

> When it was published late last year, Oprah sang its praises, tearful women called it 'the Bible', and *others* declared it had changed their lives forever.
> The book assumes all men are confident, or that if they really like a girl, they'll overcome their shyness. The *opposite* is true.
> (Cooper 2005: S38)

These are a little more complex than the other kinds of reference just described. The author proceeds, however, on the assumption that we will know 'which' people and that we will know 'which' opposite she is referring to.

A *bridging reference* (Martin and Rose 2003) is where an item refers to something that has to be inferentially derived from the text or situation; that is, something that has to be presumed indirectly. In the following example we are not told which 'blokes' Stuart is referring to. The author presumes that we can indirectly derive this:

> Stuart agrees. 'I was hopeless', he says with a laugh. 'I'm just not one of *those* blokes that finds approaching women easy.'
> (Cooper 2005: S38)

Each of these forms of reference makes a contribution to the texture of a text and the ways in which we interpret the text as we read it. The same is true of the relationship between vocabulary items in the text; that is, lexical cohesion, the subject of the next section of this chapter.

6.5 Lexical cohesion

Lexical cohesion refers to relationships in meaning between lexical items in a text and, in particular, content words and the relationship between them. The main kinds of lexical cohesion are *repetition*, *synonymy*, *antonymy*, *hyponymy*, *meronomy* and *collocation*.

i. Repetition

Repetition refers to words that are repeated in a text. This includes words which are inflected for tense or number and words which are derived from particular items such as Stuart and Stu in the following example. Although the form of these two items is (slightly) different, the author is certain that it will be clear that she is still referring to the same person:

> Jen Abydeera, 27, and *Stuart* Gilby, 22, ... are convinced they wouldn't be a couple if Jen had done things the [He's Just Not That Into You] way when they first met. '*Stu* was quiet and shy, while I was more confident and forward,' says Jen. 'He was more reluctant than I was to ask questions or to initiate a date. I would be the one to say to him: "When do you want to go out, then?"'
>
> (Cooper 2005: S38)

Thus, as she writes, Cooper (the author) exploits the readers' understanding of patterns of cohesion in her text.

ii. Synonymy

Synonymy refers to words which are similar in meaning such as 'date' and 'go out' in the above example and 'blokes' and 'men' in the following example:

> 'I'm just not one of those *blokes* that finds approaching women easy. The book assumes all *men* are confident, or that if they really like a girl, they'll overcome their shyness. The opposite is true.'
>
> (Cooper 2005: S38)

In English it is not good style to continuously repeat the same word in a text. Both 'blokes' and 'men' are referring to the same concept but in a different way.

iii. Antonymy

Antonymy describes opposite or contrastive meanings such as 'shy' and 'forward' in the earlier text and 'women' and 'men', 'real players' and 'boofheads' in the following text:

> Andy Stern, 28, a builder, says he's worried the book will drive *women* towards dodgy *men*. 'Only *real players* do full-on charm,' he says. 'The rest of us are *boofheads*. We often do nothing at all, and just hope girls notice that we like them.' (Cooper 2005: S38)

We know as we read the text which meanings contrast with each other. Part of their meaning, indeed, derives from this contrast.

134

iv. Hyponymy and meronymy

Halliday (1990) describes two kinds of *lexical taxonomies* that typically occur in texts: *superordination* and *composition*. These are words which are in a 'kind of' relationship with each other (superordination) and words that are in a 'whole-part' relationship with each other (composition). In the previous texts, Jen and Stuart are 'part of' the lexical item 'couple' whereas *He's Just Not That Into You* is a 'kind of' self-help book. The relationship between 'Jen' and 'couple' is an example of *meronymy*. The relationship between 'self-help book' and *He's Just Not That Into You* is one of *hyponymy*.

v. Hyponymy

Hyponymy, then, refers to classes of lexical items where the relationship between them is one of 'general-specific', 'an example of' or in a 'class to member' type relationship. This relationship could be represented diagrammatically as shown below in Figure 6.1. In this example, *He's Just Not That Into You, I'm Okay, You're Okay, You Can Let Go Now: It's Okay to Be Who You Are* and *Ready or Not, Here Life Comes* can also be described as *co-hyponyms* of the *superordinate* term 'self-help books'.

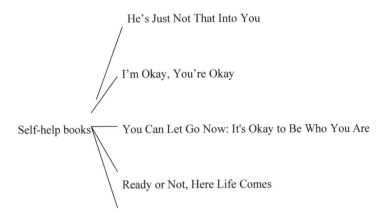

Figure 6.1 *Hyponymy*

vi. Meronymy

Meronymy is where lexical items are in a 'whole to part' relationship with each other, such as the relationship between 'Jen' and 'Stuart' in relation to the item 'couple'. 'Jen' and 'Stuart' are *co-meronyms* of the superordinate item 'couple'. These relationships could be represented diagrammatically as follows:

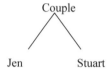

Figure 6.2 *Meronymy*

Further examples of these kinds of relationships, drawn from research reports in the area of environmental studies, are shown below.

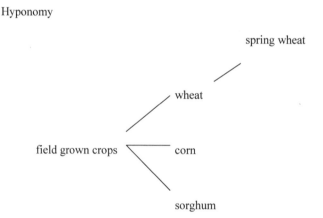

Figure 6.3 *Further example of hyponymy* (Paltridge 1998: 265)

In each kind of relationship, an understanding of one item in the taxonomy may depend on an understanding of other items and on the organization and relationship between the items in the taxonomy. As Halliday (1990: 19) points out, these taxonomies 'can become very complicated, with many layers of organisation built into them'. There is also the problem that these relationships are usually not made explicit with the result that, if someone does not already know the relationship between the items, they are left to work it out from the

Meronomy

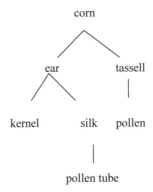

Figure 6.4 *Further example of meronymy* (Paltridge 1998: 265)

text. An example of such a taxonomy, again from the field of environmental studies, is shown in Figure 6.5. The relationship between some of these items is extremely complex and depends on a specialized knowledge of the subject being discussed, without which it could be hard to make complete sense of the text this analysis is drawn from.

6.6 Collocation

Collocation describes associations between vocabulary items which have a tendency to co-occur, such as combinations of adjectives and nouns, as in 'real-estate agent', the 'right direction' and 'Aussie men' in the following example. Collocation includes the relationship between verbs and nouns such as 'love' and 'book' and 'waste' and 'time' also in the following example. It also includes items which typically co-occur such as 'men' and 'women' and 'love' and 'hate':

> Sarah Hughes, 21, a *real-estate agent*, agrees that *Aussie men* need more help than most when it comes to romance. 'They're useless! They need a good push in the *right direction*. I *loved* the *book* and its message about not *wasting* your *time* – but if a man's shy there's no way it'll happen unless you do the asking.' (Cooper 2005: S38)

Collocation is not something that is restricted to a single text but is part of textual knowledge in general. A writer and speaker of a language draws on this knowledge of collocations as they write and speak. Expert writers (and readers) know that only certain items collocate with each other. That is, we know we can say 'real-estate agent' but not

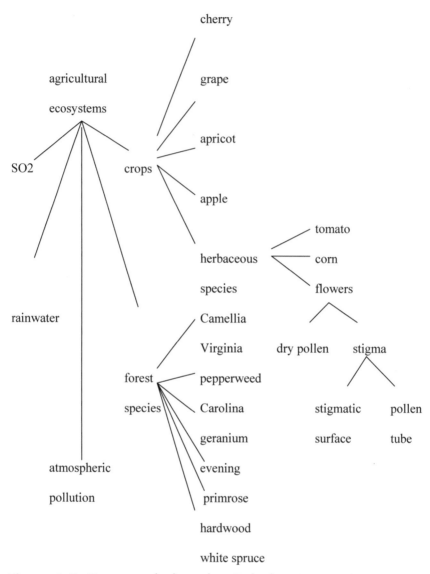

Figure 6.5 *Taxonomical relationships (Paltridge 1998: 266)*

'real-estate fruit and vegetables'. Or that we can say 'fresh fruit and vegetables' but not (with the same meaning) 'fresh real-estate agents'. This knowledge of collocation is another way in which a text has the property of texture.

i. Expectancy relations

A further kind of relationship, related to collocation, is *expectancy relations*. This occurs where there is a predictable relationship between a verb and either the subject or the object of the verb. These relations link nominal elements with verbal elements (e.g. love/book, waste/time) as in the previous example. They can also link an action with a participant (e.g. ask/guy) or an event with its location (e.g. dating/sites) as in the following examples. Expectancy can also refer to the relationship between individual lexical items and the composite nominal group that they form (e.g. art/classes, life/drawing, online/dating):

> *Art classes*
> You can do just about anything in the name of art. Try *asking* a cute *guy* to sit as your model, and if he still doesn't take the hint, you can literally draw him a picture. Take a free *life-drawing* class at the ArtHouse Hotel.

> *Online dating*
> Hand out as many kisses as you like – virtual ones, that is. *Dating sites* are all about being proactive and choosing your best match.
> (*Sun-Herald*, 6 February 2005, p. S38)

6.7 Conjunction

A further way in which language contributes to the texture of a text is through the use of *conjunction*. Conjunction refers to words, such as 'and', 'however', 'finally' and 'in conclusion' that join phrases, clauses or sections of a text in such a way that they express the 'logical-semantic' relationship between them. They are a further important part of discourse knowledge that both speakers and writers, and readers and listeners, draw on as they both produce and interpret spoken and written discourse.

Conjunctions are described by Halliday and Hasan (1976) under the groupings of additive, adversative, causal and temporal conjunctions. Martin (1992), and Martin and Rose (2003), extending Halliday and Hasan's work in this area, discuss conjunctions under the categories of *additive*, *comparative*, *temporal* and *consequential* conjunctions. Martin and Rose's work on conjunction is summarized in Table 6.1.

Additive conjunctions include 'and', 'or', 'moreover', 'in addition' and 'alternatively'. That is, they draw on the notion of 'addition' in both a positive and a contrastive sense.

Comparative conjunctions include 'whereas', 'but', 'on the other

Table 6.1 Basic options for conjunction (Martin and Rose 2003: 119)

Logical relation	Meaning	Examples
addition	addition	and, besides, in addition
	alternation	or, if not–then, alternatively
comparison	similarity	like, as if, similarly
	contrast	but, whereas, on the other hand
time	successive	then, after, subsequently, before, previously
	simultaneous	while, meanwhile, at the same time
consequence	cause	so, because, since, therefore
	means	by, thus, by this means
	purpose	so as, in order to, lest, for fear of
	condition	if, provided that, unless

hand', 'likewise' and 'equally', drawing on the notion of comparison in both a positive and negative sense. Temporal conjunctions include items such as 'while', 'when', 'after', 'meanwhile', then', 'finally' and 'at the same time'. Consequential conjunctions include items such as 'so that', 'because', 'since', 'thus', 'if', 'therefore', 'in conclusion' and 'in this way'.

The following extracts, from the review of *He's Just Not That Into You*, show 'but' being used to express a comparative point of view, 'because' to express a consequential relationship between clauses and 'and' to express addition:

> When it was published late last year, Oprah sang its praises, tearful women called it 'the Bible', and others declared it had changed their lives forever. *But* now the initial fuss has subsided, women are examining the book's philosophy a little more closely – *and* many don't like what they see.

> 'When a guy is really into you' says Behrendt ... 'he lets you know it. He calls, he shows up, he wants to meet your friends. Why would you think we would be as incapable as something as simple as picking up the phone and asking you out?' *Because*, of course, the dating game is a clumsy dance of blunders and mis-understandings. *And* sometimes, romantically challenged mean really do need a helping hand from women.   (Cooper 2005: S38)

Not all authors, however, see conjunction in this way. Vande Kopple (1985), for example, talks about *text connectives*, rather than conjunctions, which are used to indicate how parts of the text are connected to each other. Crismore *et al* (1993) discuss *textual markers* which help to organize discourse. Hyland (2005b) adds the category of *frame markers* to the discussion. Frame markers are items which sequence the material in a text (such as 'first' and 'next'), items which label the stages of text (such as 'in conclusion' and 'finally'), items which announce the goal of the discourse (such as 'my aim here is to . . .') and items which announce a change in topic (such as 'well' and 'now'). Frame markers, along with conjunction and other markers of this kind, lead the reader of a text to 'preferred interpretations' of the text as well as help form convincing and coherent texts 'by relating individual propositions to each other and to other texts' (Hyland 1998: 442). These items play an important role in holding a text together. Second language writers, for example, often under-use, over-use, or misuse conjunctive items in their texts in comparison with native speakers who tend to use them more sparingly (Basturkman 2002; Thornbury 2005).

6.8 Substitution and ellipsis

A further way in which texture is achieved in a text is through the use of substitution and ellipsis.

i. Substitution

With *substitution*, a substitute form is used for another language item, phrase or group. It can involve substituting an item for a noun. In the following example, 'one' substitutes for the noun 'book':

> Try reading this book. That *one*'s not very good.

It can involve substituting an item for a verb. In this example 'done' substitutes for the verb group 'had dinner':

> A: Has he had dinner yet?
> B: He must have *done*. There's no food in the fridge.

An item may also substitute for a clause. In the following example, 'so' substitutes for the clause 'you're still happy':

> A: That's great to hear you're still happy.
> B: Oh yes very much *so*.

ii. Ellipsis

With *ellipsis* some essential element is omitted from the text and can be recovered by referring to a preceding element in the text. Ellipsis may involve the omission of a noun or noun group, a verb or verbal group, or a clause. In the following extract, from a radio call-in show, there are examples of ellipsis in each of the caller's responses. In the caller's first response the main clause 'I want to say' is ellipsed. In the second response 'It was over' is ellipsed. In the final response a whole clause is omitted ('they usually are silly') and the main clause of the next two dependent clauses ('I want to say') are omitted. These are ellipsed as the caller's responses build on the content of what has been said before and are, thus, not necessary for an understanding of what the caller wants to say. Indeed, including these items would be unnatural in this kind of interaction:

Announcer:	Gary, what did you want to say to Allison tonight?
Caller:	[I want to say] that I'm very sorry for the fight we had the other night.
Announcer:	What was that over?
Caller:	[It was over] something rather silly actually
Announcer:	They usually are, aren't they?
Caller:	Yeah [they usually are silly] and [I want to say] that I love her very much and [I want to say that] we'll have to stick it through, you know?

iii. Differences between reference, ellipsis and substitution

It is important to point out differences between reference and ellipsis-substitution. One difference is that reference can reach a long way back in the text whereas ellipsis and substitution are largely limited to the immediately preceding clause. Another key difference is that with reference there is a typical meaning of co-reference. That is, both items typically refer to the same thing. With ellipsis and substitution, this is not the case. There is always some difference between the second instance and the first. If a speaker or writer wants to refer to the same thing they use reference. If they want to refer to something different they use ellipsis-substitution (Halliday 1985).

6.9 Patterns of cohesion: a sample analysis

Figures 6.6 and 6.7 are an analysis of the following two paragraphs of A. A. Milne's *Winnie-the-Pooh* (1965) in terms of lexical cohesion and the main reference chains in this section of the text. These two paragraphs open A. A. Milne's book:

> Here is Edward Bear, coming downstairs now, bump, bump, bump, on the back of his head, behind Christopher Robin. It is, as far as he knows, the only way of coming downstairs, but sometimes he feels that there really is another way, if only he could stop bumping for a moment to think of it ... And then he feels perhaps there isn't.

Anyhow, here he is at the bottom, and ready to be introduced to you, Winnie-the-Pooh.

When I first heard his name, I said, just as you are going to say, 'But I thought he was a boy?'   (Milne 1965: 1)

As can be seen in Figure 6.6, there are three main lexical chains in this section of the text. The first is the subject of the text, Winnie-the-Pooh. The second is the staircase and the third is the way in which Winnie-the-Pooh comes down the stairs. Winnie-the-Pooh's formal name is

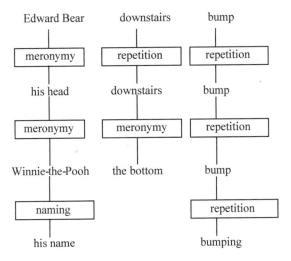

Figure 6.6 *Lexical chains: Winnie-the-Pooh* (Paltridge 2000: 146)

Edward Bear. This is what he is called the first time he is mentioned in the text. The next item (*head*) is in a part-whole relationship with Edward Bear. That is, a *head* is part of a bear, in this case *Edward Bear*. The relationship between these two items, thus, is one of meronomy. The relationship between *Winnie-the-Pooh* and *head* is exactly the same, meronymy. In order to understand this relationship it is essential for the reader to realize that Edward Bear and Winnie-the-Pooh are the same person. This relationship is made clear at the end of the first paragraph where Edward Bear's informal name is presented to the reader: Winnie-the-Pooh. The relationship between *his name* and *Winnie-the-Pooh* is one of *naming*.

The second lexical chain in the text contains an example of repetition and meronymy. *The bottom* (of the stairs) is in a whole-part relationship with the general area *downstairs*. All of the items in the

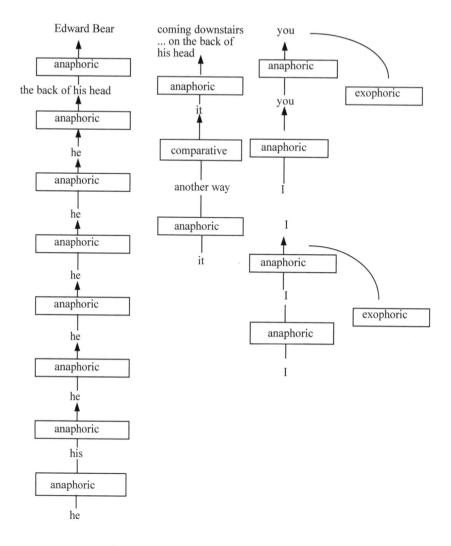

Figure 6.7 *Reference: Winnie-the-Pooh* (Paltridge 2000: 145)

third chain are an example of the same item *bump*, or the final case a grammatical variation on *bump* (*bumping*).

There are four main reference chains in this section of the text (see Figure 6.7). In the first chain, once the item *Edward Bear* is presented, all the other reference items in this chain (*his* and *he*) are examples of anaphoric reference. That is, they all refer back to Edward Bear. In the second chain, the first *it* refers to *coming downstairs on the back of his head*. *Another way* makes a comparison with *coming downstairs on the back of his head* so is an example of comparative reference. The next item in the chain, *it,* refers to this *other way* (of coming downstairs).

The third and fourth reference chains in this text are a little more complex for readers to follow. The reader needs to know who the *you* is being referred to in the text. The first *you* is the reader of the text so is thus exophoric. *You,* here, refers to someone outside the text (the reader). The following *you* and *I* refer to the same person, the reader, so are both anaphoric. They refer back to the first mention of the reader and now go back in the text, not outside it. The two instances of *I* at the beginning of the second paragraph, however, refer to someone completely different – the author of the text, A. A. Milne. The final *I* in this extract takes the reader back to the previous chain. That is, *I* refers once more to the reader of the text. In this way the author of the text involves the reader right from the beginning, by addressing them directly. This, together with the subject matter of the text, accounts for our feeling that the story is being read aloud to someone, most likely a child, the *you* in the text. As Cook explains, referring expressions thus:

> fulfil a dual purpose of unifying the text (they depend on some of the subject matter remaining the same), and of economy because they save us from having to repeat the identity of what we are talking about again and again.　　　　　　　(Cook 1989: 18)

6.10　Theme and rheme

Two further elements that contribute to the texture of a text is the relationship between *theme* and *rheme* in a clause and its contribution to the *focus* and *flow of information* in a text. An understanding of this is important, especially for the writing of successful student texts. Research has shown that different academic disciplines present information in different ways. Part of this is related to which information is given prominence, or *thematized,* in the text. Arts students, for example, have been found to more often qualify the assertions they make about other people's work in their texts than, say, do science students. They do this, especially, through what they say in the theme components of their texts (North 2005).

> *Theme* is the starting point of a clause; that is, what the clause is 'about'. The remainder of the clause is the *rheme*. Thus, in the sentence 'Hiragana represents the 46 basis sounds of the Japanese language', the theme is 'Hiragana'. The rest of the sentence is the rheme; that is, what the sentence has to say about Hiragana. In this instance 'Hiragana' is a *topical theme*. Conjunctions such as *and*

> or *but* which come at the beginning of a clause are an example of
> *textual theme*. An item that expresses a point of view on the
> content of the clause, such as *of course*, is an *interpersonal theme*.

i. Theme

Theme is 'the element which serves as the point of departure of the
message' (Halliday 1985: 38). It also introduces 'information prominence' into the clause. For example, in the sentence below from *A
Dictionary of Sociolinguistics* (Swann *et al* 2004: 123), 'genre' is the
theme of the clause and the rest of the sentence is its *rheme*. The rheme
is what the clause has to say about the theme – what it has to say about
genre. The theme in this sentence is a *topical theme*, in contrast with a
structural element such as a conjunction (such as 'and' or 'but'), which
is a *textual theme*.

An example of a textual theme can be seen in the final sentence of
the text, shown in Table 6.3, where 'but' joins two clauses together.
The rest of the themes in this extract are topical themes.

Table 6.2 *Theme and rheme*

Theme	Rheme
Genre	is a term in widespread use to indicate an approach to communication which emphasizes social function and purpose.

Table 6.3 *Textual examples of theme and rheme*

Topical theme	Textual theme	Topical theme	Rheme
Genre			is a term in widespread use to indicate an approach to communication which emphasizes social function and purpose.
Significant debate			surrounds the definition of genre, particularly the extent to which it refers to texts or activities in which texts are embedded.
It			is often vaguely defined
	but	several uses of the term	can be identified which are illustrated in different types of genre analysis

ii. Interpersonal theme

Interpersonal theme refers to an item that comes before the rheme which indicates the relationship between participants in the text, or the position or point of view that is being taken in the clause. The following example from a student essay (North 2005) shows an example of a textual theme, an interpersonal theme and a topical theme. Here the interpersonal theme expresses uncertainty about the proposition that follows:

Table 6.4 *Example of textual theme*

Textual theme	Interpersonal theme	Topical theme	Rheme
However . . .	it seems unlikely that	Descartes	would deliberately challenge the Church.

An interpersonal theme can express probability (e.g. perhaps), usuality (e.g. sometimes), typicality (e.g. generally) or obviousness (e.g. surely). It can also express opinion (e.g. to my mind), admission (e.g. frankly), persuasion (e.g. believe me), entreaty (e.g. kindly), presumption (e.g. no doubt), desirability (e.g. hopefully) or prediction (e.g. as expected) (Halliday and Matthiessen 2004).

> Patterns of theme and rheme combine in a text to give it a sense of *thematic development*. The theme of a clause, for example, may pick up, or repeat, the meaning from a preceding theme. This leads to a pattern of *theme reiteration*, where the theme of each clause is the same. Zigzag or *linear theme* is where the rheme of one clause is picked up in the theme of the next clause. These patterns may also be combined into *multiple/split rheme* patterns.

iii. Multiple theme

The following extract from the review of *He's Just Not That Into You* shows a further example of textual, interpersonal and topical themes. It is an example of *multiple theme*. That is, there is more than a single thematic element in the Theme component of the clause.

Table 6.5 *Multiple themes*

Textual theme	Interpersonal theme	Topical theme	Rheme
Because,	of course,	the dating game	is a clumsy dance of blunders and misunderstandings.

6.11 Thematic progression

The notions of theme and rheme are also employed in the examination of *thematic progression*, or *method of development* of texts (Fries 2002). Thematic progression refers to the way in which the theme of a clause may pick up, or repeat, a meaning from a preceding theme or rheme. This is a key way in which *information flow* is created in a text. There a number of ways in which this may be done. These are discussed below.

i. Constant theme

One example of thematic progression is *theme reiteration* or *constant theme*. In this pattern, 'Theme 1' is picked up and repeated at the beginning of next clause, signalling that each clause will have something to say about the theme. In Table 6.6, there are two sets of constant theme. The thematic progression of this text is shown in Figure 6.8.

Table 6.6 *Theme reiteration/constant theme* (based on Cornbleet and Carter 2001: 3)

Theme	Rheme
Text	can be used for both spoken and written language.
It	usually refers to a stretch, an extract or complete piece of writing or speech.
Discourse	is a much wider term.
It	can be used to refer to language in action, such as legal discourse, which has characteristic patterns of language.

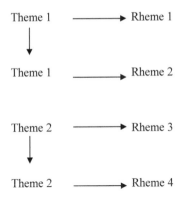

Figure 6.8 *Thematic progression: Theme reiteration/constant theme* (based on Table 6.6)

ii. Linear theme

Another common pattern of thematic progression is when the subject matter in the rheme of one clause is taken up in the theme of a following clause. The text analysed in Table 6.7 shows an example of this kind of progression. This is referred to as a *zig-zag* or *linear pattern* theme. This pattern is illustrated in Figure 6.9.

Table 6.7 *Theme and rheme: A zig-zag/linear theme pattern* (based on Knapp and Watkins 2005: 55).

Theme	Rheme
The term 'modality'	describes a range of grammatical resources used to express probability or obligation.
Generally, obligation	is used in speech, speech, especially when wanting to get things done such as 'You should keep your room tidy'.

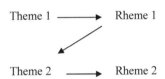

Figure 6.9 *Thematic progression: Zig-zag/linear theme* (based on Table 6.7)

iii. Split rheme

Texts may, equally, include other kinds of progression such as a 'multiple-theme' or 'split rheme' patterns. In 'multiple theme'/'split rheme' progression, a rheme may include a number of different pieces of information, each of which may be taken up as the theme in a number of subsequent clauses.

The analysis of the text in Table 6.8 and the illustration of its thematic progression in Figure 6.10 include an example of 'multiple theme'/'split rheme' progression. In this text, the two pieces of information in Rheme 2 ('two alphabets' and 'Chinese ideograms') are picked up in Themes 3 and 4 respectively. Also 'Hiragana' and 'Katakana' in Rheme 3 are picked up in Themes 5 (Hiragana), 6 and 7 (Katakana) respectively (although in the case of Theme 7 'Katakana' is ellipsed). This text also incudes examples of 'theme reiteration'/ 'constant theme' between the first two clauses and the sixth and seventh clauses and a zig-zag/linear theme pattern between a number of rhemes and subsequent rhemes.

Table 6.8 *Theme and rheme: A multiple/split theme pattern* (based on Nesbitt *et al* 1990: 21)

Theme	Rheme
When Japanese people	write their language
they	use a combination of two separate alphabets as well as ideograms borrowed from Chinese.
The two alphabets	are called hiragana and katakana.
The Chinese ideograms	are called kanji.
Hiragana	represents the 46 basic sounds that are made in the Japanese language.
Katakana	represents the same sounds as hiragana
but (Katakana)	is used mainly for words borrowed from foreign languages and for sound effects.
Kanji	are used to communicate an idea rather than a sound.

6.12 Focusing on cohesion in student texts

Focusing on patterns of cohesion can be especially useful for helping students with their writing. An important feature of a well-written text is the unity and connectedness with which individual sentences relate to each other. This is, in part, the result of how ideas are presented in the text, but also depends on the ways in which the writer has created cohesive links within and between sentences as well as within and between paragraphs in the text. Focusing on these features can help students learn how to make their texts 'hang together' in a way that

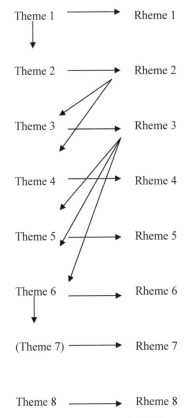

Figure 6.10 *Thematic progression: Multiple theme/split theme (based on Table 6.8)*

helps them create texts that have both unity of texture, as well as unity of structure (Celce-Murcia and Olshtain 2000). This is especially important for English writing which is *writer responsible*, as opposed to other languages (such as Japanese) where written texts are sometimes described as being *reader responsible*. That is, in English it is the writer's responsibility to make the sense of the text clear to their reader. The use of patterns of cohesion is one way in which a writer can do this.

Each of the resources described in this chapter help create unified texts; that is, texts that 'hold together' as they move from one sentence to the next. They each, thus, contribute to the texture of texts. Native speakers of a language normally use these resources without being aware they are using them. Second language students are not so necessarily aware of these resources and can benefit greatly from having their attention drawn to them.

Thornbury's (2005) *Beyond the Sentence* provides many useful suggestions for ways in which an understanding of patterns of cohesion, conjunction and thematic development, in particular, can help students deal with the discourses of work and study as well as communicate effectively in real-world situations. He argues that teachers need to move from sentence-based to 'text-based teaching' to help students achieve their real-world communicative goals. Language is not, as Thornbury argues, in its natural state, in isolated sentences. Language always occurs in texts, in discourse. An understanding of discourse grammar can help reveal the ways in which language works to create our sense of text and, in turn, our sense of connected discourse. Many textbooks focus on conjunction in the teaching of student academic writing. Many fewer focus on other aspects of textual cohesion. While coherence is as much an issue that involves a reader as the writer, coherence is very hard to achieve if the text does not, in the first place, have cohesion (Liu 2000).

6.13 Discussion questions

1. Think of an example of a grammatical feature that people use differently in conversation from the way grammar books suggest people use it. What reasons can you give for this difference?

2. Think of an experience you have had reading or listening to someone speak where you haven't understood a vocabulary or a reference item. How can the theory of cohesion help explain how you resolved this situation?

3. This chapter has discussed the topic of thematic progression. What kind of thematic progression is typical of the way you write?

4. Hasan says that unity of structure and unity of texture are two crucial attributes of texts. Think of a text you have just written. In what way does it have unity of structure and unity of texture?

6.14 Data analysis projects

1. Read Hilles (2005) and carry out a contextual analysis of a language feature you think may be useful to consider from a discourse perspective. Compare what you have found to a description of this language feature in a grammar book

you are familiar with. In what way/s is it similar and in what way/s is it different?

2. Choose a text you have written and analyse it in terms of patterns of cohesion. Refer to Bloor and Bloor (2004) Chapter 5.4 for help with your analysis. How do you think your text could be improved from the point of view of cohesion?

3. Choose a text you have written and analyse it in terms of conjunction. Read Eggins (2005) Chapter 4.5.3 for help with your analysis. Are there any ways in which you could improve the use of conjunction in your text?

4. Read Bloor and Bloor (2004) Chapter 5.3 for a discussion of thematic progression. Then do a thematic progression analysis of a text you have written. How do you think your text could be improved from this point of view?

6.15 Directions for further reading

Bloor, T. and Bloor, M. (2004), *The Functional Analysis of English: A Hallidayan Approach*. Second edition. London: Arnold. Chapter 4. Information structure and thematic structure. Chapter 5. Grammar and text.

This book is a very accessible introduction to functional grammar. Chapter 4 provides a clear outline of theme and rheme. Chapter 5 discusses patterns of cohesion and thematic progression. There are many examples and practice exercises in both chapters.

Eggins, S. (2005), *An Introduction to Systemic Functional Linguistics*. Second edition. London: Continuum. Chapter 4. Discourse-semantics: cohesion in text.

Eggin's book is a comprehensive overview of functional grammar. Chapter 4 discusses patterns of cohesion in texts and gives many examples from both spoken and written texts.

Liu, D. (2000), 'Writing cohesion: Using content lexical ties in ESOL,' *English Teaching Forum*, 38, 1, 28–35.

Liu's article gives examples of student writing that are problematic in terms of their use of patterns of cohesion. He analyses their texts and suggests ways in which they could be improved. He then gives suggestions for focusing on patterns of cohesion in language learning classrooms.

Thornbury, S. (2005), *Beyond the Sentence: Introducing Discourse Analysis*. London: Macmillan. Chapter 2. What makes a text? Chapter 3. What makes a text make sense?
Thornbury's book is an introduction to discourse analysis for language teachers. He gives examples that are drawn from real-life spoken and written data and makes good and helpful suggestions for focusing on discourse in the language learning classroom.

7 Corpus approaches to discourse analysis

There are a number of advantages in using corpora to look at the use of language from a discourse perspective. As Biber *et al* (1998) point out, until recently many discourse studies have been based on comparatively small sets of textual data and have not typically been corpus-based. As a result it is often hard to generalize from these analyses. Larger sets of data, analysed from a corpus perspective, can make these findings of discourse studies more generalizable. Corpus studies can make an important contribution to our understanding of the characteristics of spoken and written discourse.

7.1 What is a corpus?

Before discussing corpus-based approaches to discourse analysis it is necessary to define what a corpus actually is. It is generally assumed that a corpus is a collection of spoken or written authentic texts that is representative of a particular area of language use, by virtue of its size and composition. It is not always the case, however, that the corpus is representative of language use in general, or even of a specific language variety, as the data set may be very specialized (such as material collected from the Internet) and it may not always be based on samples of complete texts. The data may also be only of the spoken or written discourse of a single person, such as a single author's written work. It is important, then, to be aware of the specific nature and source of corpus data so that appropriate claims can be made from the analyses that are based on it (Kennedy 1998; Tognini-Bonelli 2004).

A corpus is usually computer-readable and able to be accessed with tools such as concordancers which are able to find and sort out language patterns. The corpus has usually (although not always) been designed for the purpose of the analysis, and the texts have been selected to provide a sample of specific text-types, or genres, or a broad and balanced sample of spoken and/or written discourse (Stubbs 2004).

Corpus studies draw on collections of texts that are usually stored and analysed electronically. They look at the occurrence and re-occurrence of particular linguistic features to see how and where they occur in the discourse. They may look at words that typically occur together (*collocations*) or they may look at the frequency of particular items. Corpus studies may look at language use in general, or they may look at the use of a particular linguistic feature in a particular domain, such as spoken academic discourse, or use of the item in a particular genre, such as university tutorial discussions.

7.2 Kinds of corpora

i. General corpora

Corpora may be general or they may be specialized. A *general corpus*, also known as a *reference corpus*:

> aims to represent language in its broadest sense and to serve as a widely available resource for baseline or comparative studies of general linguistic features. (Reppen and Simpson 2004: 95)

One use of a general corpus, for example, might be to examine words that collocate with *girl* and *lady* in English in general (Sigley and Holmes 2002) as opposed to words they collocate in particular domains of use, such as online personal ads. A further use of a general corpus might be to see to what extent hedges such as *sort of* and *kind of* are typical of English, in general, compared with what words these hedges typically collocate with in spoken academic discourse (Poos and Simpson 2002).

A general corpus, thus, provides sample data from which we can make generalizations about spoken and written discourse as a whole, and frequencies of occurrence, and co-occurrence, of particular aspects of language in the discourse. It will not, however, tell us about the language and discourse of particular genres or domain of use (unless the corpus can be broken down into separate genres or areas of use in some way). For this, we need a *specialized corpus.*

ii. Specialized corpora

A *specialized corpus*, as Hunston (2002: 14) explains is:

> a corpus of texts of a particular type, such as newspaper editorials, geography textbooks, academic articles in a particular subject, lectures, casual conversations, essays written by students etc. It aims to be representative of a given type of text. It is used to investigate a particular type of language.

Specialized corpora are required when the research question relates to the use of spoken or written discourse in particular kinds of texts or in particular situations. A specialized corpus might be used, for example, to examine the use of hedges in casual conversation or the ways in which people signal a change in topic in an academic presentation. It might look at an aspect of students' academic written discourse, and compare this with use of the same features in published academic writing, or it may look at discourse features of a particular academic genre such as theses and dissertations, or a discourse level aspect of dissertation defenses.

iii. The Michigan Corpus of Academic Spoken English

In contrast to a general corpus, then, a specialized corpus is usually designed with a particular research project in mind. An example of this is the Michigan Corpus of Academic Spoken English (MICASE) which has data from a wide range of spoken academic genres as well as information on speaker attributes and characteristics of the speech

157

events contained in the data. This is an open access corpus and is available without charge to people who wish to use it (www.lsa. umich.edu/eli/micase/index.htm).

One study carried out using the MICASE corpus was an investigation of the uses of hedges such as *sort of/sorta* and *kind of/kinda* in spoken academic discourse. These were found to be more common in some disciplines, such as the humanities, than in others, such as science (Poos and Simpson 2002). Other MICASE studies have examined the ways in which new episodes are flagged in academic lectures and group discusions by the use of frame markers such as *OK, so* and *now* (Swales and Malczewski 2001) as well as other aspects of spoken academic discourse such as hedging in the discourse of academic lectures (Mauranen 2001). In the following example from Mauranen's study the hedging is in italics:

> okay. okay, um, let me get into *sort of* the more serious stuff, and, um, what i'm hoping to do with the remainder of of this first hour, is *just* give you *some uh bit* of perspective, show where biology fits into, *sort of* the rest of your education, and *hopefully* i can, um begin this framework that we're gonna fill in in the rest of the term. so i i have entitled this lecture, philosophy of science ... or *at least* that's the point i'm talking about now.   (Mauranen 2001: 174)

Findings from MICASE projects have been integrated into training courses for international teaching assistants and for the teaching of oral presentations (Reinhart 2002). The MICASE data has also been used in the development of English language tests (MICASE online).

iv. The British Academic Spoken English

A similar spoken corpus to the Michigan corpus, the British Academic Spoken English (BASE) corpus (www.rdg.ac.uk/AcaDepts/ll/base_ corpus/), has been developed at the University of Wawick and the University of Reading in the UK. One study based on the British corpus looked at the relationship betweeen lexical density and speed in academic lectures (Nesi 2001). This study drew on data from 30 undergraduate lectures and found there was a range of speeds in the spoken discourse of the people delivering academic lectures. The lectures that were faster tended to be less lexically dense and the lectures that were slower tended to be more lexically dense. Lecturers spoke more quickly or were more lexically dense if they did not expect students to take notes, or if they were not presenting new content in their lecture. They also spoke more quickly if they were telling an anecdote which was an aside to the main content of the lecture. Nesi found, in looking at published coursebooks on listening to lectures that this range of speeds and ways of talking were not included in the books that she examined. Observations of this kind then have important implications for the development of English for academic purposes courses which aim to prepare students to study in English medium universities.

v. The British Academic Written English Corpus

Specialized corpora may also be based on written discourse alone. An example of this is the British Academic Written English (BAWE) corpus presently being developed at the University of Warwick, the University of Reading and Oxford Brookes University in the UK (www.warwick.ac.uk/fac/soc/celte/bawe/). This corpus examines students' written assignments at different levels of study and in a range of disciplines with the goal of providing a database for use by researchers and teachers to enable them to identify and describe academic writing requirements in British university settings. The BAWE corpus includes contextual information on the students' writing such as the gender and year of study of the student, details of the course the assignment was set for, and the grade that was awarded to the piece of work so as to be able to consider the relationship between these variables and the nature of the students' written academic discourse.

vi. The TOEFL Spoken and Written Academic Language Corpus

A specialized corpus may include both spoken and written discourse. An example of a corpus which does this is the *TOEFL 2000 Spoken and Written Academic Language Corpus* (a specialized corpus). This corpus aimed to provide a comprehensive linguistic description of spoken and written registers in US universities, although not, in this case, examples of student writing. The TOEFL corpus was made up of 2.7 million words and aimed to represent the spoken and academic genres that university students in the US have to participate in, or read, such as class sessions, office hour conversations, study group discussions, on-campus service encounters, text books, reading packs, university catalogues and brochures. The corpus data was collected across four academic sites, each representing a different type of university: a teacher's college, a mid-size regional university, an urban research university and a rural research university. The spoken data was mostly recorded by students, although academic and other staff recorded office hours material and service encounters. The spoken and written classroom material focused on the disciplines of business, education,

159

engineering, humanities, natural and social science, at lower and upper undergraduate and graduate levels of study (Biber *et al* 2002).

A key observation of the TOEFL study was that spoken genres in US university settings are fundamentally different from written genres. The study found, however, that classroom teaching in the US was similar in many ways to conversational genres. It found that language use varied in the textbooks of different disciplines, but not in classroom teaching in different disciplines.

7.3 Design and construction of corpora

There are, thus, a number of already established corpora that can be used for doing corpus-based discourse studies. These contain data that can be used for asking very many questions about the use of spoken and written discourse both in general, and in specific areas of use, such as academic writing or speaking. If, however, your interest is in what happens in a particular genre, or in a particular genre in a setting for which there is no available data, then you will have to make up your own corpus for your study.

Hyland's (2002a) study of the use of personal pronouns such as *I*, *me*, *we* and *us* in Hong Kong student's academic writing is an example of a corpus that was designed to answer a question about the use of discourse in a particular genre, in a particular setting. The specific aim of his study was to examine the extent to which student writers use self-mention in their texts 'to strengthen their arguments and gain personal recognition for their claims' in their written discourse, as expert writers do (Hyland 2005a: 178). His question was related to issues of discourse and identity, and the place of this writing practice in a particular academic and social community. A corpus collected at another institution or in another country would not have told him what students at his institution did. He was, however, able to use an existing corpus to compare his findings with how published academic writers use personal pronouns in their writing as a reference point for his study. Thus, by using his own custom-made corpus and an existing corpus, he was able to compare the findings of his study with the practices of the broader academic community and make observations about the way the students position themselves in the discourse, in particular, on the basis of this.

Harwood (2005) also compiled his own corpus for his study of the use of the personal pronouns *I* and *we* in journal research articles. For his study, Harwood selected research articles from electronic versions of journals as well as manually scanned articles and converted them to text format. His analysis of his data was both quantitative and qualitative. The quantitative analysis examined the frequency of writers' use of *I* and *we* in the texts and the disciplines in which this occurred. The qualitative analysis examined the use of *I* and *we* from a functional perspective; that is, what the function was of these items in the texts, as well as possible explanations for their use. He then compared his findings with explanations of the use of *I* and *we* in published academic writing textbooks.

A further example of a researcher-compiled corpus is Ooi's (2001) study of the language of personal ads on the world wide web (discussed later in this chapter). Ooi had to make up his own corpus to see how people use language in this particular genre. A large-scale corpus of language use on the world wide web, in general, would not have told him this. 'Off the shelf' corpora and custom-made corpora, then, each have their strengths, and their limitations. The choice of which to use is, in part, a matter of the research question, as well as the availability, or not, of a suitable corpus to help with answering the question.

It is not necessarily the case, however, that a custom-made corpus needs to be especially large. It depends on what the purpose of collecting the corpus is. As Sinclair (2001) has argued, small manageable corpora can be put together relatively quickly and can be honed to very specific genres and very specific areas of discourse use. They can also be extremely useful for the teaching of particular genres and for investigating learner needs.

7.4 Issues to consider in constructing a corpus

There are a number of issues that need to be considered when constructing a corpus. The first of these is what to include in the corpus; that is, the variety or dialect of the language, the genre/s to be included, whether the texts should be spoken, written or both, and whether the texts should be monologic, dialogic or multi-party. The next issue is the size of the corpus and of the individual texts, as well as the number of texts to include in each category. The issue is not, however, just corpus size, but also the way in which the data will be collected and the kinds of question that will be examined using the data (McCarthy and Carter 2001). Even a small corpus can be useful for investigating certain discourse features. The sources and subject matter of the texts may also be an issue that needs to be considered. Other issues include sociolinguistic and demographic considerations such the nationality, gender, age, occupation, education level, native language or dialect and the relationship between participants in the texts.

i. Authenticity, representativeness and validity of the corpus

Authenticity, representativeness and validity are also issues in corpus construction, as well as whether the corpus should present a static or a dynamic picture of the discourse under examination; that is, whether it should be a sample of discourse use at one particular point in time (a static, or sample corpus) or whether it should give more of a 'moving picture' view of the discourse that shows change in language use over a period of time (a dynamic, or monitor corpus) (Kennedy 1998; Reppen and Simpson 2002).

ii. Kinds of texts to include in the corpus

A key issue is what kind of texts the corpus should contain. This decision may be based on what the corpus is designed for, but it may also be constrained by what texts are available. Another issue is the permanence of the corpus; that is, whether it will be regularly updated so that it doesn't become unrepresentative, or whether it will remain as an example of the use of discourse at a particular point in time (Hunston 2002).

iii. Size of the texts in the corpus

The size of texts in the corpus is also a consideration. Some corpora aim for an even sample size of individual texts. If, for example, the corpus aims to represent a particular genre, and instances of the genre are typically long, or short, this needs to be reflected in the collection of texts that make up the corpus.

iv. Sampling and representativeness of the corpus

Sampling is also an issue in corpus design. The key issue here is defining the target population that the corpus is wishing to represent. Biber (1994: 378) points out that while any selection of texts is a sample:

> Whether or not a sample is 'representative', however, depends first of all on the extent to which it is selected from the range of text types in the target population; an assessment of this representativeness thus depends on a prior full definition of the 'population' that the sample is intended to represent, and the techniques used to select the sample from that population.

The representativeness of the corpus, further:

depends on the extent to which it includes the range of linguistic distribution in the population. That is, different linguistic features are differently distributed (within texts, across texts, across text types), and a representative corpus must enable analysis of these various distributions.   (Biber 1994: 378)

A corpus, then, needs to aim for both representativeness and balance, both of which, as Kennedy (1998) points out, are in the end matters of judgement and approximation.

All of this cannot be done at the outset, however. The compilation of the corpus needs to take place in a cyclical fashion with the original design being based on theoretical and pilot study analyses, followed by the collection of the texts, investigation of the discourse features under investigation, then, in turn, revision of the design (Biber 1994). As Reppen and Simpson (2002: 97) explain 'no corpus can be everything to everyone'. Any corpus in the end 'is a compromise between the desirable and the feasible' (Stubbs 2004: 113).

7.5 The Longman Spoken and Written English Corpus

The *Longman Spoken and Written English (LSWE) Corpus* is an important example of a corpus study. The LSWE was used at the basis for the *Longman Grammar of Spoken and Written English*. The LSWE corpus is made up of 40 million words, representing four major discourse types: conversation, fiction, news and academic prose, with two additional categories, non-conversational speech (such as lectures and public meetings) and general written non-fiction prose.

The main source of the conversational data in the corpus was British English, although a smaller sample of conversational American English data was added for comparison. The news data contained an almost equivalent amount of British English and American English data. The fiction sample drew on British English and American English, as did the academic prose. The non-conversational speech was all British English data and the general prose contained both British English and American English data.

The study was designed to contain about 5 million words of text in each discourse category. Most of the texts in the corpus were produced after 1980 so the sample is mostly of contemporary British and American English usage. The corpus was made up of 37,244 texts and approximately 40,026,000 words. The texts in the corpus varied, however, in length. The newspaper texts tended to be the shortest while fiction and academic prose were the longest.

The LSWE corpus aimed to provide a representative sampling of texts across the discourse types it contained. The conversational data in the corpus was collected in real-life settings and is many times larger than most other collections of conversational data. Both the British and American conversational data were collected from representative samples of the British and US populations. The conversational data in the corpus aimed to represent a range of English speakers in terms of age, sex, social and regional groupings (Biber *et al* 1999).

7.6 Discourse characteristics of conversational English

The major aim of the *Longman Grammar of Spoken and Written English*, which was derived from the LSWE corpus, was to provide a grammar of English based on an analysis of actual language use. The project has also made important observations about discourse characteristics of conversational English. Some of these characteristics are described below in the sections which follow. The data used to illustrate these features is a family argument from a reality television show.

i. Non-clausal units in conversational discourse

A key observation made in the Longman grammar is that conversational discourse makes wide use of *non-clausal units*; that is, utterances which do not contain an explicit subject or verb. These units are independent or self-standing in that they have no grammatical connection with what immediately precedes or follows them. The use of these units in conversational discourse is very different from written discourse where they rarely occur. Conversation, as Biber *et al* (1999) point out, is highly interactive and often avoids elaboration, or specification of meaning. The use of non-clausal units is, in part, a result of this. The non-clausal units in the following extract are in italics:

Ryan:	And ... can I have a DJ too, is that OK?
Marie:	*John?*
John:	*What?*
Marie:	Can he have a DJ ... *a DJ?*
Ryan:	Cause you won't be spending much on food so I thought ...
John:	Well, how much does a DJ cost?
Ryan:	*Yeah*, I've gotta find out.
Marie:	[to Ryan] *The DJ*, why d'you have to have a DJ? What does he do? *Just plays records all night?*

164

Ryan:	Marie: [to John] What d'you think about the DJ, is that OK with you?
John:	I just wanna know how much it is, first.
Marie:	[to Ryan] *Right*, that's what you've gotta do first, *right*?
Ryan:	I'm gonna have to get Paul to come over, too.
Marie:	*Why?*
Ryan:	So people don't crash the party.
Marie:	They won't crash the party, sweetheart, you can easily put them off.
Ryan:	*Oh yeah, yeah*, maybe twenty years ago, Mum, you know. Today ... if ... there'd be easy another forty people if you didn't have a person at the gate.
John:	[Quietly] *Bullshit.*

ii. Personal pronouns and ellipsis in conversation

Conversational discourse also makes wide use of personal pronouns and ellipsis. This is largely because in the shared context in which conversation occurs. The meaning of these items and what has been left out of the conversation can usually be derived from the context in which the conversation is taking place. In the following example, which continues on from the previous extract, the identity of *I* (John) and *you* (Ryan) are clear from the situation in which the people are speaking and cannot be derived from the text alone:

John:	Look, *I* don't want [to be embarrassed ...
Marie:	[But ... Don't *you* think it's a little dramatic saying *you*'ve gotta have a bouncer at a private [person's party?
Ryan:	[OK ... Fine ...

Later in the conversation Marie and John are alone. There is an ellipsis in John's reply to Marie as they both know what he is referring to in his reply. There is no need for him to repeat this. The ellipsis is in italics, in brackets:

Marie:	I hope you're gonna put that magazine down and give me a bit of hand in a minute.
John:	(*You want me to give you a*) Bit of a hand with what?

iii. Situational ellipsis in conversation

Some of what speakers say in conversational discourse, thus, is predictable and does not need to be fully spelled out. Speakers often use *situational ellipsis* in conversation, leaving out words of low information value where the meaning of the missing item or items can be derived from the immediate context, rather than from elsewhere in the text. For example, John leaves out the subject and the verb in the following utterance when he sums up what he thinks about the number of people that might come to the party:

> John: We've only got room for thirty people here, maximum,
>   so if you've invited thirty-seven and they're all going to
>   bring friends, we haven't got enough room, have we?
>   *Common sense.*

He does this again, later in the conversation:

> John: If you wanna have a party here, forty people is the
>   limit. *Simple as that.*

iv. Non-clausal units as elliptic replies in conversation

Non-clausal units as elliptic replies often occur in conversational discourse, as in the example below where Marie simply says 'Why (do you have to get Paul to come over)?' In the shared social situation in which the conversation is taking place both speakers know what she is asking about:

> Ryan: I'm gonna have to get Paul to come over, too.
> Marie: *Why?*

v. Repetition in conversation

Conversation also uses repetition much more than written discourse. This might be done, for example, to give added emphasis to a point being made in a conversation. One way speakers may do this is by echoing each other. An example from further in the conversation illustrates this. Marie's loud repetition of John's *I don't know why* emphasizes the point she wants to make:

> Marie: It's more drama living in this house than out of it
> John: (Quietly) *I don't know why.*
> Marie: (Loudly) *I don't know why.*

Later in the conversation Marie and John both make repeated use of parallel structures which is also typical of conversational discourse. In this case, their use of repeated structures gives emphasis to their disagreement with what Ryan has just said:

> Ryan: *You guys are livin' in the past,* I think.
> John: No we're not. No we're not.
> Marie: *We're living in our home.*
> John: *We're living in our time,* right here and now.
> Marie: *We're living in our home. We're living in our home,* Ryan
> John: *We're not living in the past.*

vi. Lexical bundles in conversational discourse

Conversational discourse also makes frequent use of *lexical bundles*; that is, formulaic multi-word sequences such as *It's going to be, If you want to* and *or something like that* (Biber *et al* 2004). Research has shown that lexical bundles occur much more frequently in spoken discourse than they do in written discourse. Speakers may, for example, use them to give themselves time to think what they will say next. They do this as conversation occurs in real time and speakers often take and hold on to the floor at the same time as they are planning what to say next. Ryan uses the lexical bundle *I'm just saying*, then the utterance launcher *well* to take and hold on to his turn while he plans what to say to Marie:

> Marie: Why do you need a bouncer at the gate? Come on.
>
> Ryan: *I'm just saying, well* say I invite three guys, they bring a friend along. He's ... a guy that I don't like...

John gives himself thinking time with *All I'm saying is* in the following example:

> John: *All I'm saying is* if you've invited thirty-seven people and ... they're all going to bring friends, you can't bring friends

A speaker may also use lexical bundles to give the person they are speaking to time to process what they have just said. Ryan does this with his use of *you know* when he says:

> Ryan: Maybe twenty years ago, Mum, *you know*. Today ... if...

As does John in:

> John: I don't want to be embarrassed, *you know*

Lexical bundles can also function as *discourse organizers* in conversation. Ryan uses the lexical bundle *Here we go again* to show the conversation has gone back to the original topic in:

> John: Well, if you've got any idea that there's gonna be trouble here ... then we don't want trouble.
>
> Ryan: Ah, *here we go again*. I didn't...

7.7 Performance phenomena of conversational discourse

The Longman grammar discusses *performance phenomena* that are characteristic of conversational discourse. Speakers need to both plan what they are going to say and speak at the same time as they are doing this, meaning that their speech contains pauses, hesitations and repetitions while this happens.

i. Silent and filled pauses in conversation

Performance phenomena that are characteristic of conversational discourse include silent and filled pauses, in the middle of a turn or a grammatical unit. In the following example Marie uses a silent pause to hold on to her turn. As she has not completed a syntactic unit, she is less in danger of losing the turn than if she were to pause at the end of the unit:

> Marie: You are being ... a sixteen-year-old twit. Sit down and write down your guests.

ii. Utterance launchers and filled pauses

Filled pauses at transition points in conversational discourse typically use *utterance launchers* such as 'well', 'and' and 'right' as the speaker prepares what they will say. At the beginning of the conversation Ryan uses 'and' as an utterance launcher:

> Ryan: *And ...* can I have a DJ too, is that OK?

John and Marie both use *Well* as utterance launchers to take follow-up turns and fill potential pauses as they discuss how many people are coming to the party:

> John: How many people's coming?
> Marie: *Well*, he wrote the invitations yesterday
> John: *Well*, how many's he invited?
> Marie: I don't know.
> John: *Well*, find out how many he's invited!
> Marie: Will we need a bouncer?
> John: *Well*, we'll have to find out how many's comin'

Later, Marie uses *Right* as an utterance launcher to both take the turn, to fill a pause and to affirm the point she is about to make:

> Marie: *Right*, so we get out there and we do the twist and the bop and the shimmy shimmy and whatever, do we?

iii. Attention signals in conversation

Speakers often use another person's name as an *attention signal* to make it clear who they are speaking to as in:

> Marie: *John*?
> John: What?

iv. Response elicitors in conversation

There are a number of typical ways of eliciting a response in conversational discourse. A question tag, for example, can function as a *response elicitor* as in:

> Marie: We'll keep an orderly party for Saturday night ... *All right?*

as can a single item as in the example below:

> Marie: We had your damn party over at the park. We didn't have any gatecrashers.
> Ryan: Party over at the park. How old was I Mum? *Eight?*
> Marie: Six.

v. Non-clausal items as response forms

Non-clausal items such as *uh huh, mm, yeah* and *OK* often operate as *response forms* in conversation as in:

> Marie: The DJ, why d'you have to have a DJ? What does he do? Just plays records all night?
> Ryan: *Yeah.*

vi. Extended co-ordination of clauses

Conversational discourse often includes long extended turns. These turns may be extended by co-ordination where one clausal unit is added to another and then another with items such as *and* and *but*, or by the direct juxtaposition of clauses as in:

> Ryan: We'll leave the gate open. We'll leave the pontoon there, *and* you'll see just see. You ... you think I'm so stupid. *But* if you ... you look around and open your eyes, you'll see.

7.8 Constructional principles of conversational discourse

The Longman grammar discusses three key principles which underlie the production of conversational discourse. The principle of *keep talking* refers to the need to keep a conversation going while planning for the conversation is going on. The principle of *limited planning ahead* refers to human memory limitations on planning ahead; that is, restrictions on the amount of syntactic information that can be stored in memory while the planning is taking place. The principle of *qualification of what has been said* refers to the need to qualify what has been said 'after the event' and to add things which otherwise would have already been said in the conversation. This may be done by the use of digressions inserted in the middle of something else, or by the use of 'add-ons' to what has been said.

In the following example, a main clause is added on, retrospectively, to make the first part of the sentence a dependent clause:

Ryan: You guys are livin' in the past, *I think.*

i. Prefaces in conversation

In conversation, the main part of a speaker's message is often preceded by a preface which connects what they have to say to the previous utterance as well as giving the speaker time to plan what they will say next. Prefaces may include fronting of clausal units, noun phrase discourse markers and other expressions such as interjections, response forms, stance adverbs, linking adverbs, overtures, utterance launchers and the non-initial use of discourse markers. Below is an example of a noun phrase, the object of the sentence, used as a preface:

Marie: *The DJ,* why d'you have to have a DJ?

In the next example Marie uses a single word (*Truly*) as a preface to orient John to what she is about to say:

Marie: *Truly,* it's more drama living in this house than out of it.

The following is an example of a lexical bundle (*All I'm saying is*) being used as an overture to preface what John wants to say:

John: *All I'm saying is,* if you've invited thirty-seven people ... and they're all going to bring friends, you can't bring friends.

ii. Tags in conversation

Speakers add tags in many ways as an afterthought to a grammatical unit in conversational discourse. They can do this by use of a question tag at the end of a sentence. The effect of this is to turn a statement into a question. Ryan does this in his reply to John and Marie:

Marie: Well, there's not going to be any trouble.
John: Well, Ryan seems to think there is.
Ryan: Oh yeah, there's gonna be gang warfare in my backyard, *is there?*

A tag can also be added to the end of a statement to reinforce what has just been said. This can be done by repeating a noun phrase, by paraphrasing what has been said, or by adding a clausal or non-clausal unit retrospectively to what has just been said. In the following example Marie paraphrases *now* as *right this minute*:

> Marie: You can cut it out now, *right this minute*.

Conversational discourse, then, has many features which are not typical of more formal kinds of spoken discourse, or of written discourse. Because conversation takes place in a shared context, and in real time, there is often less specification of meaning than there is in other spoken and written genres. Also, because conversation take place between people who usually know each other it is less influenced by traditional views of accuracy and correctness that is associated with more publicly available texts. The need to keep talking while planning what to say next also has an influence on the nature of conversational discourse.

7.9 Corpus studies of the social nature of discourse

Corpus studies have also considered what the use of the discourse means in wider social terms. Using the MICASE corpus, Swales (2003), for example, asks whether the use of spoken language in academic settings can help us understand whether the university is a single community of practice or a set of 'tribalized coteries' of communities of practice. He found (as did Biber *et al*, in the TOEFL study, although the framework for their analysis was quite different) that, in the area of academic speaking (in contrast to academic writing), there were fewer differences between disciplines than he had expected and that many spoken academic interactions had a lot in common with general conversational English. He found academic speaking across the university tended to be informal and conversational, guarded rather than evaluative and deferential rather than confrontational. He found spoken discourse to be unpretentious in terms of vocabulary choice. It also generally avoided name-dropping and the use of obscure references. He concludes, as a result of his analysis, that from a language point of view, there are fewer barriers to cross-disciplinary oral communication than there perhaps might be in written academic communication because of the convergence of spoken discourse styles. Swales found, for example, the same use of non-clausal units such as *um* and *uh* being used as fillers in spoken academic discourse as did Biber *et al* (1999) in their study of conversational discourse. The following example from a research talk illustrates this:

171

> You remember I mentioned *um*, that *uh* Sir William B. Hardy, in
> nineteen twenty-five or thereabout, *uh* did an experiment dropping
> fatty acid in water ...   (Swales 2003: 208)

Swales also found the same level of informality and casualness in
academic speech as in conversational discourse. The following
example from the opening of an ecology colloquium is an example of
this. This example shows the extended co-ordination of clausal units
by the use of *and* referred to above. The hedge *sort of* at the beginning
is also typical of conversational discourse, as well as spoken academic
discourse:

> what we plan to here is uh i'll talk for a little bit, um, about *sort of*
> the underlying theoretical framework that we think we are oper-
> ating under here *and* then when I finish that, there'll be just five
> minutes or so *and* then i'll talk about the work that we're doing in
> Nicaragua *and* when I finish talking about the work that we're
> doing in Nicaragua, why Ivette will talk about the work that we're
> doing in Mexico, *and* then finally when fe- she finished why i'll
> come back up here to talk uh, um a little bit s- more reflective about
> how the, uh theoretical framework fits into the work that we're
> doing *and* what we plan to do in the future *and* how people might
> be, might b- uh be wanting to join us, okay?   (Swales 2003: 209)

Hyland's (2004b) study of the generic structure of second language students' dissertation acknowledgements is a further example of
a corpus study which examines the discourse structure of part of a
genre, as well as the social role of this part of the discourse. His analysis shows not only the typical ways in which these texts are organized but also how students use their texts to display their disciplinary
membership and networks at the same time as they express gratitude to
the people that have helped them in their academic undertaking. As
Hyland (2004b: 323) points out, these short and seemingly simple texts
'bridge the personal and the public, the social and the professional,
and the academic and the moral'. Through these texts, students balance debts and responsibilities at the same time as give their readers 'a
glimpse of a writer enmeshed in a network of personal and academic
relationships'. The following is an example of how one of the students
in Hyland's study expressed gratitude in their dissertation acknowledgements section:

> *The writing of an MA thesis is not an easy task.* During the time of
> writing I received support and help from many people. In parti-
> cular, *I am profoundly indebted to* my supervisor, Dr James Fung,
> who was very generous with his time and knowledge and assisted
> me in each step to complete the thesis. *I am grateful to* The School

of Humanities and Social Sciences of HKUST whose research travel grant made the field work possible. *Many thanks* also *to* those who helped arrange the field work for me. And finally, but not least, *thanks* go *to* my whole family who have been an important and indispensable source of spiritual support. However, *I am the only person responsible for errors in the thesis.*

(Hyland 2004b: 309)

In this acknowledgements section, the student shows disciplinary membership and allegiances at the same time as thanking people for their support. The acknowledgement observes appropriate academic values of modesty (*The writing of an MA thesis is not an easy task*), gratitude (*I am profoundly indebted to, I am grateful to, Many thanks to*, etc.) and self-effacement (*I am the only person responsible for errors in the thesis*). This study then, as with the Swales study, reveals not only important characteristics of academic discourse, but also what the use of this discourse means in social and interpersonal terms.

7.10   Collocation and corpus studies

Corpus studies have also been used to examine collocations in spoken and written discourse. Hyland and Tse's (2004) study of dissertation acknowledgements, for example, found the collocation 'special thanks' was the most common way in which dissertation writers expressed gratitude in the acknowledgements section of their dissertations. This was followed by 'sincere thanks' and 'deep thanks'. They found this by searching their corpus to see how the writers typically expressed gratitude, and then what items typically occur to the left of the item 'thanks'. Through their use of language, Hyland and Tse (2004: 273) argue, dissertation students 'display their immersion in scholarly networks, their active disciplinary membership, and their observance of the valued academic norms of modesty, gratitude and appropriate self-effacement', as the example in the previous section shows.

Ooi (2001) carried out a corpus-based study of the language of personal ads on Internet sites in the US and in Singapore, while Bruthiaux (1994) carried out a corpus-based study of the language of ads in personal columns in the *LA Weekly*. Ooi used the concordance program *WordSmith Tools* to examine word frequency and lexical and grammatical collocations in his sample texts. His interest was in how people in different cultures communicate on the Internet on the same topic and in the same genre, as well as what gender differences there might be in the ways that they do this. He found, for example, that many US writers used the terms 'attractive' and 'great' as descriptive devices whereas the Singaporean writers largely did not. When writers

173

used the item 'old' many more men preceded this with a specification of age (as in '39 years old') than did women. The verb 'looking for' predominated the data and commonly collocated with an item which represented the writer's 'hope or dream', as in 'someone special', 'that special woman', 'a discreet relationship', etc. Ooi then goes on to suggest ways in which students can carry out studies of this kind, looking for features of the language of romance, dating, intimacy and desire.

Bruthiaux (1994) found in his study that writers frequently used *personal chaining* and *hyphenated items* in personal advertisements; that is, strings of adjectives and nouns such as *artistic, athletic, adorable 18–32 year old* (personal chaining) and hyphenated items such as *good-looking* (hyphenated items) that collocate with nouns such as *man* and *woman* and synonyms of these items. There was also a high use of *conventionalized abbreviations* for collocations such as SAM for single Asian male and SWF for single white female. The following contains an example of the use of a conventionalized abbreviation (*SWF*) and examples of personal chaining (in italics):

> *Serene, cerebral beauty*, SWF, 34 journalist, wants to turn new page with *sage, intrepid, winsome, commitment-minded* professional. (Bruthiaux 1994: 149)

The genre of personal ads, further, commonly uses *linguistic simplification* and an economy of language that is characteristic of other discourse types, such as newspaper headlines, academic note taking and conversational discourse. The following example has an abbreviated 'heading' (*SWF*), personal chaining (*attractive, young* 40, *cool, off-beat guy*) and a non-clausal unit (*Secure and laid back*) as an add-on, a feature which is also characteristic of conversational discourse:

> *SWF, attractive, young* 40, seeks *cool, off-beat* guy 30–45 who likes film, literature, music, outdoors. *Secure and laid back.* (Bruthiaux 1994: 149)

7.11 Criticisms of corpus studies

There have, however, been criticisms of corpus studies. Flowerdew (2005) provides a summary of, and response to some of these criticisms. One criticism is that the computer-based orientation of corpus studies leads to atomized, bottom-up investigations of language use. Another criticism is that corpus studies do not take account of contextual aspects of texts. Tribble (2002) counters these views by providing a detailed discussion of contextual features, such as the social context of the text, communicative purpose of the text, roles of readers and writers of the text, shared cultural values required of readers and writers of the text and knowledge of other texts that can be considered in corpus studies to help address this issue. Each of these features, he argues, can be drawn on to locate the analysis and to give the findings a strong contextual dimension. As he argues, understanding language use includes understanding social and contextual knowledge, not just knowledge of the language system. Table 7.1 presents the contextual and linguistic components of Tribble's framework.

Table 7.1 Contextual and linguistic framework for analysis (adapted from Tribble 2002).

Contextual analysis	
Name	What is the name of the genre of which the text is an example?
Social context	In what social setting is this kind of text typically produced? What constraints and obligations does this impose on the text?
Communicative purpose	What is the communicative purpose of the text?
Role	What roles may be required of writers and readers/speakers and their audience in the use of this genre?
Cultural values	What cultural values are shared by writers and readers/speakers and their audience in the performance of this genre?
Text context	What knowledge of other texts may be required by writers and readers/speakers and their audience in this example of the genre?
Formal text features	What shared knowledge of written or spoken conventions are required to effectively use this genre?
Linguistic analysis	
Lexico-grammatical features	What lexico-grammatical features of the text are statistically prominent and stylistically salient?
Text relations/ textual patterning	Can textual patterns be identified in the text? What is the reason for such textual patterning?
Text structure	How is the text organized as a series of units of meaning? What is the reason for this organization?

One way of gaining contextual information for an analysis is by the use of interviews and focus group discussions with users of the genre and consideration of the textual information revealed in the corpus study in relation to this information, as Hyland (2004c) did in his *Disciplinary Discourses*. The analysis can also be combined with other contextual information available on the data such as information on the speech event and speaker attributes and other information that is available on the data, such as the information that accompanies the MICASE and BAWE corpora. A further approach is to read more widely on the topic of the discourse to see if this might help explain or provide insights on the analysis. Each of these strategies can help offset the argument that corpus studies are, necessarily, decontextualized and only of interest at the item, rather than the discourse level.

7.12 Discussion questions

1. Make a note of how people around you speak. To what extent is how they speak typical of the characteristics of conversational discourse described in this chapter?

2. Choose a sample of a written text you often read. What are some discourse features that are typical of this kind of text? How could a corpus study help you examine this?

3. Have a look at the findings of a discourse-oriented corpus study. How do you think an ethnographic examination of the texts that were examined would help explain its findings? Read Tribble (2002) for suggestions on this.

7.13 Data analysis projects

1. Look at Bruthiaux's (1994) corpus-based study of personal advertisements in the *LA Weekly*. Collect a similar set of data from a newspaper, magazine or Internet site. Carry out a similar kind of analysis of one or more of the features that Bruthiaux examined. In what ways are your results similar to his and in what ways are they different? Why do you think this might be the case?

2. Read Ooi's (2001) chapter on investigating genres using the world wide web. Think of a genre you would like to investigate and carry out a similar investigation. Use Tribble's (2002) framework for considering the contextual aspects of your analysis. Develop a set of interview questions from Tribble's framework, then interview people who you think could help explain the findings of your analysis.

3. Record, then analyse a conversation between yourself and a friend for features which are characteristic of it being an example of conversational discourse in the terms outlined in

the *Longman Grammar of Spoken and Written English* (Biber *et al* 1999).

7.14 Directions for further reading

Flowerdew, L. (2005), 'An integration of corpus-based and genre-based approaches to text analysis in EAP/ESP: Countering criticisms against corpus-based methodologies,' *English for Specific Purposes*, 24, 321–32.

Flowerdew's article presents common criticisms of corpus studies and makes suggestions for ways in which these criticisms can be countered. She suggests drawing together genre, corpus and contextual views of discourse as a way of doing this.

Hunston, S. (2002), *Corpora in Applied Linguistics*. Cambridge: Cambridge University Press.

Hunston's book is a thorough overview of the use of corpus studies in applied linguistics. Topics covered include design and methods in corpus studies, and the application of corpus studies in language teaching and applied linguistics.

Ooi, V. B. Y. (2001), 'Investigating and teaching genres using the World Wide Web', in M. Ghadessy, A. Henry and R. L. Roseberry (eds), *Small Corpus Studies and ELT*. Amsterdam: John Benjamins, pp. 175–203.

Ooi's chapter is an excellent example of a small-scale researcher-compiled corpus study that examines a very particular research question. He discusses the merits of small versus large corpora and representativeness in the collection of corpus data. He also suggests ways in which corpora can be used in the teaching and learning of genres.

Reppen, R. and Simpson, R. (2004), 'Corpus linguistics', in N. Schmitt (ed.), *An Introduction to Applied Linguistics*. London: Arnold, pp. 92–111.

This chapter provides an overview of issues in corpus design and compilation. It discusses the marking up and annotation of corpora, differences types of corpus studies and ways of using corpora in the classroom. The chapter includes websites to refer to for further information on corpus studies.

8 Critical discourse analysis

Chapter overview

The norms and values which underlie texts are often 'out of sight' rather than overtly stated. As Hyland (2005b: 4) observes, acts of meaning making (and in turn discourse), are 'always *engaged* in that they realize the interests, the positions, the perspectives and the values of those who enact them'. The aim of a critical approach to discourse analysis is to help reveal some of these hidden and 'often out of sight' values, positions and perspectives. As Rogers (2004: 6) puts it, discourses 'are always socially, politically, racially and economically loaded'. Critical discourse analysis examines the use of discourse in relation to social and cultural issues such as race, politics, gender and identity and asks why the discourse is used in a particular way and what the implications are of this kind of use.

> *Critical discourse analysis* explores the connections between the use of language and the social and political contexts in which it occurs. It explores issues such as gender, ethnicity, cultural difference, ideology and identity and how these are both constructed and reflected in texts. It also investigates ways in which language constructs and is constructed by social relationships. A critical analysis may include a detailed textual analysis and move from there to an explanation and interpretation of the analysis. It might proceed from there to deconstruct and challenge the text/s being examined. This may include tracing underlying ideologies from the linguistic features of a text, unpacking particular biases and ideological presuppositions underlying the text, and relating the text to other texts and to people's experiences and beliefs.

Critical discourse analysis starts with the assumption that 'language use is always social' and that 'discourse both reflects and constructs the social world' (Rogers 2004: 5). A critical analysis might explore issues such as gender, ideology and identity and how these are reflected in particular texts. This might commence with an analysis of the use of discourse and move from there to an explanation and interpretation of the discourse. From here, the analysis might proceed to deconstruct and challenge the texts, tracing ideologies and assumptions underlying the use of discourse, and relating these to different views of the world, experiences and beliefs (Clark 1995).

8.1 Principles of critical discourse analysis

There is no single view of what critical discourse analysis actually is, so it is difficult to present a complete, unified view on this. Fairclough and Wodak (1997), however, describe a number of principles for critical discourse analysis which underlie many of the studies done in this area. These include:

- social and political issues are constructed and reflected in discourse;
- power relations are negotiated and performed through discourse;
- discourse both reflects and reproduces social relations;
- ideologies are produced and reflected in the use of discourse.

Each of these is discussed in the sections which follow.

i. Social and political issues are constructed and reflected in discourse

The first of Fairclough and Wodak's principles is that critical discourse analysis addresses social and political issues and examines ways in which these are constructed and reflected in the use of discourse. An example of this is Teo's (2005) study of slogans for Singapore's 'Speak Mandarin' campaign. In this campaign there is clearly a view that Singaporeans of Chinese decent should speak Chinese, despite the fact that, at the time of the launch of the campaign, only a small percentage of them actually spoke Mandarin as their first language. The aim of the campaign was to connect Chinese Singaporeans with Chinese cultural traditions as well as help counter 'negative effects of westernisation' (Teo 2005: 123). The campaign was also motivated by an economic policy which aimed at attracting foreign investment, especially from China. These arguments were captured in slogans such as *Mandarin: Window to Chinese Culture, Speak Mandarin, It's an Asset* and *Speak Mandarin: Your Children's Future Depends on Your Effort*. Mandarin was also presented as cool and of contemporary relevance, as well as a 'stepping-stone to greater business opportunities' with the Chairman of the Promote Mandarin Council saying that Mandarin is '"cool" in more ways than one', 'Mandarin is definitely "in"' and Mandarin is 'a store of linguistic and cultural treasure waiting to be explored' (Teo 2005: 134). The discourse of the campaign, thus, constructs the view of Mandarin as a language that has both cultural, social and, in particular, economic value for the people of Singapore.

ii. Power relations are negotiated and performed through discourse

The next principle of critical discourse analysis is that power relations are both negotiated and performed through discourse. One way in which this can be looked at is through an analysis of who controls conversational interactions, who allows a person to speak, and how they do this. Hutchby (1996) examined this in his study of arguments in British radio talk shows. As Hutchby and Wooffitt (1998) point out, the person who speaks first in an argument is often in a weaker position than the person who speaks next. The first person has to set their opinion on the line whereas the second speaker merely has to challange their opponent to expand on, or account for their claims. In a radio talk back programme it is normally the host that comes in the second position and has the power to challenge the caller's claim, or to ask them to justify what they have just said. The following example shows how a talk back show host does this simply by saying *Yes* and *So?*:

Caller:	I: have got three appeals letters here this week. (0.4) All a:skin' for donations. (0.2). hh Two: from tho:se that I: always contribute to anywa:y,
Host:	*Yes?*
Caller:	.hh But I expect to get a lot mo:re.
Host:	*So?*
Caller:	.h Now the point is there is a limi[t to . . .
Host:	[What's that got to do – what's that got to do with telethons though.
Caller:	hh Because telethons . . .

(Hutchby 1996: 489)

The host does this again in the next example where *What's that got to do with it?* challenges the caller and requires them to account for what they just said:

Caller:	When you look at e:r the childcare facilities in this country, hh we're very very low, (.) i-on the league table in Europe of (.) you know of you try to get a child into a nursery it's very difficult in this country.. hh An' in fa:ct it's getting wor::se.
Host:	*What's that got to do with it.*
Caller:	.phh Well I think whu- what 'at's gotta d-do with it is . . . .

(Hutchby 1996: 490)

The caller can take the second speaking part in this kind of interaction only when the host has moved, or been manoeuvred, into first position by giving an opinion of their own. If this does not happen, it is hard for the caller to take control of the conversation, and challenge the control of the host. This kind of analysis, then, shows how power is brought into play, and performed, through discourse (Hutchby 1996) (see Cameron 1998; Barton and Tusting 2005 for further discussions of power and discourse).

iii. Discourse both reflects and reproduces social relations

A further principle of critical discourse analysis is that discourse not only reflects social relations but is also part of, and reproduces, social relations. That is, social relations are both established and maintained through the use of discourse. Page's (2003) study of representations in the media of Cherie Blair, wife of the British Prime Minister Tony Blair, illustrates this. Page shows how representations of Cherie Blair in the media as a lawyer, a wife and, especially, a working mother aim to establish a certain relationship between her and the public and, in particular, other working mothers. While Cherie Blair is largely presented by the media as a success story for managing her role as a working mother, as Page points out, working mothers are more typically presented in negative terms in everyday discourse, in a way that produces quite different readings of the term, and in turn, different views of women with children who work. Stokoe's (2003) study of neighbourhood disputes shows, equally, how terms such as *mother* and *single women* can be used to make moral assessments about women as well as perpetuate 'taken-for-granted "facts" about women's appropriate behaviour' (p. 339) and social relations with other people. The use of language in this way both reflects and reproduces certain social views and relations. It, equally, reinforces social and gendered stereotypes and inequalities (Page 2003).

iv. Ideologies are produced and reflected in the use of discourse

Another key principle of critical discourse analysis is that ideologies are produced and reflected in the use of discourse. This includes ways of representing and constructing society such as relations of power, and relations based on gender, class and ethnicity. Mallinson and Brewster's (2005) study of how stereotypes are formed in everyday spoken discourse illustrates this. As they point out, negative attitudes towards non-standard social dialects of English are often transferred to negative views of the people who speak these dialects. A job applicant who speaks a non-standard dialect, for example, may not be hired when an employer uses this use of discourse as a way of predicting the applicant's future occupational performance; that is, the view that 'good workers' speak standard English and 'bad workers' don't.

In their study of US restaurant workers' views of their customers, Mallinson and Brewster found that the (white) workers viewed all black customers as the same, in negative terms, using stereotypes to form their expectations about future interactions with black customers, and the broader social group of African Americans. This was clear in the 'discourse of difference' (Wodak 1997) that they used as they spoke about their black customers and distanced themselves from them. The workers' views of rural white Southerner customers were similarly stereotyped, although they talked about this group in somewhat different ways, referring to where they lived, the ways they dressed and their food and drink preferences as a way of justifying their claims about them. In both cases, the workers' use of discourse privileged their own race and social class, reflecting their ideological, stereotyped views of both groups of customer.

Critical discourse studies, then, aim to make connections between social and cultural practices and the values and assumptions that underlie the discourse. That is, it aims to unpack what people say and do in their use of discourse in relation to their views of the world, themselves and relationships with each other. Critical discourse analysis takes the view that the relationship between language and meaning is never arbitrary in that the choice of a particular genre or rhetorical strategy brings with it particular presuppositions, meanings, ideologies and intentions (Kress 1991). As Eggins (1994: 10) argues:

> Whatever genre we are involved in, and whatever the register of the situation, our use of language will also be influenced by our ideological positions: the values we hold (consciously or unconsciously), the biases and perspectives we adopt.

Thus, if we wish to complain about a neighbour we may chose a genre such as a neighbour mediation session, or we may decide to air our complaint in a television chat show, as some of the speakers did in Stokoe's (2003) study of neighbour complaints. We may also do this by complaining to another neighbour about them. Our intention in speaking to the other neighbour may be to build up a 'neighbourhood case' against the person we are unhappy with. If the neighbour we are complaining about is a single mother we may draw on other people's prejudices against single mothers, and our own biases and moral judgements about them as an added rationale for complaining about the neighbour. The woman being complained about may pick up on this, as did one of Stokoe's subjects, Macy, in a neighbour mediation session where she says 'if I had a big bloke living with me ... none of this would happen' (Stokoe 2003: 329). Macy does not allow her single status to be used as a reason to complain about her.

In a further extract Stokoe shows how speakers may draw on the fact that their neighbour has *boyfriends* (more than one) as added ammunition against her; that is, the view that women should be monogamous (but not men) and if a woman breaches this rule, they should be held morally accountable for their behaviour. The following example illustrates this. In this example Terry (T) is the chat show host and Margaret (M) is a member of the audience who is complaining about her neighbour:

T: I want to know (.) what happened to you↓
           (0.5)

M: after living very happily (.) in my (.) one bedroom flat
           for thirteen years (.) it was a *three* storey block of flats

and I was on the top floor (.) and the young woman was
put in the flat below me (0.5) I them had (.) seven and a
half *ye:ars* (.) of sheer hell

T: *what so*rt of hell?

M: loud music (.) night *and* day (.) it just depended=

T: =well that wasn't the worst was it?

M: = (0.5) it was boyfriends (.) and lovemaking that...

(Stokoe 2003: 333)

The rhetorical strategy here, then, is to draw on a moralizing discourse
about women (and especially, single women who have sex) as a way of
legitimating complaints about female neighbours, as well as building a
defence for making the complaint (Stokoe 2003).

A key focus, then, of critical discourse studies is the uniting of
texts with the discourse and sociocultural practices that the text
reflects, reinforces and produces (Fairclough 1995). The chart in Figure
8.1 summarizes this. Discourse, in this view, simultaneously involves
each of these dimensions.

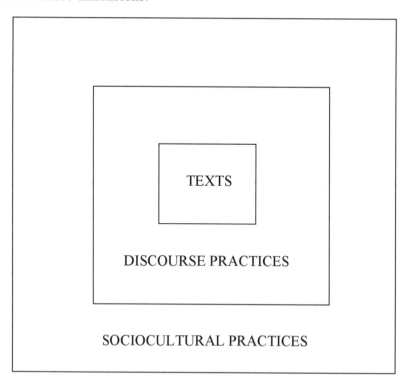

Figure 8.1 *The relationship between texts, discourse practices and socio-cultural practices in a critical perspective* (adapted from Fairclough 1992: 73)

8.2 Doing critical discourse analysis

Critical discourse analysis 'includes not only a description and interpretation of discourse in context, but also offers an explanation of why
and how discourses work' (Rogers 2004: 2). Researchers working
within this perspective:

> are concerned with a critical theory of the social world, the relation-
> ship of language and discourse in the construction and represen-
> tation of the social world, and a methodology that allows them to
> describe, interpret and explain such relationships. (Rogers 2004: 3)

A critical analysis, then, might commence by deciding what discourse
type, or genre, the text represents and to what extent and in what way
the text conforms to it (or not). It may also consider to what extent the
producer of the text has gone beyond the normal boundaries for the
genre to create a particular effect.

The analysis may consider the *framing* of the text; that is, how the
content of the text is presented, and the sort of angle or perspective the
writer, or speaker, is taking. Closely related to framing is the notion of
foregrounding; that is, what concepts and issues are emphasized, as
well as what concepts and issues are played down or *backgrounded* in
the text. Equally important to the analysis are the background knowledge, assumptions, attitudes and points of view that the text presupposes (Huckin 1997).

At the sentence level, the analyst might consider what has been
topicalized in each of the sentences in the text; that is, what has been
put at the front of each sentence to indicate what it is 'about'. The
analysis may also consider who is doing what to whom; that is, *agent-
patient relations* in the discourse, and who has the most authority and
power in the discourse. It may also consider what agents have been left
out of sentences, such as when the passive voice is used, and why this
has been done (Huckin 1997).

At the word and phrase level, connotations of particular words
and phrases might be considered as well as the text's degree of formality or informality, degree of technicality, and what this means for
other participants in the text. The choice of words which express
degrees of certainty and attitude may also be considered and whether
the intended audience of the text might be expected to share the views
expressed in the text, or not (Huckin 1997).

The procedure an analyst follows in this kind of analysis depends
on the research situation, the research question and the texts that are
being studied. What is essential, however, is that there is some

attention to the *critical, discourse* and *analysis* in whatever focus is taken up in the analysis (Rogers 2004).

Critical discourse analysis, then, takes us beyond the level of description to a deeper understanding of texts and provides, as far as might be possible, some kind of explanation of why a text is as it is and what it is aiming to do. It looks at the relationship between discourse and society and aims to describe, interpret and explain this relationship (Rogers 2004). As van Dijk (1998) has argued, it is through discourse that many ideologies are formulated, reinforced and reproduced. Critical discourse analysis aims to provide a way of exploring this and, in turn, challenging some of the hidden and 'out of sight' social, cultural and political ideologies and values that underlie texts.

8.3 Critical discourse analysis and genre

One way in which a question might be approached from a critical perspective is by considering the genres that have been chosen for achieving a particular discourse goal. Flowerdew (2004) did this in his study of the Hong Kong government's promotion campaign of Hong Kong as a 'world-class city'. He discusses the various genres that were involved in constructing this view of Hong Kong. These included committee meetings, policy speeches, commission reports, an inception report, public fora, exhibitions, focus group discussions, presentations, a website, consultation documents, information leaflets, consultation digests and videos. He discusses how each of these genres played a role in the construction of this particular view of Hong Kong. He then carries out an analysis of three different genres which made this claim: a public consultation document, the Hong Kong annual yearbook and a video that was produced to promote Hong Kong as 'Asia's World City'.

Flowerdew shows how the Hong Kong bureaucracy developed and constructed this particular view, from the generation of an initial idea through to the public presentation of this view. He also shows that while the official aim of the consultation process was to gain feedback on the proposal, it was as much designed to win over the public to this view. The public consultation document, Flowerdew shows, used a language of 'telling' rather than a language of 'asking' (or indeed consulting). The tone of the text was prescriptive in its use of the modal verb *will*, for example, as in *every Hong Kong resident will, HK 2030 will involve* and *This will ensure*. The voice of authority, thus, was dominant in the use of the genre and discouraged dissent from the view that it promoted.

186

The yearbook that Flowerdew examined extolled the virtues of Hong Kong and was overtly promotional in nature. Other voices were brought in to give authority to this view such as 'perceptions of Hong Kong internationally' and 'our review on international perspectives of Hong Kong'. Who these views actually belong to was not stated. This text, interestingly, was produced before the actual public consultation process commenced and suggests the government had already decided on the outcome of its consultation, before it had actually commenced.

The voice on the video that was examined, as with the yearbook, was overwhelmingly promotional. The difference between this and the yearbook was that the video used the discourse of advertising and public relations to make its point, rather than the discourse of bureaucracy. The video used short sharp pieces of text such as *The pace quickens* and *Horizons expand*. These statements were accompanied by series of images of technology, architecture and night-life that presented Hong Kong as a vibrant and fast-paced modern city. The mix of traditional Chinese and Western music on the soundtrack of the video gave both an Asian and an international feel to the video. The video was also produced before the public consultation actually took place. As Flowerdew points out, this is consistent with branding theory which emphasizes the importance of gaining support and the belief of the public in the promotion of a brand, or product. It is not, however, the sequence of genres that might be expected to conform with a public consultation process. Flowerdew, then, shows how the voices of three very different genres come together to impose, rather than negotiate, a certain point of view on the readers and viewers of the texts that formed part of the campaign.

8.4 Critical discourse analysis and framing

A further way of doing a critical analysis is to examine the way in which the content of a text is *framed*; that is, the way in which the content of the text is presented to its audience, and the sort of perspective, angle and slant the writer or speaker is taking. Related to this is what is foregrounded and what is backgrounded in the text; that is, what the author has chosen to emphasize, de-emphasize or, indeed, leave out of the text (Huckin 1997).

Huckin (1997) looks at a newspaper report on a demonstration at a nuclear test site in the US in just this way. Figure 8.2 is the opening section of the text he examined.

The demonstration described in this report is framed as a confrontation between the group of protesters and law-officials. The report does not discuss the issue that motivated the protest. The protesters

> MERCURY, NV (AP) – More than 700 people were arrested Saturday during an anti-nuclear, anti-Persian Gulf buildup protest at the Nevada Test Site, an official said.
>
> Thousands turned out for the demonstration. Those arrested on misdemeanour trespass charges were taken to holding pens, then transported by bus it Beatty, 54 miles north of the remote nuclear proving ground.
>
> An Energy Department spokesman estimated the crowd at 2,200 to 2,500 people. A sponsor of the protest, American Peace Test, said the crowd was 3,000 to 4,000 strong.
>
> The turnout was one of the largest since anti-nuclear demonstrations began at the test site nearly a decade ago, but it failed to match a turnout of 5,000 demonstrators in 1987, when 2,000 people were arrested on trespass charges.
>
> The DOE spokesman, Darwin Morgan, said more than 700 people were arrested and would be released in their own recognizance.
>
> 'Some of the demonstrators were a bit more aggressive, kicking at the guards when they were brought out of the pens' Morgan said. . . .

Figure 8.2 *A newspaper report on an anti-nuclear demonstration* (Huckin 1997: 85)

and how many were arrested is presented to the readers. The protesters are presented negatively, as trespassers, rather than as people with a concern for the environmental future of their country. A 'police vs. protesters' frame is foregrounded, and also presented, rather than the social, public health or environmental issues they are protesting about. There is much that is backgrounded, or omitted from the text. Information on nuclear testing planned for the site is left out, nor is anything mentioned of the health issues faced by people living near the site. The role of the government is also omitted from the text. The story, thus, presupposes that the most interesting and important aspect of the story is the number of protesters that were arrested, not the issues they were protesting about (Huckin 1997).

Huckin goes on to examine topicalization in the text. As he shows, the topic of the sentences support his claim that the text is 'about' protesters vs. officials, not the issues that prompted the demonstration. In the following examples the topic of each sentence is in italics:

> *More than 700 people* were arrested Saturday during an antinuclear, anti-Persian Gulf buildup protest at the Nevada Test Site
> *Thousands* turned out for the demonstration.
> *A sponsor of the protest, American Peace Test*, said the crowd was 3,000 to 4,000 strong.

Throughout the text, it is the officials that largely have the *agency*; that is, it is they who initiate the action. They do the arresting and decide if the protestors will be released. The protesters only have agency when they are engaged in anti-social behaviour, such as kicking the guards.

The text is mostly written in the semi-formal register of 'objective' news reporting. Events are presented as factual, 'without the slightest trace of uncertainty'. This has the effect of making the issues that underlie the protest 'completely closed to discussion and negotiation' (Huckin 1997: 89–90). As Huckin shows, the tactics used by the writer put a particular slant on the text and encourage the reading of the text in a particular way. Analyses of this kind, thus, aim to bring hidden meanings to the surface by unpacking the assumptions, priorities and values that underlie texts.

8.5 Critical discourse analysis and multimodality

Many readings of texts are constructed not just by the use of words but by the combination of words with other modalities, such as pictures, film or video images and sound. The ways in which people reacted to the events of 11 September, for example, were very much affected by the images they saw on television as they were by verbal reports of the events. This use of *multimodal discourse* both established a 'proximity' to the events and engaged people in the events. Street shots from Manhattan helped to create proximity and involvement with the events. They compressed distance and brought images and experiences into people's homes that would otherwise be unavailable to them. This moved the viewer from a position of 'spectator' to a position of 'witness' of the events. The use of video footage to accompany the reports put the viewer 'right there' in the scene of suffering, as the events were unfolding. The viewers were 'both there' yet powerless to act (Chouliaraki 2004).

The multimodal use of discourse is as much a feature of print genres as it is of television genres. The presentation of women in magazines, for example, relies not just on words on the page but as much on the images that are used to accompany the words. These representations are not necessarily just local and in the case of magazines with a worldwide network of distribution and publication are just as much global. The magazine *Cosmopolitan* is a case in point. *Cosmopolitan* is published in 44 different versions across the world in countries such as the UK, The Netherlands, Germany, Spain, Greece, Finland, India, Taiwan, the US, Brazil and others. While there are local differences in these editions of the magazine, there is also a global brand to the magazine and presentation of women in the magazine (Machin and Thornborrow 2003).

Cosmopolitan, Machin and Thornborrow argue, is not just about selling magazines to its readers. It is also about selling values of independence, power and fun. The multimodal use of discourse in the magazine highlights this. Women appear in the magazine as playful fantasies. Images of the cafés they go to, and the clothes they wear are presented and discussed in the pages of the magazine. *Cosmopolitan*, thus, has a 'brand' which it promotes via the magazine, as well as through other products such as television programmes, clothes, fashion and *Cosmo* cafés. Central to this branding are the discourses it draws on, and the strategies it employs for the presentation of its view of women and its underlying values of independence, power and entertainment. It does this through the background, setting, use of colour and lighting in the images it displays. It also does this through the agency it gives to women in their pursuit of men and sex.

Women are presented in *Cosmopolitan* as fun and fearless with 'a take charge attitude that's totally you' (Machin and Thornborrow 2003: 462). Terms such as 'powerful' and 'go-getting' are used to describe women in bed. Sex in the office is described as 'exciting and fun', and as a way in which a woman can achieve or maintain power. Women in the magazine, Machin and Thornborrow argue, 'rely on acts of seduction and social manoeuvring, rather than on intellect, to act in and on the world' (p. 453). The power they have, however, 'is always connected to their body, rather than their professional competence' (p. 466).

Cosmopolitan, thus, presents women as advancing themselves through the use of particular social and discourse strategies, rather than through technical or intellectual skills. Women are aligned with the values and views of the magazine as well as with the other products that it sells. These values are expressed not just in words, but through the clothes that *Cosmo* women wear, the lipstick they use, the way they do their hair, the places they shop and the places they go for lunch (Machin and Thornborrow, 2003). These are all presented to readers of the magazine through a range of *multimodal discourse practices*, each of which contributes to a particular reading of the text.

8.6 Critical discourse analysis and identity

The issue of how identity is constructed in the use of discourse is also an area of interest in critical discourse analysis. Gordon (2004), for example, discusses how a family in the US use language to create and socialize each other into a shared family political identity as

190

Democrats, and supporters of Al Gore. They do this by the way they refer to Al Gore, using terms which express closeness and alignment such as *Al, our President, our guy* and *my friend.* By contrast, they refer to Gore's opponent, George W. Bush, in ways which express social distance such as *Bush* and *that alcoholic car-driving man.*

In the following extract from one of their conversations their four-year-old son, Jason, is positioned (well before he can vote) by his parents as a voting Democrat. His parents, Neil and Clara, ask Jason which ice cream he voted for as his favourite at school:

Neil:	Well did you – what did you pick?
	What kind of ice cream [did you vote on]?
Jason:	[U:::m] vanilla [and] chocolate
Neil:	[Van-]
	You picked BOTH of them?
Clara:	[[He had-]] strawberry was the odd man out.
Neil:	[Oh.]
	Well see he's a good Democrat
	he votes several times

(Gordon 2004: 623)

Through their use of discourse Neil and Clara, thus, socialize their son into their political views, at the same time as they create their family political identity. As Gordon shows, these identities are co-constructed, moment by moment, through the use of discourse and the process of conversational interactions.

Online communities are a further example of where social relations and identities are constructed through people's participation in the community's activities and their interactions with each other. In Thomas's (forthcoming) study of children's online interactions in a virtual community called a palace, she found children's talk and their technical ability helped to give them authority and a sense of belonging to the particular group. One boy, Face Off, spent days away from the palace preparing highly complex images for the site so that he could project an identity as a highly capable online participant to new people in the group. On his return the other members noticed he had been away and on seeing what he has done described him as a 'Paint master', saying they wanted to work him as a team on creating new scripts for the palace.

The shared sense of belonging in online communities is also created by the use of screen names and emoticons which express emotions such as laughing, smiling, amazement and excitement. At points in their interactions some members in Thomas's study, however, switched identities. Face Off, for example, takes on the identity of his mother on one occasion. Here, he adopts a voice of authority and control saying:

> Face Off: i hear you want to interview my son
> well i give you my upmost permission
> nobody talk
> ok now ask me questions

The other members of the group fall in with the game and change the way they interact with him, while he is being his mother.

Thomas observes that to speak (or in this case to write) in an online environment is to have an identity and to not write is not to have an identity. In this setting, she argues 'to write is to exist, and that writing is an essential component for identity construction'. As one of her participants commented:

> Violetta: to make friends online you need to be around a lot and be willing to talk ... to be 'real' in a virtual kind of way

As Thomas comments, the ways in which children establish friendships and identities offline is very different from how they do it online. Online, it is very much through the use of discourse and proficiency in use of the online environment. The discourse of this environment is very much a multimodal one, using not just words, but also images, layout, design, a different view of grammar, spelling and punctuation and a different way of reading texts.

The identities that online participants explore, further, may be in conflict with offline socially encouraged identities. Davies (2004), for example, found this in her study of girls' interactions in an online game called *Babyz*, a game which encourages girls to take on identities which express stereotyped mothering values. She found that many of the girls in her study resisted the maternal child-rearing identity promoted by the game and developed multiple identities that were in conflict with the overarching theme of the game. The girls in her study used the web as a place in which they could 'explore identities, confide, confess and challenge' social roles and identities (Davies 2004: 44). They created their sense of community through the shared use of discourse strategies such as heavy punctuation (*CUTE*!), the use of text-messaging type language (*LOL*), colloquialisms (*so* sweet!), shorthand expressions (*i.e.*) and their own created *Babyz* jargon. This shared use of a discourse style, Davies argues, all contributes to the feeling of a discrete community with a shared (although sometimes contested) set of values and identities. Within this setting, the girls experimented 'with voices and viewpoints which would be taboo elsewhere'. They, thus, were able 'to connect with each other, to role play a range of attitudes, stances and identities and to explore ideas in a free space' that they may not have been able to do many other places (Davies 2003b: 2).

Thomas and Davies show that the use of particular discourse strategies is one way in which identities can be established online. Technical capacity is another way in which this can be done. The amount of knowledge a person shows about the topic under discussion is a further way in which identity, and in turn, authority might be established online. Indeed, content knowledge and expertise in this kind of environment may be more important than factors such as age, gender and social status which might matter more in an offline environment. Matsuda (2002) found this in his study of the online interactions of a Japanese email language teacher's group.

In Japanese, hierarchies in relations are marked by the use of address forms such as *chan* and *san* and verb endings such as *desu* and *masu*. In order to know how to address someone in an online environment in Japanese a person clearly needs to know something about that person, such as their age, gender and social standing. The members of the group Matsuda examined tried to work this out from the email address the message had come from (such as the school or university address), or by reading the signature at the end of the message. As the discussions continued, however, changes in hierarchies occurred on the basis of the amount of knowledge an online member showed of the topic under discussion. That is, those that showed they had more knowledge tended to be given higher status in the discussion than those who showed they were there more to learn from the others. This change in hierarchies was then reflected in the way the members of the group both constructed and positioned themselves in relation to each other in the discourse. The online setting, thus, became an alternate site for members to negotiate identity and relationships, in a way that was different from their offline worlds. This negotiation, importantly, was done through the use of discourse.

8.7 Critical discourse analysis and the world wide web

Much of the work in critical discourse analysis draws its discussion from the analysis of often only a few texts which have sometimes been criticized for being overly selective and lacking in objectivity. One way in which the scale of texts used for a critical analysis can be expanded is through the use of texts that are available on the world wide web. Using material from the world wide web is not without its problems, however. It is not always possible to identify the source of texts on the web. It is also not always possible to determine which texts have more authority on a topic than others on the web. It is also difficult to see sometimes who in fact is writing on the web. Texts on the web, further, also often rely on more than just words to get their message across. Their multimodal nature, thus, needs to be taken account of in any analysis of material from the web. Texts on the web are also more subject to change than many other pieces of writing. Each of these issues needs to be considered when using data from the world wide web for a critical (or indeed any kind of) discourse study (Mautner 2005a).

The world wide web has, however, been used productively to carry out critical discourse studies which draw on the strengths of the web's capacity to collect a lot of relevant data. Mautner's (2005b) study of 'the entrepreneurial university' is an example of this. Mautner did a search of the web for the term 'entrepreneurial university' to see who is using this term, what genres it typically occurs in, and how it is typically used. She used a search engine to do this as well as carried out a trawl through the websites of 30 top UK universities to find further uses of the term. She also used a reference corpus to see what words 'entrepreneurial' typically collocated with, outside of her particular area of interest.

Mautner observes that the use of the term entrepreneurial university brings together the discourses of business and economics with the discourse of the university. It is not just the newer, seemingly more commercially driven universities, however, that are doing this. The following example from the Oxford University website illustrates this:

> Oxford is one of Europe's most innovative and *entrepreneurial universities*. Drawing on an 800-year tradition of discovery and invention, modern Oxford leads the way in creating jobs, skills and innovation for the 21st century.   (Mautner 2005b: 109)

The term 'entrepreneurial university' was not, however, used positively in all the texts that Mautner examined. On occasions writers purposely distanced themselves from the term by putting scare quotes around these words. Even those who are advocates of the entrepreneurial university also showed they are aware of the potentially contentious nature of the term by adding qualifying statements to their use of it, such as 'we still care about eduction and society' and 'it isn't about commercialisation' (Mautner 2005b: 111). Studies such as this, then, show the enormous potential of using the world wide web for the critical study of the use of discourse.

8.8 Criticisms of critical discourse analysis

Critical discourse analysis has not been without its critics, however. One argument against critical discourse analysis has been that it is very similar to earlier stylistic analyses that took place in the area of literary criticism. Widdowson (1998, 2004) for example, argues that a critical analysis should include discussions with the producers and consumers of texts, and not just rest on the analyst's view of what a text might mean alone. Others have suggested that critical discourse analysis does not always consider the role of the reader in the consumption and interpretation of a text, sometimes mistaking themselves for a member of the audience the text is aimed at (van Noppen 2004). Critical discourse analysis has also been criticized for not always providing sufficiently detailed, and systematic, analyses of the texts that it examines (Schegloff 1997).

There have been calls for critical discourse analysts to be more critical and demanding of their tools of analysis, as well as aim for more thoroughness and strength of evidence for the claims that they make (Toolan 1997). Others, however, have come to the defence of critical discourse analysis arguing that its agenda is important and of considerable social significance but that there are important details and arguments that still need to be carefully worked out (Stubbs 1997).

Writers such as Cameron (2001) discuss textual interpretation in critical discourse analysis saying it is an exaggeration to say that any reading of a text is a possible or valid one. She does, however, agree with the view that a weakness in critical discourse analysis is its reliance on just the analyst's interpretation of the texts. She suggests drawing more on recipients' interpretations in the analysis and interpretation of the discourse as a way of countering this. As Cameron (2001: 140) suggests, a critical discourse analysis:

> is enriched, and the risk of making overly subjective or sweeping claims reduced, by going beyond the single text to examine other related texts and to explore the actual interpretations recipients make of them.

As she points out, all discourse and all communication is interactive, and this needs to be accounted for in the analysis.

Benwell (2005) aimed to deal with this in his study of the ways in which men respond to the discourse of men's lifestyle magazines. Drawing on a *textual culture* approach, two groups of readers were interviewed about their reading habits, practices and dispositions with reference to issues such as gender, sexism, humour and irony in articles and images in the magazines. Conversation analysis and *membership categorization analysis* were used for the analysis of the data. One of the interviewees said, laughing, *Lucky this is anonymous!* when admitting that he had responded to the influence of an advertisement in a magazine and had gone and bought a skin care product, more commonly associated with women. In his hesitation in revealing this, he also showed his alignment with the constructions of masculinity promoted by the magazine as well as his affiliation with the view that ' "real" mean do not use grooming products' (Benwell 2005: 164). The combination, thus, of Benwell's reading of the texts, with readers' views in relation to the texts, tells us more about the texts themselves, as well as about how many men may read them.

A further way in which critical discourse studies could be enhanced is through a more detailed linguistic analysis of its texts than sometimes occurs. Systemic functional linguistics has been proposed as a tool for one way in which this could be done (Martin 2000; Fairclough 2003). Corpus approaches have also been proposed as a way of increasing the quantitative dimension of critical discourse analyses (Mautner 2005a). Others have proposed expanding critical discourse studies by drawing on work such as schema theory and work in the area of language and cognition (McKenna 2004).

Threadgold (2003) proposes a greater bringing together of work in the area of cultural studies with work in the area of critical discourse analysis, suggesting the issue of *performativity* (see Chapters 1 and 2 of this book) be given greater prominence in this work to give greater explanation and understandings of what people 'do' in their use of spoken and written discourse. Trautner (2005) did this in her examination of how exotic dancers do both gender and social class in their presentations of themselves to their clients. She found that gender and social class are a central feature of the interactions that take place in dance clubs. They are reflected, she found, 'in very concrete ways: in the appearance of dancers and other staff, dancing and performance styles, and the interactions that take place between dancers and customers' (Trautner 2005: 786). The notion of performativity, thus, provides an important way for thinking about language, identity, class, social memberships and, in turn, the critical analysis of discourse.

8.9 Discussion questions

1. To what extent do you think texts reflect hidden and 'often out of sight' values? Choose a text which you think illustrates this and explain in what way you think this is done through the use of the discourse.

2. To what extent do you think that the way a text is 'framed' encourages a certain reading of it. Choose a text which you think illustrates this. Discuss framing, foregrounding, backgrounding and the presuppositions that underlie the way the text is presented to its audience.

3. Choose a text which you feel encourages a certain reading from its use of illustrations, pictures, layout and design, etc. How do you feel each of these resources aim to 'position' the reader in a particular way?

8.10 Data analysis projects

1. Choose a text which you feel would be useful to examine from a critical perspective. Analyse it from the point of view of genre and framing. Link your analysis to a discussion of how you feel the text aims to 'position' its readers. Read Huckin (1997) on critical discourse analysis to help with this.

2. Choose a text which you feel uses multimodal discourse such as layout, design and images to communicate its message to its audience. Analyse your text highlighting the ways in which it does this. Look at Van Leeuwen's (2005) *Introducing Social Semiotics* for suggestions on how to do this.

8.11 Directions for further reading

Blommaert, J. (2005), *Discourse: A Critical Introduction*. Cambridge: Cambridge University Press. Chapter 2. Critical discourse analysis. This chapter of Blommaert's book outlines the origins and theoretical background to critical discourse analysis. It discusses pros and cons of critical discourse analysis as well as its potential and its limitations. The remainder of his book offers suggestions for countering the problems presented in this chapter.

Cameron, D. (2001), *Working with Spoken Discourse*. London: Sage. Chapter 9. Hidden agendas? Critical discourse analysis. Cameron's chapter discusses central themes in the area of critical discourse analysis. These include discourse and the construction of reality, the relationship between discourse and social change, as the well as the issue of interpretation of analyses carried out from a critical perspective.

McKenna, B. (2004), 'Critical discourse studies: Where to from here?' *Critical Discourse Studies*, 1, 1, 9–39.

In this article, McKenna gives an overview of the theory and methodology of critical discourse analysis. He then surveys some of the major issues in critical discourse studies. The article presents suggestions for interdisciplinary research as a way of moving critical discourse studies forward.

9 Doing discourse analysis

The previous chapters in this book have outlined a number of different perspectives on discourse analysis as well as described a range of approaches to the analysis of discourse data. This chapter discusses issues that need to be considered when planning and carrying out a discourse analysis project. A number of sample studies are discussed to give you an idea of how previous students have gone about answering discourse analysis questions that have interested them. The chapter concludes with a discussion of issues to consider in evaluating the quality of a discourse analysis project.

9.1 Developing a discourse analysis project

There are a number of issues that need to be considered when planning a discourse analysis project. The first of these is the actual research question. The key to any good research project is a well-focused research question. It can, however, take longer than expected to find this question. Cameron (2001) has suggested that one important characteristic of a good research project is that it contains a 'good idea'; that is, the project is about something that is worth finding out about. As Cameron and others have pointed out, deciding on and refining the research question is often the hardest part of the project. It is, thus, worth spending as much time as necessary to get it right.

i. Criteria for developing a discourse analysis project

In her book *Qualitative Methods in Sociolinguistics*, Johnstone (2000) lists a number of criteria that contribute to the development of a good and workable research topic. In her case, she is talking about research in the area of sociolinguistics. What she says, however, applies equally to discourse analysis projects. These criteria include:

- a well-focused idea about spoken or written discourse that is phrased as a question or set of closely related questions;
- an understanding of how discourse analytic techniques can be used to answer the research question/s you are asking;
- an understanding of why your question/s about spoken or written discourse are important in a wider context; that is, why answering the question/s will have practical value and/or be of interest to the world at large;
- familiarity with and access to the location where your discourse analysis project will be carried out;
- ability to get the discourse data that is needed for the research project;
- the time it will realistically take to carry out the discourse analysis project, analyse the results, and write up the results of the project;
- being comfortable with and competent in the ways of collecting the discourse data required by the project;
- being competent in the method/s of analysis required for the project.

9.2 Choosing a research topic

A good place to start in choosing a research question is by drawing up a shortlist of topics that interest you. You can do this by speaking to other students, by asking colleagues, by asking teachers and by asking potential supervisors, as well as by looking up related research in the library. As Cameron (2001: 183) points out, good ideas for research don't 'just spring from the researcher's imagination, they are suggested by previous research'. It is important, then, to read widely to see what previous research has said about the topic you are interested in, including what questions can be asked and answered from a discourse perspective. This reading will also give a view of what the current issues and debates are in the approach to discourse analysis you are interested in, as well as how other researchers have gone about answering the question you are interested in from a discourse perspective.

Choosing and refining a research topic is not, however, a linear process. As one of my students explained:

> It is, rather, a process of going back-and-forth between the research questions, the analytical framework, and the data until a balance has been struck between each of these. A high level of consistency needs to be achieved between the research questions, the analytical framework, the analysis of the data and the conclusions reached in the study. The research question, thus, can be refined [and often is] at any stage of the research. This may be the result of further reading of the literature, the analysis of the data, or simply getting some new ideas from somewhere else.

A good example of this can be seen in how this student chose and refined his research questions. His point of departure was his interest in contrastive rhetoric and second language writing. He had first met contrastive rhetoric in a course he had done on literacy and language education. As a Chinese writer of English he had often been surprised, in his first English academic writing, by some of the different conventions and expectations between Chinese and English academic writing. He wondered if contrastive rhetoric could help him understand these differences. He was also interested in discourse analysis having done a course on this as well, so some sort of discourse analysis of Chinese and English writing seemed to him to be a useful, as well as an interesting topic to investigate. As he read on this topic he saw that Chinese and English writing had indeed been investigated from a contrastive rhetoric perspective. He also saw that there were differing views on whether Chinese writing has an influence on Chinese students' second language writing in English. So he had an area of interest, but not yet a topic. And he had an area of interest that, at this point, was still very wide and not yet focused.

9.3 Focusing a research topic

My student, then, needed to focus his research topic. Often beginning researchers start off with a project that is overly large and ambitious. Stevens and Asmar (1999: 15) suggest that 'wiser heads' know that a good research project is 'narrow and deep.' In their words, 'even the simplest idea can mushroom into an uncontrollably large project'. They highlight how important it is for students to listen to more experienced researchers in their field and to be guided by their advice in the early stages of their research. They suggest starting off by getting immersed in the literature and reading broadly and widely to find a number of potential research topics. This can be done by making heavy use of the library, as well as by reading the abstracts of recent theses and dissertations, some of which are available on the world wide web (see *Directions for further reading* at the end of this chapter for some of these URLs).

Once the reading has been done, it is useful to write a few lines on each topic and use this as the basis to talk to other people about the research. Often one topic may emerge as the strongest contender from these conversations, not only because it is the most original or interesting, but also because it is the most doable in terms of access to data and resource facilities, your expertise in the use of discourse analysis techniques, as well as supervision support.

Here are some of the ideas my student interested in comparing Chinese and English writing started off with.

Topic 1:   A comparison of Chinese students' essay writing in Chinese and English written in their first year of undergraduate studies

Topic 2:   A comparison of students' Master's theses in Chinese and English

Topic 3:   An examination of newspaper articles in Chinese and English from a contrastive rhetoric perspective

Each of these questions is influenced by previous research on the topic. Each of them, however, has their problems. The first question is an interesting one. It would be difficult, however, to get texts written by the same students in their first year of undergraduate studies in the two different settings. It is also not certain (or perhaps not even likely) that they will be asked to do the same or even comparable pieces of writing in the two sets of first-year undergraduate study. It is also not likely that a Chinese student who has completed an undergraduate degree in a Chinese university would then do the same undergraduate degree in an

English medium university. There is also no suggestion in the first topic as to how the pieces of writing would be analysed.

The second question is more possible as some Chinese students do go on to do a degree that includes a thesis in English after having done a degree with a thesis component in Chinese. There would, however, be many more students writing coursework essays and assignments in English who had done something similar in Chinese. So there is a problem of gaining sufficient pieces of writing for the study. There is also the problem of gaining access to the students, and hoping the students will still have the pieces of writing that they did when they were students in China. It is, of course, possible to do both of these first two studies with writing done by different students, as most studies of this kind have done. There is still, however, the problem of getting comparable pieces of writing so that the same, or at least similar things, can be compared.

The third topic, in some ways, solves the data collection issue as newspaper texts are publicly available as long as you have access to a library, or an electronic database where previous copies of newspapers are held. The theoretical framework in this topic, contrastive rhetoric, however, in the sense of cultural influences of ways of writing in one language on another, has not been used to examine newspaper articles as it is probably not very common that Chinese writers of newspaper articles are required to write a newspaper article in English. So while the third topic is practical in many ways, the theoretical framework had not at this stage been used to approach it. My student who was working on this topic decided the notion of genre, rather than contrastive rhetoric, might be a better place to start. He still retained an interest in contrastive rhetoric, however, and wanted to include this in some way in his study. His re-focused topic, then, became:

> A contrastive study of letters to the editor in Chinese and English.

9.4 Turning the topic into a research question

My student had settled on his topic, but it still needed to be turned into a research question. A possible first attempt at this question might be:

> What are the differences between letters to the editor in Chinese and English?

This question however pre-supposes an outcome before the study has been carried out; that is, that there would indeed be differences between the two sets of writings. The question also does not capture anything of the theoretical models that might be used to answer this question. The re-focused set of questions that my student ended up with was:

1) In what ways are Chinese and English letters to the editor similar or different?
2) Can we use genre theory and contrastive rhetoric to understand these similarities and differences?

His question, thus, became more focused. It did not yet state exactly what aspects of genre theory he would draw on for his analysis, however. These became clearer as he read further on his topic and carried out trial analyses. He then decided to look at the *schematic structures* in the two sets of texts and the typical *rhetorical types* (such as problem-solution, compare and contrast, etc.) present in the texts. He also decided to look at the use of *logico-semantic relations* (Martin 1992) between clauses in the two sets of texts as his reading had told him this was an aspect of writing, in some genres at least, that differs in Chinese and English writing. His plan was then to see to what extent previous research in the area of contrastive rhetoric into other genres might help him explain whatever similarities and differences he might observe in his two sets of data.

His questions, thus, were now *worth asking* and *capable of being answered* from a discourse analysis perspective. As he argued, most studies of Chinese and English writing either looked at Chinese, or English writing, but not at both. Also few studies used the same textual criteria for the two sets of analyses. Many previous studies of this kind, further, focused on 'direct' or 'indirect' aspects of Chinese and English writing and did not go beyond this to explore how the various parts of the texts combine together to create coherent texts. So what he was doing was theoretically useful, it was possible to collect the texts, and he was capable of analysing the data in the way that he proposed.

It is important, then, as my student did, to strike a balance between the value of the question and your ability to develop a discourse analysis project you are capable of carrying out; that is, a project that you have the background, expertise, resources and access to data that are needed for the project (see *A written discourse project* below for further discussion of this project).

9.5 Kinds of discourse analysis projects

There are a number of different kinds of projects that can be carried out from a discourse analysis perspective. A number of these are described below, together with examples of previous discourse projects and details of the data that were collected for each of these projects.

i. Replication of previous discourse studies

One kind of study to consider is a replication study. As Santos (1989) points out, the findings of many studies are often not tested by further studies which follow the same methodology and a similar data set, either at the same point in time or at some stage later when the findings may be different. Santos describes this lack of replication studies as a serious weakness in applied linguistics research. Such studies provide both the accumulation and consolidation of knowledge over time. They can confirm, or call into question, previous findings in the research literature.

Samraj's (2005) study of research article abstracts and introductions is an example of a replication study. Her aim was to test the results of previous research into the discourse structure of research article introductions to see whether they apply to articles written in the area of conservation biology and wildlife behaviour. She also wished to look at whether the discourse structure of the research article abstracts was as different from the discourse structure of research article introductions as previous research had claimed them to be. To carry out her study, she randomly selected 12 research article abstracts and 12 research article introductions from two key journals in the area of conservation biology and wildlife behaviour. She analysed her data using models that had been used in previous research on this topic, namely Swales' (1990) research into research article introductions and Bhatia's (1993) and Hyland's (2004c) research on research article abstracts. Once she had compared her findings with the results of previous research, she then compared her two data sets with each other to examine the extent to which they were similar in terms of discourse organization and function, also the focus of previous research.

ii. Using different discourse data but the same methodology

A further way of using previous research is to carry out a study which uses different discourse data from a previous study, but the same methodology so as to be able to compare and contrast your findings with those of the original study. Yang's (1997) study of the opening sequences in Chinese telephone calls did this. She collected 80 Chinese telephone conversations made by three Chinese families living in Beijing. She analysed the opening sequences of these conversations, then compared her findings with the findings of previous research into opening sequences in telephone calls in the United States and a number of other countries and, in particular, published claims about 'canonical' openings of telephone conversations in English.

iii. Analysing existing data from a discourse analysis perspective

Channell's (1997) study of telephone conversations took already published data, a conversation purported to be between the Prince of Wales and Camilla Parker-Bowles, and analysed it to see in what way the speakers expressed love and desire, what the effect of the telephone was on their talk and what features of the conversation mark it as being the talk of two people who are in a close and intimate relationship. She looked at topic choice and topic management, ways of expressing love and caring, the language of desire and the way in which the speakers said goodbye to each other. Her study confirmed previous work on telephone closings in that both speakers employed an elaborate set of pre-closings and continued repetitions (such as 'love you', 'love you forever' and 'love you too') before concluding their conversation. She did not follow the conversation analysis procedure of transcribing the data herself as the data had already been published (and was not, in any case, available in audio form). It had also been tidied up to some extent when it was originally published. Notwithstanding, her study does show the value of taking already existing data to see how discourse analytic techniques can help to further understand already published data.

iv. Analysing discourse data from a different perspective

Another possibility is to take data that has already been analysed from one discourse perspective and analyse it from another. Orr (1996) did this in her study of arguments in a reality TV show. Her particular interest was in using conversation analysis as an alternate way of looking at data that had already been examined from a frame semantics perspective (Lee 1997) to see what this other perspective might reveal about the nature of the interactions. Her study followed the philosophy of conversation analytic studies in that she started with the data and allowed the details of the analysis to emerge from her transcriptions. Through repeated listenings to the data she saw how the speakers challenged and countered each other's points of view in a series of cyclical moves until one or the other speaker accepted the point of the argument. She then compared her findings with the findings of the study that had used frame semantics as its framework for analysis.

v. Considering the validity of a previous claim

A further possibility is to design a project which considers the validity of a previous claim in the research. Liu's (2004, forthcoming) study of Chinese ethnic minorities' and Han Chinese students' expository writing in English aimed to examine an existing claim in his particular setting. He examined, in particular, the claim that the typical Chinese rhetorical structure of *Qi-cheng-zhuan-he* would influence his students' expository writing in English. He collected texts from a preparation test in which the students were asked to produce a piece of expository writing in English. The data was made up of English texts written by Tibetan students, Mongolian students and Han Chinese students. He examined both the schematic structure and thematic structure of the students' texts. He then examined these structures to see to what extent they were influenced by the Chinese rhetorical structure he was interested in. Finally, he made a comparison of the three student groups' writing to see if there were any differences in the discourse structures of their writing.

vi. Focusing on unanalysed genres

Another possibility is to focus on data that has not been analysed before and describe characteristic features of the particular discourse. This could, for example, be an analysis of one of the many new genres that are emerging through the use of new technologies, or it may be examples of a genre that has not been analysed before from a discourse perspective. Ooi (2001) looked at a new and emerging genre in his study of personal advertisements on the Internet. His study was based on data collected from Internet dating sites in the US and Singapore. He broke his data up into three groupings based on three types of 'sought after relationship': 'romance', 'dating' and 'intimate'. He found his data by doing an Internet search, typing in the keywords 'personal ads', 'personal advertisements' and 'personal classifieds'. He collected 12 files of texts for his study, with ten texts in each file, based on further subcategories of his groupings. He then carried out a lexical analysis of the texts, looking at word frequency and collocations by gender and country of origin to see to what extent males and females differ in their expectations of each other in writing this kind of advertisement, and the kinds of words and expressions they use to express these expectations.

Shalom (1997) carried out a similar study in her examination of personal advertisements in London's *Time Out* entertainment guide. She collected 766 ads from the Lonely Hearts section of *Time Out* over a period of four months. Her interest was in the attributes of the person the writers were seeking to meet. She broke up her corpus of texts into four groupings for her analysis: straight men (367 texts), straight women (186 texts), gay men (155 texts) and gay women (58 texts) to see in what ways each of these groups typically described the person of their desire.

vii. Mixed-methods discourse studies

Mixed-methods studies which combine research techniques can increase the validity as well as to help gain greater insights into a topic under investigation. Eckert's (2000) *Linguistic Variation as Social Practice* is an example of a study which combines both quantitative and qualitative analyses for the analysis of spoken discourse. She carried out a study of phonemic variation in the speech of two polarized groups of students in a Midwestern high school in the US: 'jocks' (students with a high level of participation in athletics or other school activities and generally from the upper half of the local socioeconomic continuum) and 'burnouts' (students who are generally from the lower half of the local socioeconomic continuum and who are more likely to go into the workforce than to university at the end of high school).

Eckert looked, not just at language variation, but also the way the identity of the speakers was constructed in their use of language. Her data included interviews in which she collected speech samples that she then analysed for the particular linguistic features she was interested in. She also carried out day-to-day observations in and around the school where she carried out her study. She walked around and took notes on who was where, what they were doing and who they were doing it with. She took notes from extracurricular activities, in the park, in the neighbourhood and at McDonalds. She interviewed people separately and in groups, both in and out of school hours. She kept notes on how the students dressed, how they did their hair and makeup, as well as where they hung out, who they hung out with and when. Working with *social network theory*, the notion of *communities of practice* and *friendship clusters*, she discusses her observations about stylistic variation, the social meaning of that variation and the social and linguistic construction of identity through the use of spoken discourse.

Ohashi's (2000) study of the speech act of thanking in Japanese is a further example of a discourse study which combines a number of different research techniques. He combined elicited data in the form of discourse completion tasks, role plays and letter writing tasks with actual examples of language use. He looked at his data from both cross-cultural pragmatic and interlanguage pragmatic perspectives. His interest was in the notion of a debt–credit equilibrium in thanking as an expression of politeness in Japanese. He carried out four data-based studies, each of which examined this issue. The real-life data was drawn from telephone conversations recorded at the time of the *seibo* season, one of two major gift-giving seasons in Japan. This was then contrasted with the findings of the other data: discourse completion tasks completed by native speakers of Japanese, native speakers of English and adult learners of Japanese; role-plays performed by native speakers of Japanese; and letters of request and letters of thanks written by native and non-native speakers of Japanese. By comparing both elicited and real-life data he contributes to cross-cultural discussions of politeness as well as shows the strength of methodological *triangulation* in this sort of investigation.

9.6 Two sample discourse studies

The two projects which follow are both examples of studies which combine approaches to research in the analysis of discourse. The first is a mixed-methods study. The second is a study which draws on both discourse and non-discourse analysis perspectives on its particular topic. The use of triangulation is a particular strength of these two studies, as is the detail of analysis that each of the students carried out in their discourse analysis projects.

9.7 A spoken discourse project

Silence in Japanese students' tutorial interactions in English.

i. Summary of the study

Nakane's (2003, 2005) examination of silence in Japanese students' interactions in university tutorials in English looked at the students' actual performance in the university classrooms as well as the students', other students and lecturer's perceptions of the Japanese students' performance. She combined the techniques of conversation analysis with ethnographic data in order to get multiple perspectives on the question she was investigating.

ii. Aim of the study

The aim of Nakane's study was to examine the communication problems faced by Japanese students in mainstream English medium university classrooms. She also wanted to see whether there were characteristic discourse patterns of Japanese students which could be sources of their communication problems. This question drew from her own experience as an English teacher in Japan, where she had begun to wonder how Japanese students would cope with academic interactions in an English-speaking country. She discovered, from her research, that we know very little about what happens to these students in mainstream university classrooms. Her study looked at the actual performance of these students in mainstream university classes, as well as exploring other people's perceptions of these students' performances in these classes.

iii. Methodology

Nakane carried out a conversation analysis of the students' classroom interactions. She also conducted individual interviews, focus group discussions and administered questionnaires. She combined this data with three case studies which drew on video and audio recordings, field notes and artifacts from her classroom observations. The case studies used stimulated recall interviews and follow-up interviews with the Japanese students, fellow English-speaking students and their teachers. A large-scale survey that had been independently carried out at another university was also used as a data source for the study. Nakane also collected data from classrooms in Japan in order to make a comparison between her observations of the English medium classrooms and how Japanese students might typically behave in a similar kind of setting in Japan. The Japanese data consisted of video recordings, field notes and artifacts from the Japanese classrooms.

Apart from the conversation analyses of the English classroom data, a content analysis was carried out of the interview and stimulated recall data where Nakane allowed categories and sub-categories to emerge from the data, rather than using a set of pre-determined categories as the starting point for her analysis. The video and audio material were coded following patterns that had emerged from the students' and staff's self reports in the stimulated recall interviews and the follow-up interviews. The conversation analysis component of the data was counter-checked by another analyst, a native speaker of English.

iv. Results of the study

Nakane's study showed that silence was one of the major problems for the Japanese students in the English medium classrooms, both for themselves and for their lecturers. She found, however, that the degree and type of silence varied among the students. She found that gaps in assumptions about classroom communication between the Japanese students, fellow English-speaking students and their lecturers contributed to the students' silence in each of her three cases. She also considered the results of her study in relation to other issues such as teacher–student interactional modes, teacher control of classroom discourse, timing in the taking of turns and the Japanese students' perceptions of politeness and, in particular, the hierarchy-oriented politeness system they were used to in their interactions with teachers in Japan. She also considered her findings in relation to the issue of the Japanese students' language proficiency and their different schema, or interpretive frames, for classroom interactions.

Nakane found that the Japanese students' silence in class seemed to prevent the establishment of rapport between them and their lecturers. She found there was a conflict between the lecturers' view of the Japanese students' personalities (for example, as being shy) when this was not the case for the students outside of the classroom. She also found that the students' silence in class was interpreted as a negative attitude and lack of commitment to their studies, where in fact, for one of the students she examined, this was not at all the case.

v. Commentary

A particular strength of Nakane's study was the multiple perspectives she took on her research question in order to provide both validity and depth to her research findings. These multiple data sources provided for a detailed and fine-grained analysis of the research questions. The project showed a good understanding of the importance of triangulation in this sort of study by combining different perspectives on the research questions that she examined. Her ethnographic data provided insights into her findings that would not have been possible by looking at the spoken interactions alone. It is an example of a project that was well conceived, well designed and well carried out. Further, it provided answers to questions that are of value to both university teaching staff and to students that may help, in the future, to provide solutions to the kinds of communication problems the students in her study were experiencing.

vi. Further research

Nakane is well aware of the limits to the claims that can be made on the basis of her study and argues for the accumulation of further data and analyses of the kind that she had carried out. In particular she points to the need to further explore the types and aspects of silence that she observed. She argues that these analyses need to be at both the micro and the macro levels; that is, by a detailed analysis of the actual interactions, as well as a broader analysis of the situation and circumstances that surround the interactions. She also suggests the examination of student interactions in different types of study situations to see to what extent students' interactions in these situations are similar to, or different from, the interactions that she observed. She suggests looking at the reverse kind of situation as well; that is, looking at the interactions of English-speaking students in Japanese university settings to see to what extent the English-speaking students' experiences in a Japanese university classroom are similar to, or different from, the Japanese students' interactions that she examined in her study.

9.8 A written discourse project

A contrastive analysis of letters to the editor in Chinese and English.

i. Summary of the study

Wang's (2002, 2004) contrastive study of letters to the editor in English and Chinese is an example of a written discourse project that drew on different, yet complementary, theoretical frameworks for his study: contrastive rhetoric and the systemic functional view of genre. He also read outside of these two areas to try to find socio-cultural explanations for the similarities and differences that he observed in his study.

ii. Aim of the study

Wang's study had several research questions: in what ways are Chinese and English letters to the editor similar or different in terms of their rhetorical structures, to what extent can systemic functional genre theory and contrastive rhetoric be used to explore and understand these similarities and differences and what are the reasons for the similarities and differences in the performance of this genre in the two different linguistic and cultural settings.

212

iii. Methodology

The data Wang collected for this study consisted of ten letters to the editor in Chinese and ten letters to the editor in English published in two sets of widely read Chinese and English newspapers. He looked at the schematic structure of each of the two sets of data, the rhetorical types (such as 'problem/solution', 'evaluation' and 'exposition') represented in the two data sets and logico-semantic relationships between the clauses and clauses complexes in the two sets of texts. He then read discussions of differences in collectivism and individualism in Chinese and Western cultures in order to try to understand the findings of his study.

iv. Results of the study

Wang found that the Chinese and English letters to the editor shared some similarities at the level of schematic structures. Notwithstanding, he found that there was often an editor's preview to the Chinese letters to the editor that was absent in the English letters. He found that appeals to values and needs were used to support claims in the Chinese letters whereas the English letters used evidence to do this. He also found that while consequential and additive logico-semantic relations were used in both the Chinese and English texts, consequential relations occurred more frequently in the Chinese texts than in the English texts.

Wang argues that the notion of evidence is deeply rooted in Western culture so therefore finds it way into English texts, whereas appeals to values and needs is especially important in Chinese culture and so is strongly present in the Chinese letters to the editor. He also argues that the editor's preview in the Chinese letters plays the role of presenting a societal norm, or point of view, that individuals in Chinese society are expected to follow. He suggests that the greater use of consequential relations in the Chinese texts is a reflection of the commonly used inductive style of Chinese writing as well as the typical subordinate–main sequences that often occur.

v. Commentary

By employing approaches to analysis from systemic functional genre studies and contrastive rhetoric, Wang was able to able to carry out a detailed examination of the similarities and differences between letters to editors in English and Chinese at different levels of analysis. He also looked outside of the texts to try to gain an understanding of why they had been written the way they were. There were, however, aspects in which the project could have been strengthened. The process of text sampling could have been wider and the number of texts could have been larger. He saw from his study, however, the value of combining linguistic and non-linguistic analyses in order to understand not just what occurs when the same genre is written in different linguistic and cultural contexts, but also why this occurs. This is something he decided to explore in more detail in his subsequent contrastive genre study of newspaper commentaries in Chinese and English on the events of September 11 (see below).

vi. Further research

Wang was aware of the limitations of the claims he could make from the size and particular geographical location of his data set and suggests further data be collected from a wider range of Chinese and English language newspapers than he did in his original study. He tried to address this issue in his subsequent contrastive genre study of newspaper commentaries in Chinese and English on the events of September 11. This study is based on an examination of 50 Chinese newspaper commentaries and 50 English language newspaper commentaries. The data he chose for his study of newspaper commentaries are drawn from national general, national specialist and regional newspapers in both Chinese and English (Wang 2006a, 2006b).

His study, in his current project, draws on the strengths of two different perspectives on genre analysis: the view of genre based in systemic functional linguistics and the view of genre represented by researchers in the *new rhetoric* (Freedman and Medway 1994) school of genre studies. His study incorporates textual, intertextual and contextual analyses of the two sets of texts. At the textual level, he examines the schematic structure of the two sets of texts, the rhetorical types they typically represent and the ways in which key participants are introduced into and kept track of in the texts. At the intertextual level he explores the ways in which the texts draw on other sources, and other voices, in the production of the texts. He then combines this analysis with a discussion of the notion of intertextuality across communities of practice as a way of both broadening and giving greater depth to his analysis. His contextual analysis considers the textual and intertextual findings of the study in relation to their respective socio-cultural and socio-political contexts, and, in particular, the role of the media and discourses of terrorism in each of the particular settings.

Wang's second study shows how the results and insights that have been gained in one discourse analysis project can be drawn on for the development of a further, more substantial, discourse analysis project. In his particular case, he learnt how much a contextual analysis has to contribute to genre analysis projects, making this a critical focus of his second project on the topic of Chinese/English writing.

9.9 Combining discourse and other research perspectives

Both the Nakane and the Wang studies that have just been described drew on a number of different discourse analysis and other research perspectives to work towards answers to their research questions. When combining perspectives in this way, it is important to understand the basis of the perspectives being drawn on to understand what this placing together implies and, indeed, if it is possible to do this. People working in the area of conversation analysis, for example, would consider Nakane's combination of conversation analytic techniques and ethnography impossible as for a conversation analyst the evidence is in the data, and the closest an analyst is able to get to understanding an event is in the transcription and analysis of the data. For them, insiders' views are only intuitions and not, in their view, admissible in the analysis and interpretation of the data. My view, however, is that Nakane strengthened, rather than weakened her study by combining perspectives in the way that she did.

Cameron (2005b: 125) discusses the problems associated with what she calls 'theoretical and methodological eclecticism'. She points out that sometimes this carries a high risk of superficiality as the researcher may be trying to do too many things at once and not end up doing any of them properly (which is not the case in either the Nakane or the Wang studies). It is not impossible to mix discourse analysis and other methods. What this requires, however, is 'a clear rationale for putting approaches together, a sophisticated understanding of each approach, and an account of how the tensions between approaches will be handled in [the] study' (Cameron 2005b: 127).

A researcher can, then, combine an approach to discourse analysis with a non-discourse analytic perspective on the research, as both Nakane and Wang have done in their studies. Both Nakane and Wang have shown how doing this can provide more of an account of the issue they are examining than might have been possible with just the one, single discourse analysis (or other research) perspective. It is crucial, however, in the planning of this kind of project, that each of the approaches are weighed up against each other, identifying what kind of information each approach can (and cannot) supply. By doing this the use of one approach to discourse analysis in combination with another approach to discourse analysis, or other approach to research, can be justified. Indeed, often an approach of this kind can provide a fuller, and more explanatory perspective on the question under investigation than might be provided with just the one single perspective.

9.10 Evaluating a discourse analysis project

Each of the studies described in this chapter suggest ways in which discourse analysis can provide insights into social, pedagogic and linguistic questions. Taylor (2001) suggests a number of criteria by which discourse studies can be evaluated. These criteria, she argues, should be an integral part of any discourse analysis project and should guide readers of the project in their evaluation of it. Three key issues to consider in this are the *reliability, validity* and *replicability* of the project that has been carried out.

i. Reliability

Reliability refers to the consistency of the results obtained in the project. This is comprised of two kinds of reliability, internal reliability and external reliability. *Internal reliability* refers to the consistency of the data collection, analysis of the data and interpretation of the results; that is, the extent to which the researcher was consistent in what they did and whether someone else would get the same results if they carried out the same analysis of the data.

In his study of Chinese and English letters to the editor referred to earlier in this chapter, Wang decided which newspapers would best represent the genre he wanted to investigate in terms of their circulation and which of them were the most widely read in the particular social and cultural setting. Once he had decided which newspapers to select his texts from he chose his texts from only these two sets of newspapers. He then analysed each of his texts in the same way. That is, he looked at the schematic structure, rhetorical types and logico-semantic relations in each of the 20 texts in his study. He then analysed and interpreted the results of his analyses in the same way for each of the texts he examined. He looked for typical patterns in each of the sets of texts and considered the extent to which the use of the patterns he observed reflected particular socio-cultural views of the relationship between the writers and their audience in the particular settings in which the texts were produced.

External reliability (or *replicability*) refers to the extent to which another researcher could reproduce the study, using the same dis-course analysis procedures, and obtain the same or similar results to those obtained in the study. In order to ensure the replicability (and thereby external reliability) of his study, Wang provided his sample texts and detailed analyses of each of the aspects he examined in the appendix to his study. In the methodology section of his study he both explained and gave details of each of his categories of analysis so that readers of his study could then take these categories and re-analyse his data in the same way, if they so wished to. In the presentation of his Chinese data he provided English translations for each of his texts and glossed each of his Chinese examples in English so that a reader who cannot read Chinese would be able to follow his analysis and the arguments and claims he was making. That is, he provided sufficient information about the approach he used and his categories of analysis so that someone else approaching his data, in the same way, would come up with the same findings.

ii. Validity

Validity refers to the extent to which a piece of research actually investigates what it says it will investigate, and 'the truth or the accuracy of the generalizations being made by the researcher'. *Internal validity* refers to 'how far claims about cause are "true" in the situation being studied' (Taylor 2001: 318). *External validity* refers to the extent to which the results of the study can be generalized from the sample used in the study to a broader population.

In Wang's case he was careful to caution that his observations were limited to the set of texts that he had chosen for his study. Even though his texts were chosen at random, he was well aware that another set of 20 texts may reveal something different from what he observed, as indeed may an analysis of a larger set of texts. In terms of generalizability, then, he was well aware that this is not possible from the size of his sample. He did, however, provide sufficient details on the nature and source of his texts and his analyses of the texts, so that a reader could consider the extent to which his findings could be *transferred* or *compared* to what might be found in another, similar set of texts. By doing this, he aimed to provide *credibility*, *dependability* and *transferability* to his study. He, thus, left an *audit trail* that other people reading his research could follow by making as clear as possible what he did, how he did it and how he reached the conclusions that he did.

9.11 Planning a discourse analysis project

The final task in this book asks you to draw on the issues presented in this and previous chapters to develop a proposal for a discourse analysis project. The readings, websites and journals that follow are suggestions for places to look to read further and to help you choose a topic that you would like to investigate.

Task

> Draw up a shortlist of possible research topics, writing a sentence or two about each topic. Discuss this list with an academic, considering issues which might arise with each of the topics, such as practicality, originality, focus and scale of the project. Once you have selected a topic from your list, consider the advice presented in this chapter on developing a research project. Start writing a proposal for your project, then take it to the person you spoke with for further discussion. Once you have had this discussion, read further on your topic. Now write a research proposal using the following set of headings.
>
> • title of the discourse analysis project;
> • purpose of the discourse analysis project;
> • research question/s the discourse analysis project will aim to answer;
> • background literature relevant to the discourse analysis project;
> • research method/s and discourse analysis techniques that will be used for the project;
> • significance of the discourse analysis project;
> • resources that will be required for the discourse analysis project.

9.12 Directions for further reading

Cameron, D. (2001), *Working with Spoken Discourse*. London: Sage.
    Chapter 12. Designing your research project
This chapter of Cameron's book discusses the planning of a discourse analysis project from an initial idea to the final stage of writing up the project. Different kinds of studies are suggested, with examples from Cameron's students' work.

218

Hughes, R. (2002), *Teaching and Researching Speaking*. Harlow, UK: Longman. Section III: Researching speaking, Section IV: References and further information
Hughes's book discusses issues in researching spoken discourse. It gives examples of spoken discourse projects, discusses new directions in researching spoken discourse as well as gives ideas for spoken discourse projects. The book concludes with a chapter on resources for investigating spoken discourse.

Hyland, K. (2002b), *Teaching and Researching Writing*. Harlow, UK: Longman. Section III: Researching writing, Section IV: References and resources
This section of Hyland's book discusses issues and practices in the researching of written texts. It describes a number of sample studies as examples of different kinds of research and research methods. The book includes a list of key sources for reading further on researching written discourse.

Wray, A., Trott, K. and Bloomer, A. (eds) (1998), *Projects in Linguistics: A Practical Guide to Researching Language*, London: Arnold/New York: Oxford University Press.
This book provides advice on how to choose a research topic, how to collect data, how to analyse data and how to write up the results. Many ideas are given for possible research projects and lists of key references are provided for following up on each of the topics discussed.

Websites for looking for theses and dissertations which take a discourse perspective:

> The Networked Digital Library of Theses and Dissertations (www.ndltd.org/)
> UMI Pro Quest Digital Dissertations (www.lib.umi.com/dissertations/)
> The Australian Digital Theses Program (adt.caul.edu.au/)

Journals for looking for examples of studies which take a discourse perspective:

> Annual Review of Applied Linguistics
> Applied Linguistics
> Australian Review of Applied Linguistics
> Critical Inquiry in Language Studies
> Discourse Processes
> Discourse and Society
> Discourse Studies
> Educational Linguistics

English for Specific Purposes
Functions of Language
International Journal of Applied Linguistics
International Journal of Corpus Linguistics
Journal of English for Academic Purposes
Journal of Politeness Research
Journal of Second Language Writing
Journal of Pragmatics
Journal of Sociolinguistics
Language and Communication
Language and Education
Language, Identity and Education
Language in Society
Language Teaching
Pragmatics
TESOL Quarterly
Text and Talk
Written Communication

References

Abell, J. and Stokoe, E. (1999), '"I take full responsibility, I take some responsibility, I'll take half of it but no more than that": Princess Diana and the negation of blame in the Panorama interview', *Discourse Studies*, 1, 297–310.

Aoki, N. (2005), 'Japanese dialling up Dalian call centers,' *The Japan Times Online*. 5 October 2005, available at: www.japantimes.co.jp/cgi-bin/getarticle.pl5?nn20051005f3.htm – accessed 27 December 2005.

Asahi Newspaper (1993), 'Crown Prince and Masako's engagement press conference', 20 January 1993, p. 1.

Askehave, I. and Swales, J. M. (2000), 'Genre identification and communicative purpose: A problem and possible solution, *Applied Linguistics*, 22, 195–212.

Atkinson, J. M. and Drew, P. (eds) (1979), *Order in Court: The Organisation of Verbal Interaction in Judicial Settings*. London: Social Sciences Research Council.

Austin, J. L. (1962), *How to Do Things With Words*. Oxford: Clarendon Press.

Austin, T. (1998), 'Cross-cultural pragmatics. Building in analysis of communication across cultures and languages: Examples from Japanese', *Foreign Language Annals*, 31, 3, 326–41.

Australian.idolblog.com (2004), Casey Donovan. Australian Idol Blog. www.australian.idolblog.com/contestant/casey_donovan.php – accessed 30 November 2004.

Bartolome, L. (1998), *The Misteaching of Academic Discourses: The Politics of Language in the Classroom*. Boulder, Co: Westview Press.

Barton, D. and Tusting, K. (eds) (2005), *Beyond Communities of Practice: Language, Power and Social Context*. Cambridge: Cambridge University Press.

Basturkman, H. (2002), 'Clause relations and macro patterns: Cohesion, coherence and the writing of advanced ESOL students', *English Teaching Forum*, 38, 50–6.

Baxter, J. (2002), 'Is PDA really an alternative? A reply to West', *Discourse and Society*, 13, 853–9.

Bazerman, C. (1988), *Shaping Written Knowledge*. Madison, Wi: University of Wisconsin Press.

BBC (1995), 'The BBC Panorama interview' available at: www.bbc.co.uk/politics97/diana/panorama.html – accessed 14 January 2005.

Béal, C. (1992), '"Did you have a good weekend?" or why there is no such thing as a simple question', *Australian Review of Applied Linguistics*, 15, 23–52.

Becher, T. and Trowler, P. (2001), *Academic Tribes and Territories: Intellectual*

Enquiry and the Cultures of Discipline. Buckingham, UK: Open University Press.

Beebe, L. and Waring, H. Z. (2005), 'Pragmatic development in responding to rudeness', in J. Frodesen and C. Holten (eds), *The Power of Context in Language Teaching and Learning.* Boston, Mass: Thomson/Heinle, pp. 67–80.

Behrendt, G. and Tuccillo, L. (2004), *He's Just Not That Into You: The No-excuses Truth to Understanding Guys.* London: Element.

Benwell, B. (2005), ' "Lucky this is anonymous!" Ethnographies of reception in men's magazines: A "textual culture" approach', *Discourse and Society*, 16, 147–72.

Bhatia, V. K. (1993), *Analysing Genre: Language Use in Professional Settings.* London: Longman.

—— (1997), 'Genre-mixing in academic introductions', *English for Specific Purposes.* 16, 181–95.

—— (1998), 'Integrating products, processes, purposes and participants in professional writing', in C. N. Candlin and K. Hyland (eds), *Writing: Texts, Processes and Practices.* London: Longman, pp. 21–39.

—— (2004), *Worlds of Written Discourse: A Genre-Based View.* London: Continuum.

Biber, D. (1986), 'Spoken and written textual dimensions in English: Resolving the contradictory findings', *Language*, 62, 384–414.

—— (1988), *Variation Across Speech and Writing.* Cambridge: Cambridge University Press.

—— (1994), 'Representativeness in corpus design', in A. Zampolli, N. Calzolari, N. and M. Palmer (eds), *Current Issues in Computational Linguistics: In Honour of Don Walker.* Pisa: Giardini; Norwell, MA: Kluwer, pp. 377–407.

Biber, D., Conrad, S. and Cortes, V. (2004), '*If you look at . . . :* Lexical bundles in university teaching and textbooks', *Applied Linguistics*, 25, 371–405.

Biber, D., Conrad, S. and Reppen, R. (1994), 'Corpus-based approaches to issues in applied linguistics', *Applied Linguistics*, 15, 169–89.

—— (1998), *Corpus Linguistics: Investigating Language Structure and Use.* Cambridge: Cambridge University Press.

Biber, D., Conrad, S., Reppen, R., Byrd, P. and Helt, M. (2002), 'Speaking and writing in the University: A multidimensional comparison', *TESOL Quarterly*, 36, 9–48.

Biber, D., Johansson, S., Leech, G., Conrad, S. and Finegan, E. (1999), *Longman Grammar of Spoken and Written English.* London: Longman.

Big Brother (2004) www.bigbrother.com.au/ accessed 30 July 2004.

Billig, M. (1999), 'Critical discourse analysis and conversation analysis: An exchange between Michael Billig and Emanuel A. Schegloff', *Discourse and Society*, 10, 543–82.

Blommaert, J. (2005), *Discourse: A Critical Introduction.* Cambridge: Cambridge University Press.

Bloor, T. and Bloor, M. (2004), *The Functional Analysis of English: A Hallidayan Approach* (2nd edn). London: Arnold.

Borg, E. (2003), 'Key concepts in ELT: Discourse community', *ELT Journal*, 57, 398–400.

Brown, G. and Levinson, S. (1987), *Politeness. Some Universals in Language Usage*. Cambridge: Cambridge University Press.

Brown, R. (1992), 'Foreword', in H. Koch (ed.), *Casablanca. Script and Legend*. Woodstock, NY.: Overlook Press, pp. 7–10.

Bruthiaux, P. (1994), 'Me Tarzan, you Jane: Linguistic simplification in "personal ads" register', in D. Biber and E. Finegan (eds), *Sociolinguistic Perspectives on Register*. Oxford: Oxford University Press, pp. 136–54.

Burns, A. and Joyce, H. (1997), *Focus on Speaking*. Sydney: National Centre for English Language Teaching and Research, Macquarie University.

Butler, J. (1990), *Gender Trouble: Feminism and the Subversion of Identity*. New York: Routledge.

—— (2004), *Undoing Gender*. London: Routledge.

Button, G. (1987), 'Moving out of closings', in G. Button and J. R. E. Lee (eds), *Talk and Social Organization*. Clevedon: Multilingual Matters pp. 101–51.

Cadman, K. (1997), 'Thesis writing for international students: A question of identity?' *English for Specific Purposes*, 16, 3–14.

Cahill, D. (2003), 'The myth of the "turn" in contrastive rhetoric', *Written Communication*, 20, 170–94.

Cameron, D. (1998), ' "Is there any ketchup, Vera?": Gender, power and pragmatics,' *Discourse and Society*, 9, 437–55.

—— (1999), 'Performing gender identity: Young men's talk and the construction of heterosexual masculinity', in A. Jaworski and N. Coupland (eds), *The Discourse Reader*. London: Routledge, pp. 442–58.

—— (2000), 'Styling the worker: Gender and the commodification of language in the globalized service economy', *Journal of Sociolinguistics*, 4, 323–47.

—— (2001), *Working with Spoken Discourse*. London: Sage.

—— (2005a), 'Language, gender, and sexuality: Current issues and new directions', *Applied Linguistics*, 26, 482–502.

—— (2005b), 'Review of Allyson Jule: Gender, participation and silence in the language classroom: Sh-shusing the girls', *Applied Linguistics*, 26, 125–38.

Cameron, D. and Kulick, D. (2003), *Language and Sexuality*. Cambridge: Cambridge University Press.

Canagarajah, A. S. (2002), *Critical Academic Writing and Multilingual Students*. Ann Arbor: The University of Michigan Press.

Canale, M. (1983), 'From communicative competence to communicative language pedagogy', in J. C. Richards and R. W. Schmidt (eds), *Language and Communication*. London: Longman, pp. 2–27.

Canale, M. and Swain, M. (1980), 'Theoretical bases of communicative approaches to second language teaching and testing', *Applied Linguistics*, 1, 1–47.

Casanave, C. P. (2002), *Writing Games: Multicultural Case Studies of Academic Literacy Practices in Higher Education*. Mahwah: NJ: Laurence Erlbaum.

Cazden, C. (1998), 'The meanings of 'discourse'. Applied Linguistics Association of America Plenary Panel of Past Presidents, Seattle.

223

Celce-Murcia, M. (1997), 'Describing and teaching English grammar with reference to written discourse', in T. Miller (ed.), *Functional Approaches to Written Text: Classroom Applications*. Washington, DC: United States Information Agency, pp. 174–85.

Celce-Murcia, M. and Olshtain, E. (2000), *Discourse and Context in Language Teaching. A Guide for Language Teachers*. Cambridge: Cambridge University Press.

Channell, J. (1997), 'I just called to say I love you: Love and desire on the telephone', in K. Harvey and C. Shalom (eds), *Language and Desire: Encoding Sex, Romance and Intimacy*. London: Routledge, pp. 143–69.

Chimombo, M. and Roseberry, R. L. (1998), *The Power of Discourse: An Introduction to Discourse Analysis*. Mahwah, NJ: Lawrence Erlbaum.

Cho, H. (Executive producer) (1992), 'The last appeal: The murder case of a Korean immigrant', Seoul: Seoul Broadcasting System, broadcast 13 September 1992.

Chouliaraki, L. (2004), 'Watching 11 September: The politics of pity', *Discourse and Society*, 15, 185–98.

Christie, C. (2002), 'Politeness and the linguistic construction of gender in parliament: An analysis of transgressions and apology behaviour', *Working Papers on the Web*, 3, available at: www.shu.ac.uk/wpw/politeness/christie. htm – accessed 27 December 2005.

Christie, F. (1993), 'The "received" tradition of literacy teaching: The decline of rhetoric and the corruption of grammar', in B. Green (ed.), *The Insistence of the Letter: Literacy Studies and Curriculum Theorizing*. London: Falmer Press, pp. 75–106.

Cicourel, A. V. (1992), 'The interpenetration of communicative context: Examples from medical encounters', in A. Duranti and C. Goodwin (eds), *Rethinking Context: Language as an Interactive Phenomenon*. Cambridge: Cambridge University Press, pp. 1–42.

Clark, R. J. (1995), 'Developing critical reading practices', *Prospect*, 10, 65–80.

Conduit, A. M. and Modesto, D. V. (1990), 'An investigation of the generic structure of the materials/methods section of scientific reports', *Australian Review of Applied Linguistics*, Series S, No 6, 109–34.

Connor, U. (1996), *Contrastive rhetoric: Cross-cultural aspects of second language writing*. Cambridge: Cambridge University Press.

—— (2004), 'Intercultural rhetoric research: Beyond texts', *Journal of English for Academic Purposes*, 3, 291–304.

Cook, G. (1989), *Discourse*. Oxford: Oxford University Press.

Cooper, A. (2005), 'Make the first move', *The Sun-Herald*, 6 February 2005, p. S38.

Corliss, R. (1992), 'Casablanca: An analysis of the film', in H. Koch (ed.), *Casablanca: Script and Legend*. Woodstock: Overlook Press, pp. 233–47.

Cornbleet, S, and Carter, R. (2001), *The Language of Speech and Writing*. London: Routledge.

Crismore, A., Markkanen, R. and Steffensen, R. (1993), 'Metadiscourse in persuasive writing: A study of texts written by American and Finnish university students', *Written Communication*, 5, 184–202.

Cutting, J. (2002), *Pragmatics and Discourse. A Resource Book for Students*. London: Routledge.

Davies, J. (2003a), 'Expressions of gender: An analysis of pupils' gendered discourse styles in small group classroom discussions', *Discourse and Society*, 14, 115–32.

—— (2003b), 'Negotiating femininities online: *"Babyz"*, cyber bedrooms and scandalous talk', Children's Literacy and Popular Culture seminar, University of Sheffield, 1 July 2003, available at: www.sheffield.ac.uk/ literacy/ ESRC/seminar4.html – accessed 8 December 2005.

—— (2004), 'Negotiating femininities online', *Gender and Education*, 16, 35–49.

Davies, R. and Ikeno, O. (2002), *The Japanese Mind: Understanding Contemporary Japanese Culture*. Boston and Tokyo: Tuttle Publishing.

Devitt, A. (1997), 'Genre as a language standard', in W. Bishop and H. Ostrum (eds), *Genre and Writing*. Portsmouth, NH: Boynton/Cook, pp. 45–55.

—— (2004), *Writing Genres*. Carbondale, Ill: Southern Illinois University Press.

Downes, S. (1995), 'Eating Out', *The Sunday Age*, 23 April 1995, Life, p. 4.

Eckert, P. (2000), *Linguistic Variation as Social Practice*, Oxford: Blackwell.

—— (2002), 'Demystifying sexuality and desire', in K. Campbell-Kibler, R. J. Podesva, S. J. Roberts and A. Wong (eds), *Language and Sexuality: Contesting Meaning in Theory and Practice*. Stanford, Cal: CSLI Publications, pp. 99–110.

Eckert, P. and McConnell-Ginet, S. (2003), *Language and Gender*. Cambridge: Cambridge University Press.

Eco, U. (1987), *Travels in Hyperreality*. London: Picador.

Eelen, G. (2001), *A Critique of Politeness Theories*. Manchester, UK/Northampton, MA: St Jerome Publishing.

Eggins, S. (1994), *An Introduction to Systemic Functional Linguistics*. London: Pinter.

—— (2005), *An Introduction to Systemic Functional Linguistics* (2nd edn). London: Continuum.

Eggins, S. and Slade, D. (1997), *Analysing Casual Conversation*. London: Cassell. (Republished 2005, London: Equinox Publishers).

Engardio, P. and Roberts, D. (2004), 'Special report: The China price', *Business Week*, Asian edition, 6 December 2004, pp. 48–58.

Eslami-Rasekh, Z. (2005), 'Raising the pragmatic awareness of language learners', *ELT Journal*, 59, 199–208.

Fairclough, N. (1992), *Discourse and Social Change*. Cambridge: Polity Press.

—— (1995), *Critical Discourse Analysis*. London: Longman.

—— (2003), *Analyzing Discourse: Textual Analysis for Social Research*. London: Routledge.

Fairclough, N. and Wodak, R. (1997), 'Critical discourse analysis: An Overview', in T. A. van Dijk (ed.), *Discourse as Social Interaction*. London: Sage, pp. 67–97.

225

Farrer, J. (2002), *Opening Up: Youth Sex Culture and Market Reform in Shanghai*. Chicago: University of Chicago Press.

Flowerdew, J. (1990), 'Problems of speech act theory from an applied perspective', *Language Learning*, 40, 79–105.

—— (2002), 'Genre in the classroom: A linguistic approach', in A. Johns (ed.), *Genre in the Classroom: Multiple Perspectives*. Mahwah, NJ: Lawrence Erlbaum Publishers, pp. 91–102.

—— (2004), 'The discursive construction of a world-class city', *Discourse and Society*, 15, 579–605.

Flowerdew, L. (2005), 'An integration of corpus-based and genre-based approaches to text analysis in EAP/ESP: Countering criticisms against corpus-based methodologies', *English for Specific Purposes*, 24, 321–32.

Fox H. (1994), *Listening to the World: Cultural Issues in Academic Writing*. Urbana, Ill: National Council of Teachers of English.

Fraser, B. (1980), 'Conversational mitigation', *Journal of Pragmatics*, 14, 341–50.

Freedman, A. (1989), 'Reconceiving genre', *Texte*, 8, 279–92.

—— (1999), 'Beyond the text: Towards understanding the teaching and learning of genres,' *TESOL Quarterly*, 33, 764–8.

Fries, P. H. (2002), 'The flow of information in a written text', in P. H. Fries, M. Cummings, D. Lockwood and W. Spruidell (eds), *Relation and Functions Within and Across Language*. London: Continuum, pp. 117–55.

Gardner, R. (1994), 'Conversation analysis: Some thoughts on its applicability to applied linguistics', *Australian Review of Applied Linguistics*, Series No 11, 97–118.

—— (2001), *When Listeners Talk: Response Tokens and Listener Stance*. Amsterdam: John Benjamins.

—— (2004), 'On delaying the answer: Question sequences extended after the question', in R. Gardner and J. Wagner (eds), *Second Language Conversations*. London: Continuum, pp. 246–66.

Gee, J. P. (1993), *An Introduction to Human Language: Fundamental Concepts in Linguistics*. Englewood Cliffs, NJ: Prentice Hall.

—— (1996), *Social Linguistics and Literacies: Ideology in Discourses*. London: Taylor and Francis.

—— (2004), 'Discourse analysis: What makes it critical?' in R. Rogers (ed.), *An Introduction to Critical Discourse Analysis in Education*. Mahwah, NJ: Laurence Erlbaum, pp. 19–50.

—— (2005), *An Introduction to Discourse Analysis: Theory and Method* (2nd edn). London: Routledge.

Gee, S. (1997), 'Teaching writing: A genre-based approach', in G. Fulcher (ed.), *Writing in the English Language Classroom*. Hertfordshire, UK: Prentice Hall Europe ELT, pp. 24–40.

Gibson, R. (2000), *Intercultural Business Communication*. Oxford: Oxford University Press.

Goffman, E. (1967), *Interaction Ritual: Essays on Face to Face Behaviour*. New York: Garden City.

226

Gordon, C. (2004), '"Al Gore's our guy": Linguistically constructing a family political identity', *Discourse and Society*, 15, 607–31.

Grice, H. P. (1975), 'Logic and conversation', in P. Cole and J. L. Morgan (eds), *Syntax and Semantics 3: Speech Acts*. New York: Academic Press. Reprinted in A. Jaworski and N. Coupland (eds) (1999), *The Discourse Reader*. London: Routledge, pp. 76–88.

Gu, Y. (1990), 'Politeness phenomena in modern Chinese', *Journal of Pragmatics*, 14, 237–57.

Hall, K. (1995), 'Lip service on the fantasy lines', in K. Hall and M. Bucholtz (eds), *Gender Articulated: Language and the Socially Constructed Self*. London: Routledge, pp. 183–216.

Halliday, M. A. K. (1985), *An Introduction to Functional Grammar*. London: Edward Arnold.

—— (1989), *Spoken and Written Language*. Oxford: Oxford University Press.

—— (1990), 'Some grammatical problems in scientific English', *Australian Review of Applied Linguistics*, Series S, 6, 13–37.

Halliday, M. A. K. and Hasan, R. (1976), *Cohesion in English*. London: Longman.

Halliday, M. A. K. and Matthiessen, C. (2004), *An Introduction to Functional Grammar* (3rd edn). London: Edward Arnold.

Hammersley, M. (2003), 'Conversation analysis and discourse analysis: Methods or paradigms?' *Discourse and Society*, 14, 751–81.

Hammond, J. and Macken-Horarick, M. (1999), 'Critical literacy: Challenges and questions for ESL classrooms,' *TESOL Quarterly*, 33, 528–44.

Harris, Z. (1952), 'Discourse analysis', *Language*, 28, 1–30.

Hartford, B. and Mahboob, A. (2004), 'Models of discourse in the letter of complaint', *World Englishes*, 23, 585–600.

Harwood, N. (2005), '"We do not seem to have a theory ... the theory I present here attempts to full this gap": Inclusive and exclusive pronouns in academic writing', *Applied Linguistics*, 26, 343–75.

Hasan, R. (1989a), 'The structure of a text', in M. A. K. Halliday and R. Hasan, *Language, Context and Text: Aspects of Language in a Social-Semiotic Perspective*. Oxford: Oxford University Press, pp. 52–69.

—— (1989b), 'The texture of a text', in M. A. K. Halliday and R. Hasan, *Language, Context and Text: Aspects of Language in a Social-Semiotic Perspective*. Oxford: Oxford University Press, pp. 70–96.

Hilles, S. (2005), 'Contextual analysis a la Celce-Murcia', in J. Frodesen and C. Holten (eds), *The Power of Context in Language Teaching and Learning*. Boston, Mass: Thomson/Heinle, pp. 3–12.

Hirvela, A. and Belcher, D. (2001), 'Coming back to voice: The multiple voices and identities of mature multilingual writers', *Journal of Second Language Writing*, 10, 83–106.

Holmes, J. (1995), *Women, Men and Politeness*. London: Longman.

—— (1997), 'Women, language and identity', *Journal of Sociolinguistics*, 1, 195–223.

—— (2001), *An Introduction to Sociolinguistics* (2nd edn). Harlow: Longman.

227

—— (2004), 'Power, *lady*, and linguistic politeness in *Language and Women's Place*', in M. Bucholtz (ed.) *Language and Woman's Place: Text and Commentaries*. Oxford: Oxford University Press, pp. 151–7.

Huckin, T. N. (1997), 'Critical discourse analysis', in T. Miller (ed.), *Functional Approaches to Written Text: Classroom Applications*. Washington, DC: United States Information Agency, pp. 78–92.

Hughes, R. (2002), *Teaching and Researching Speaking*. Harlow, UK: Longman.

Hughes, R. and McCarthy, M. (1998), 'From sentence to discourse: Discourse grammar and English language teaching', *TESOL Quarterly*, 32, 263–87.

Hunston, S. (2002), 'Pattern grammar, language teaching, and linguistic variation', in R. Reppen, S. M. Fitzmaurice and D. Biber (eds), *Using Corpora to Explore Linguistic Variation*. Amsterdam: John Benjamins, pp. 167–83.

Hutchby, I. (1996), 'Power in discourse: The case of arguments on a British talk radio show', *Discourse and Society*, 7, 481–97.

Hutchby, I. and Wooffitt, R. (1998), *Conversation Analysis: Principles, Practices and Applications*. Cambridge: Polity Press.

Hyland, K. (1998), 'Persuasion and context: the pragmatics of academic metadiscourse,' *Journal of Pragmatics*, 30: 437–55.

—— (2002a), 'Authority and invisibility: Authorial identity in academic writing', *Journal of Pragmatics*, 34, 1091–112.

—— (2002b), *Teaching and Researching Writing*. Harlow, UK: Longman.

—— (2002c), 'Options of identity in academic writing', *ELT Journal*, 56, 4, 351–8.

—— (2004a), *Genre and Second Language Writing*. Ann Arbor: The University of Michigan Press.

—— (2004b), 'Graduates' gratitude: The generic structure of dissertation acknowledgements', *English for Specific Purposes*, 23, 303–24

—— (2004c), *Disciplinary Discourses: Social Interactions in Academic Writing* (2nd edn). Ann Arbor: The University of Michigan Press.

—— (2005a), 'Digging up texts and transcripts: Confessions of a discourse analyst', in P. K. Matsuda and T. Silva (eds), *Second Language Writing Research: Perspectives on the Process of Knowledge Construction*. Mahwah, NJ: Lawrence Erlbaum, pp. 177–89.

—— (2005b), *Metadiscourse: Exploring Interaction in Writing*. London: Continuum.

Hyland, K. and Tse, P. (2004), '"I would like to thank my supervisor" Acknowledgments in graduate dissertations', *International Journal of Applied Linguistics*, 14, 259–75.

Hymes, D. (1964), 'Introduction: Towards ethnographies of communication', in J. J. Gumperz and D. Hymes (eds), *The Ethnography of Communication*. *American Anthropologist*, 66, 1–34.

—— (1972), 'On communicative competence', in J. B. Pride and J. Holmes (eds), *Sociolinguistics: Selected Readings*. Harmondsworth: Penguin, pp. 269–93.

228

Hyon, S. (1996), 'Genre in three traditions: Implications for ESL,' *TESOL Quarterly*, 30, 693–722.

—— (2001), 'Long term effects of genre-based instruction: A follow up study of an EAP reading course', *English for Specific Purposes*, 20, 417–38.

Ide, S. (1982), 'Japanese sociolinguistics: Politeness and women's language', *Lingua*, 57, 49–89.

Jaworski, A. and Coupland, N. (1999), 'Editors' introduction to Part 1', in A. Jaworski and N. Coupland (eds), *The Discourse Reader*. London: Routledge, pp. 47–53.

Jefferson, G. (2004), 'Glossary of transcript symbols with an introduction', in G. H. Lerner (ed.), *Conversation Analysis: Studies from the First Generation*. Amsterdam: John Benjamin, pp. 13–31.

Johns, A. M. (1993), 'Written argumentation for real audiences: Suggestions for teacher research and classroom practice', *TESOL Quarterly*, 27, 75–90.

—— (1997), *Text, Role and Context: Developing Academic Literacies*. Cambridge: Cambridge University Press.

—— (forthcoming), 'Research and L2 writing instruction,' in E. U. Juan and A. Martinez (eds), *Current Issues in the Development of the Four Language Skills*. Berlin: Mouton de Gruyter.

Johnstone, B. (2000), *Qualitative Methods in Sociolinguistics*. New York: Oxford University Press.

—— (2002), *Discourse Analysis*. Oxford: Blackwell.

Kaplan, R. B. (1966), 'Cultural thought patterns in intercultural education', *Language Learning*, 16, 1–20.

Kasper G. (1997), 'Can pragmatic competence be taught?', Second Language Teaching and Curriculum Center, University of Hawaii, available at: http://nflrc.hawaii.edu/NetWorks/NW06/ – accessed 23 November 2004.

Kay, H. and Dudley-Evans, T. (1998), 'Genre: What teachers think', *ELT Journal*, 52, 308–14.

Kennedy, G. (1998), *An Introduction to Corpus Linguistics*. London: Longman.

Kiesling, S. F. (2002), 'Playing the straight man: Displaying and maintaining male heterosexuality in discourse', in K. Campbell-Kibler, R. J. Podesva, S. J. Roberts and A. Wong (eds), *Language and Sexuality: Contesting Meaning in Theory and Practice*. Stanford, Cal: CSLI Publications, pp. 249–66

Kitzinger, C. (2000), 'Doing feminist conversation analysis', *Feminism and Psychology*, 10, 163–93.

Kitzinger, C. and Frith, H. (1999), 'Just say no? The use of conversation analysis in developing a feminist perspective on sexual refusal', *Discourse and Society*, 10, 293–316.

Knapp, P. and Watkins, M. (2005), *Genre, Text, Grammar: Technologies for Teaching and Assessing Writing*. Sydney: University of New South Wales Press.

Koch, H. (1996), *Casablanca: Script and Legend*. Woodstock, NY: Overlook Press.

Kowal, S. and O'Connell, D. C. (1997), 'Theoretical ideals and their violation:

Princess Diana and Martin Bashir in the BBC interview', *Pragmatics*, 7, 309–23.

Kress, G. (1991), 'Critical discourse analysis,' *Annual Review of Applied Linguistics*, 11, 84–99.

Kubota, R. (1997), 'A reevaluation of the uniqueness of Japanese written discourse: Implications for contrastive rhetoric', *Written Communication*, 14, 460–80.

Kurzon, D. (1996), 'The maxim of quantity, hyponymy and Princess Diana', *Pragmatics*, 6, 217–27.

Labov, W. (1966), *The Social Stratification of New York City*. Washington, DC: Centre for Applied Linguistics.

Lakoff, R. T. (1973), 'The logic of politeness: Minding your Ps and Gs', *Chicago Linguistics Society*, 9, 292–305.

—— (1975), *Language and Women's Place*. New York: Harper and Row.

—— (1990), *Talking Power*. New York: Basic Books.

Larsen-Freeman, D. (2003), *Teaching Language: From Grammar to Grammaring*. Boston, MA: Thomson Heinle.

Lee, D. A. (1997), 'Frame conflicts and competing construals in family argument', *Journal of Pragmatics*, 27, 339–60.

Leech, G. (1983), *Principles of Pragmatics*. London: Longman.

Leki, I. (1997), 'Cross-talk: ESL issues and contrastive rhetoric, in C. Severino, J. C. Guerra and S. E. Butler (eds), *Writing in Multicultural Settings*. New York: Modern Language Association of America, pp. 234–44.

Lemke, J. L. (1992), 'Intertextuality and educational research', *Linguistics and Education*, 4, 257–67.

—— (1995), *Textual Politics. Discourse and Social Dynamics*. London: Taylor and Francis.

Liu, D. (2000), 'Writing cohesion: Using content lexical ties in ESOL', *English Teaching Forum*, 38, 28–35.

Liu, J. (2004), 'A study of Chinese ethnic minorities English writing from a contrastive rhetoric perspective'. (MEd TESOL dissertation, University of Sydney).

—— (forthcoming), 'Generic and rhetorical structures of Chinese minority nationalities' English expositions: An intra-cultural contrastive-rhetoric perspective', *Language and Intercultural Communication*.

Lo Castro, V. (2003), *An Introduction to Pragmatics. Social Action for Language Teachers*. Ann Arbor: The University of Michigan Press.

Luke, A. (1996), 'Genres of power? Literacy education and the production of capital', in R. Hasan and G. Williams (eds), *Literacy in Society*. London: Longman, pp. 308–38.

Machin, D. and Thornborrow, J. (2003), 'Branding and discourse: The case of *Cosmopolitan*', *Discourse and Society*, 14, 453–71.

Mallinson, C. and Brewster, Z. W. (2005), ' "Blacks and bubbas": Stereotypes, ideology, and categorization processes in restaurant servers' discourse', *Discourse and Society*, 16, 787–807.

Mao, L. R. (1994), 'Beyond politeness theory: "Face" revisited and renewed', *Journal of Pragmatics*, 21, 451–86.

Markee, N. (2000), *Conversation Analysis*. Mahwah, NJ: Lawrence Erlbaum.

Martin, J. R. (1984), 'Language, register and genre', in F. Christie (ed.), *Language Studies: Children's Writing: Reader*. Geelong, Vic: Deakin University Press, pp. 21–9. Reprinted with revisions in A. Burns and C. Coffin (eds) (2001), *Analyzing English in a Global Context*. London: Routledge, pp. 149–66.

—— (1992), *English Text. System and Structure*. Amsterdam: John Benjamins.

—— (1993), 'Genre and literacy – modelling context in educational linguistics', *Annual Review of Applied Linguistics*, 13, 141–72.

—— (2000), 'Close reading: Functional linguistics as a tool for critical discourse analysis', in L. Unsworth (ed.), *Researching Language in Schools and Communities: Functional Linguistic Perspectives*. London: Cassell, pp. 275–302.

Martin, J. R. and Rose, D. (2003), *Working with Discourse: Meaning Beyond the Clause*. London: Continuum.

Matsuda, P. K. (2002), 'Negotiation of identity and power in a Japanese online discourse community', *Computers and Composition*, 19, 39–55.

Matsumoto, Y. (1989), 'Politeness and conversational universals – observations from Japanese', *Multilingua*, 8, 207–22.

Mauranen, A. (2001), 'Reflexive academic talk: Observations from MICASE', in R. C. Simpson and J. M. Swales (eds), *Corpus Linguistics in North America: Selections from the 1999 Symposium*. Ann Arbor: The University of Michigan Press, pp. 165–78.

Mautner, G. (2005a), 'Time to get wired: Using web-based corpora in critical discourse analysis', *Discourse and Society*, 16, 809–28.

—— (2005b), 'The entrepreneurial university: A discursive profile of a higher education buzzword', *Discourse and Society*, 2, 95–120.

McCarthy, M. (1994), '*It*, *this*, and *that*', in M. Coulthard (ed.), *Advances in written text analysis*. London: Routledge, pp. 266–75.

—— (1998), *Spoken Language and Applied Linguistics*. Cambridge: Cambridge University Press.

—— (2001), *Issues in Applied Linguistics*. Oxford: Oxford University Press.

McCarthy, M. and Carter, R. (2001), 'Size isn't everything: Spoken English, corpus, and the classroom', *TESOL Quarterly*, 35, 337–40.

McKenna, B. (2004), 'Critical discourse studies: Where to from here?', *Critical Discourse Studies*, 1, 9–39.

Mean, L. (2001), 'Identity and discursive practice: Doing gender on the football pitch', *Discourse and Society*, 12, 789–815.

MICASE (nd), 'Research and development activities', available at www.lsa.umich.edu/eli/micase/index.htm – accessed 22 November 2005.

Mills, S. (1997), *Discourse*. London: Routledge.

—— (2003), *Gender and Politeness*. Cambridge: Cambridge University Press.

Milne, A. A. (1965), *Winnie-the-Pooh*. London: Methuen & Co.

Milroy, J. and Milroy, L. (1978), 'Belfast: Change and variation in an urban vernacular', in P. Trudgill (ed.), *Sociolinguistic Patterns in British English.* London: Arnold, pp. 19–36.

Milroy, J. and Milroy, L. (1997), 'Varieties and variation', in F. Coulmas (ed.), *The Handbook of Sociolinguistics.* Oxford: Blackwell, pp. 47–64.

Milroy, L. (1987), *Language and Social Networks* (2nd edn). Oxford: Basil Blackwell.

Mitchell, T. F. (1957), 'The language of buying and selling in Cyrenaica', *Hesperis*, 44, 31–71.

Morton, A. (1999), *Monica's Story.* New York: St Martin's Press.

Mullany, L. (2002), ' "I don't think you want me to get a word in edgeways do you John?" Re-assessing (im)politeness, language and gender in political broadcast interviews', *Working Papers on the Web*, 3, available at www.shu.ac.uk/wpw/politeness/mullany.htm – accessed 14 November 2005.

Nakane, I. (2003), 'Silence in Japanese-Australian Classroom Interaction: Perceptions and Performance'. (PhD dissertation, Department of Linguistics, University of Sydney).

—— (2005), 'Negotiating silence and speech in the classroom', *Multilingua*, 24, 75–100.

Nakanishi, M. (1998), 'Gender enactment on a first date: A Japanese sample', *Women and Language*, 21, 10–17.

Nesbitt, D., Nesbitt, J. and Uchimaru, K. (1990), *Contact Japanese: Communicating in Japanese.* Auckland: New House Publishers.

Nesi, H. (2001), 'A corpus-based analysis of academic lectures across disciplines', in J. Cotterill and Ife, A. (eds), *Language Across Boundaries.* London: BAAL in association with Continuum Press, pp. 201–18.

Norris, S. (2004), *Multimodal Interaction: A Methodological Framework.* London: Routledge.

North, S. (2005), 'Disciplinary variation in the use of theme in undergraduate essays', *Applied Linguistics*, 26, 431–52.

O'Loughlin, K. (1989), 'Routine beginnings: Telephone openings in Australia', *Melbourne Papers in Applied Linguistics*, 1, 27–42.

O'Shannessy, C. (1995), 'Pre-court barrister–client interactions: An investigation' (MA thesis, Department of Linguistics and Applied Linguistics, University of Melbourne).

Ohashi, J. (2000), 'Thanking, giving and receiving in Japanese: A cross-cultural pragmatic investigation' (PhD thesis, Department of Linguistics and Applied Linguistics, University of Melbourne).

Ooi, V. B. Y. (2001), 'Investigating and teaching genres using the World Wide Web', in M. Ghadessy, A. Henry and R. L. Roseberry (eds), *Small Corpus Studies and ELT.* Amsterdam: John Benjamins, pp. 175–203.

Orr, J. (1996), 'A comparative investigation into the structure of arguments: Frame semantics and conversation analysis' (MA thesis, Department of Linguistics and Applied Linguistics, University of Melbourne).

Page, R. E. (2003), ' "Cherie: lawyer, wife, mum": Contradictory patterns of representation in media reports of Cherie Booth/Blair', *Discourse and Society*, 14, 559–79.

Paltridge, B. (1998), 'Get your terms in order', in P. Master and D. Brinton (eds), *New Ways in English for Specific Purposes*. Alexandra, Va: TESOL, pp. 263–6.

—— (2000), *Making Sense of Discourse Analysis*. Gold Coast, Queensland: Antipodean Educational Enterprises.

—— (2001), *Genre and the Language Learning Classroom*. Ann Arbor: The University of Michigan Press.

—— (2002), 'Thesis and dissertation writing: An examination of published advice and actual practice', *English for Specific Purposes*, 21, 125–43.

—— (2004), 'The exegesis as a genre: An ethnographic examination,' in L. Ravelli and R. Ellis (eds), *Analyzing Academic Writing: Contextualised Frameworks*. London: Continuum, pp. 84–103.

Poos, D. and Simpson, R. C. (2002), 'Cross-disciplinary comparisons of hedging: Some findings from the Michigan Corpus of Academic Spoken English', in R. Reppen, S. M. Fitzmaurice and D. Biber (eds), *Using Corpora to Explore Linguistic Variation*. Amsterdam: John Benjamins, pp. 3–23.

Prince, A. (2000), 'Writing through cultures: The thesis writing experiences of five postgraduate research students from non-English speaking backgrounds and cultures' (MA thesis, Department of Linguistics and Applied Linguistics, University of Melbourne).

Reinhart, S. (2002), *Giving Academic Presentations*. Ann Arbor: The University of Michigan Press.

Reppen, R. and Simpson, R. (2002), 'Corpus linguistics', in N. Schmitt (ed.), *An Introduction to Applied Linguistics*. London: Arnold, pp. 92–111.

Richards, J. C. and Schmidt, R. (2002), *Longman Dictionary of Language Teaching and Applied Linguistics* (3rd edn). Harlow, UK: Longman.

Richardson, K. (2000), ' "Suffer in your jocks, ya dickhead": Solidarity and the construction of identity in an Australian university cricket club magazine' (MA thesis, Department of Linguistics and Applied Linguistics, University of Melbourne).

Riggenbach, H. (1999), *Discourse Analysis in the Language Classroom*. Volume 1: The Spoken Language. Ann Arbor: The University of Michigan Press.

Rogers, R. (2004), 'Setting an agenda for critical discourse analysis in education', in R. Rogers (ed.), *An Introduction to Critical Discourse Analysis in Education*. Mahwah, NJ: Laurence Erlbaum, pp. 237–54.

Sacks, H. (2004), 'An initial characterisation of the organisation of turn taking for conversation', in G. H. Lerner (ed.), *Conversation Analysis: Studies from the First Generation*. Amsterdam: John Benjamin, pp. 35–42.

Sacks, H., Schegloff, E. A. and Jefferson, G. (1974), 'A simplest systematics for the organisation of turn taking for conversation', *Language*, 50, 696–735.

Samraj, B. (2005), 'An exploration of a genre set: Research article abstracts and introductions in two disciplines', *English for Specific Purposes*, 24, 141–56.

Santos, T. (1989), 'Replication in applied linguistics research', *TESOL Quarterly*, 23, 699–702.

Sartain, S. (1995), 'Letter to the editor', *The Sunday Age*, 30 April 1995, p. 16.

Saville-Troike, M. (1996), 'The ethnography of communication', in S. L. McKay and N. H. Hornberger (eds), *Sociolinguistics and Language Teaching*. Cambridge: Cambridge University Press, pp. 351–82.

—— (2003), *The Ethnography of Communication: An Introduction* (3rd edn). Malden, Mass: Blackwell.

Schegloff, E. (1986), 'The routine as achievement,' *Human Studies*, 9, 111–52.

—— (1997), 'Whose text? Whose context?' *Discourse and Society*, 8, 2, 165–87.

—— (2004), 'Answering the phone', in G. H. Lerner (ed.), *Conversation Analysis: Studies from the First Generation*. Amsterdam: John Benjamins, pp. 63–107.

Schegloff, E. A., Koshik, I., Jacoby, S. and Olsher, D. (2002), 'Conversation analysis and applied linguistics,' *Annual Review of Applied Linguistics*, 22, 3–31.

Schegloff, E. and Sacks, H. (1973), 'Opening up closings', *Semiotica*, 7, 289–437.

Schiffrin, D. (1994), *Approaches to Discourse*. Oxford: Blackwell.

Scollon, R. and Wong-Scollon, S. (2001), *Intercultural Communication: A Discourse Approach*. Second edition. Oxford: Blackwell.

Scott, M. and Groom, N. (1999), 'Genre-based pedagogy: Problems and possibilities', in P. Thompson (ed.), *Issues in EAP Research and Writing Instruction*. Reading: Centre for Applied Language Studies, University of Reading, pp. 18–27.

Searle, J. R. (1969), *Speech Acts*. London: Cambridge University Press.

Shalom, C. (1997), 'That great supermarket of desire: Attributes of the desired other in personal advertisements', in K. Harvey and C. Shalom (eds), *Language and Desire: Encoding Sex, Romance and Intimacy*. London: Routledge, pp. 186–203.

Sigley, R. and Holmes, J. (2002), 'Looking at *girls* in corpora of English', *Journal of English Linguistics*, 30, 138–57.

Sinclair, J. (2001), 'Preface', in M. Ghadessy, A. Henry and R. L. Roseberry (eds), *Small Corpus Studies and ELT*. Amsterdam: John Benjamins, pp. vii–xv.

Spender, D. (1980), *Man Made Language*. London: Routledge and Kegan Paul.

Spolsky, B. (1998), *Sociolinguistics*. Oxford: Oxford University Press.

Stevens, K. and Asmar, C. (1999), *Doing Postgraduate Research in Australia*. Melbourne: Melbourne University Press.

Stokoe, E. H. (2003), 'Mothers, single women and sluts: Gender, morality and membership categorization in neighbour disputes', *Feminism & Psychology*, 13, 317–44.

Storch, N. (2001a), 'How collaborative is pair work? ESL tertiary students composing in pairs', *Language Teaching Research*, 5, 29–53.

—— (2001b), 'An investigation into the nature of pair work in an ESL classroom and its effect on grammatical development'. (PhD thesis Department of Linguistics and Applied Linguistics, University of Melbourne).

Stubbs, M. (1997), 'Whorf's children: Critical comments on critical discourse analysis (CDA)', in A. Ryan and A. Wray (eds), *Evolving Models of Language*. Clevedon: Multilingual Matters, pp. 100–16.

—— (2004), 'Corpus-assisted text and corpus analysis: Lexical cohesion and communicative competence', in D. Schiffrin, D. Tannen and H. E. Hamilton (eds), T*he Handbook of Discourse Analysis*. Oxford: Blackwell, pp. 304–20.

Sunderland, J. and Litosseliti, L. (2002), 'Gender identity and discourse analysis: Theoretical and empirical considerations', in J. Sunderland and L. Litosseliti (eds), *Gender Identity and Discourse Analysis*. Amsterdam: John Benjamins, pp. 1–39.

Swales, J. M. (1981), 'Aspects of article Introductions', *Aston ESP Research Reports*, No 1. Language Studies Unit. The University of Aston at Birmingham.

—— (1990), *Genre Analysis: English in Academic and Research Settings*. Cambridge: Cambridge University Press.

—— (1993), 'Genre and engagement', Revue Belge de Philologie et d'Histoire, 71, 689–98.

—— (1996), 'Occluded genres in the academy: The case of the submission letter', in E. Ventola and A. Mauranen (eds), *Academic Writing: Intercultural and Textual Issues*. Amsterdam and Philadelphia: John Benjamins, pp. 45–58.

—— (1998), *Other Floors, Other Voices: A Textography of a Small University Building*. Mahwah, NJ: Lawrence Erlbaum.

—— (2000), 'Languages for specific purposes', *Annual Review of Applied Linguistics*, 20, 59–76.

—— (2002), 'On models of applied discourse analysis', in C. N. Candlin (ed.), *Research and Practice in Professional Discourse*. Hong Kong: City University of Hong Kong Press, pp. 61–77.

—— (2003), 'Is the university a community of practice?' in S. Sarangi and T. van Leeuwen (eds), *Applied Linguistics and Communities of Practice*. London: Continuum, pp. 203–16.

—— (2004), *Research Genres: Explorations and Applications*. Cambridge: Cambridge University Press.

Swales, J. M. and Feak, C. B. (2000), *English in Today's Research World: A Writing Guide*. Ann Arbor: The University of Michigan Press.

Swales, J. M. and Malczewski, B. (2001), 'Discourse management and new episode flags in MICASE', in R. Simpson and J. M. Swales (eds), *Corpus Linguistics in North America: Selections from the 1999 Symposium*. Ann Arbor: The University of Michigan Press, pp. 145–64.

Swann, J. (2002), 'Yes, but is it gender?' in L. Litosseliti and J. Sunderland (eds), *Gender Identity and Discourse Analysis*. Amsterdam: John Benjamins, pp. 43–67.

Swann, J., Deumert, A., Lillis, T. and Mesthrie, R. (2004), *A Dictionary of Sociolinguistics*. Edinburgh: Edinburgh University Press.

Tan, R. (2005), 'So steady pom pi pi', *Sunday Times*, Singapore, 27 February 2005, p. 38.

Tanaka, K. (1997), 'Developing pragmatic competence: A learners-as-researchers approach', *TESOL Journal*, 6, 14–18.

Tannen, D. (ed.) (1982), *Spoken and Written Language: Exploring Orality and Literacy*. Norwood, NJ: Ablex.

Tannen, D. (1990), *You Just Don't Understand: Women and Men in Conversation*. New York: William Morrow.

Tardy, C. (2003), 'A genre system view of the funding of academic research', *Written Communication*, 20, 7–36.

Taylor, S. (2001), 'Evaluating and applying discourse analytic research', in M. Wetherall, S. Taylor and S. J. Yates (eds), *Discourse as Data: A Guide for Analysis*. London: Sage, pp. 311–30.

Teo, P. (2005), 'Mandarinizing Singapore: A critical analysis of slogans in Singapore's "Speak Mandarin" Campaign', *Critical Discourse Studies*, 2, 121–42.

Thomas, A. (2000), 'Textual construction of children's online identities', *CyberPsychology and Behavior*, Special issue: 'Case Studies in Cyberspace', 3, 665–72.

—— (2004), 'Digital literacies of the cybergirl', *E-Learning*, 1, 358–82.

—— (forthcoming), 'discourse@virual-community.com: Literacy and identity online', *Critical Discourse Studies*.

Thomas, J. (1983), 'Cross cultural pragmatic failure', *Applied Linguistics*, 4, 91–112.

—— (1995), *Meaning in Interaction. An Introduction to Pragmatics*. London: Longman.

Thornborrow, J. (2001), 'Questions, control and the organization of talk in calls to a radio phone-in', *Discourse Studies*, 1, 119–43.

Thornbury, S. (2005), *Beyond the Sentence: Introducing Discourse Analysis*. London: Macmillan.

Threadgold, T. (1989), 'Talking about genre: Ideologies and incompatible discourses', *Cultural Studies*, 3, 101–27.

—— (2003), 'Cultural studies, critical theory and critical discourse analysis" Histories, remembering and futures', *Linguistik Online*, 14, 2, available at www.linguistik-online.de/14_03/threadgold.html – accessed 29 November 2005.

Thurlow, C., Lengel, L. and Tomic, A. (2004), *Computer Mediated Communication: Social Interaction and the Internet*. London: Sage.

Tognini-Bonelli, E. (2004), 'Working with corpora: Issues and insights', in C. Coffin, A. Hewings and K. O'Lalloran (eds), *Applying English Grammar: Functional and Corpus Approaches*, London: Arnold, pp. 11–24.

Toolan, M. (1997), 'What is critical discourse analysis and why are people saying such terrible things about it?', *Language and Literature*, 6, 83–103.

Trautner, M. N. (2005), 'Doing gender, doing class: The performance of sexuality in exotic dance clubs', *Gender and Society*, 19, 771–88.

Tribble, C. (2002), 'Corpora and corpus analysis: New windows on academic writing', in J. Flowerdew (ed.), *Academic Discourse*. London: Longman, pp. 131–49.

Truss, L. (2003), *Eats, Shoots & Leaves*. London: Profile Books.

Tsang, D. (2000), 'Notes on queer "n" asian virtual sex', in D. Bell and B. Kennedy (eds), *The Cybercultures Reader*. London: Routledge, pp. 432–7.

Uchida, A. (1992), 'When "difference" is "dominance": A critique of the "anti-power-based" cultural approach to sex differences', *Language in Society*, 21, 547–68.

van Dijk, T. A. (1998), *Ideology*. London: Sage.

van Leeuwen, T. (2005), *Introducing Social Semiotics*. London: Routledge.

van Noppen, J.-P., (2004), 'CDA: A discipline come of age?', *Journal of Sociolinguistics*, 8, 107–26.

Vande Kopple, W. (1985), 'Some exploratory discourse on metadiscourse', *College Communication and Composition*, 36, 82–93.

Verschueren, J. (1999), *Understanding Pragmatics*. London: Arnold.

Walker, J. (1997), 'Restaurateur shows food critic the door', *The Weekend Australian*, 7–8 June 1997.

Wang, W. (2002), 'A contrastive analysis of letters to the editor in English and Chinese' (MEd dissertation, The University of Sydney).

—— (2004), 'A contrastive analysis of letters to the editor in Chinese and English', *Australian Review of Applied Linguistics*, 27, 72–88.

—— (2006a), 'Newspaper commentaries in China and Australia: A contrastive genre study', in U. Connor and E. Nagelhout (eds), *From Contrastive to Intercultural Rhetoric*. London: Equinox.

—— (2006b), 'Editorials on terrorism in Chinese and English: A contrastive genre study' (PhD thesis, University of Sydney).

Wardhaugh, R. (1998), *An Introduction to Sociolinguistics* (3rd edn). Oxford: Blackwell.

Watts, R. (2003), *Politeness*. Cambridge: Cambridge University Press.

Weatherall, A. (2002), *Gender, Language and Discourse*. London: Routledge.

Wenger, E. (1998), *Communities of Practice: Learning, Meaning and Identity*. Cambridge: Cambridge University Press.

West, C. and Zimmerman, D. H. (1983), 'Small insults: A study of interruptions in cross-sex conversations between unacquainted persons', in B. Thorne, C. Kramerae and N. Henley (eds), *Language, Gender and Society*. Rowley, Mass: Newbury House, pp. 103–18.

Wetherell, M. (1998), 'Positioning and interpretative repertoires: Conversation analysis and post-structuralism in dialogue', *Discourse and Society*, 19, 387–412.

—— (2001), 'Themes in discourse research: The case of Diana', in M. Wetherell, S. Taylor and S. J. Yates (eds), *Discourse Theory and Practice: A Reader*. London: Sage, pp. 14–28.

Widdowson, H. (1998), 'Review article: The theory and practice of critical discourse analysis,' *Applied Linguistics*, 19, 136–51.

—— (2004), *Text, Context, Pretext: Critical Issues in Discourse Analysis*. Oxford: Blackwell.

Wierzbicka, A. (2003), *Cross-Cultural Pragmatics: The Semantics of Human Interaction* (2nd edn). Berlin and New York: Mouton de Gruyter.

Wiseman, R. (1994), *Defending Ourselves: A Guide to Prevention, Self-Defence, and Recovery from Rape*. New York: Farrar, Straus and Giroux.

Wodak, R. (1996), *Disorders of Discourse*. London: Longman.

—— (1997), 'Das Ausland and anti-Semitic discourses: The discursive construction of the Other', in S. Riggens (ed.), *The Language of Politics and Exclusion*. London: Sage, pp. 65–87.

Wooffitt, R. (2005), *Conversation Analysis and Discourse Analysis: A Comparative and Critical Introduction*. London: Sage.

Wray, A., Trott, K. and Bloomer, A. (eds) (1998), *Projects in Linguistics: A Practical Guide to Researching Language*. London: Arnold/New York: Oxford University Press.

Yang, L. (1997), 'An Analysis of Opening Sequences in Chinese Telephone Calls' (MA thesis, Department of Linguistics and Applied Linguistics, University of Melbourne).

Zhang, J. (1986), *Love Must Not be Forgotten*. Beijing: China Books and Periodicals.

Zhang, Y. (2005), House of Flying Daggers: director's statement: www.sonyclassics.com/houseofflyingdaggers/flashsite.html – accessed 4 May 2005.

Index

Page numbers in *italics* refer to figures and tables.